Their Lives and Numbers

Documents in American Social History

A series edited by
Nick Salvatore

A complete list of titles
in the series appears at
the end of the book.

THEIR LIVES
AND
NUMBERS

The Condition of Working People
in Massachusetts, 1870–1900

EDITED WITH AN INTRODUCTION BY

HENRY F. BEDFORD

Cornell University Press

ITHACA AND LONDON

Copyright © 1995 by Cornell University

All rights reserved. Except for brief quotations in a review, this book, or parts thereof, must not be reproduced in any form without permission in writing from the publisher. For information, address Cornell University Press, Sage House, 512 East State Street, Ithaca, New York 14850.

First published 1995 by Cornell University Press.

Printed in the United States of America

♾ The paper in this book meets the minimum requirements of the American National Standard for Information Sciences— Permanence of Paper for Printed Library Materials, ANSI Z39.48-1984

Library of Congress Cataloging-in-Publication Data

Their lives and numbers : the condition of working people in Massachusetts, 1870–1900 / edited with an introduction by Henry F. Bedford.
    p. cm.
Includes index.
ISBN 0-8014-3032-1 (cloth)
ISBN 0-8014-8258-5 (paper)
    1. Working class—Massachusetts—History—19th century. 2. Blue collar workers—Massachusetts—History—19th century. 3. Working class families—Massachusetts—History—19th century. 4. Factories—Massachusetts—History—19th century. 5. Labor—Massachusetts—History—19th century. 6. Massachusetts—Social conditions.
HD8083.M4F33   1995
305.5′62—dc20
                                            94-23402

To the memory of
Ken and Jack

Contents

Illustrations

Tables

Preface

Peter Drucker, a guru of modern business management, has complained that "only a very few social historians have even an inkling of the material conditions" in which ordinary people existed and worked in the American past. His lament echoes the concern more than a century earlier of Massachusetts legislators, who established the Bureau of Statistics of Labor to provide reliable data about the lives and circumstances of their working constituents. Indeed, the agency collected considerable information about the very elements among "the great masses—the domestic servants, the shop girls, the manual workers" that Drucker specified.[1]

The bureau's research began to appear in 1870 in annual reports to the Massachusetts General Court. This book samples material from the first thirty of those reports. Selections indicate the range of the agency's interests, though they do not reflect every item examined or attempt to recreate some typical volume. Staff changes and the need to reply to specific legislative inquiries resulted in unproductive investigations and data of marginal significance that are not included here. But in the course of three decades, the bureau considered the major groups that made up the state's diverse working population—men, women, children, Yankees, immigrants, and, by the end of the century, blacks—and the array of tasks those people performed, from making

1. Peter F. Drucker, *Managing for the Future* (New York: Dutton, 1991), 114.

beds to manufacturing sheets, blankets, and the bedsteads themselves. Moreover, the bureau also reported periodically about the way working families lived: their residences, schools, marriages, amenities, worship, and bad habits.

Those examples reflect the bureau's own emphasis and suggest the importance of, and variety in, its work. They also constitute much of the agenda of contemporary students of the social history of the later nineteenth century. To facilitate use of this rich resource, I have organized material topically, often combining related surveys from several years in one chapter; the requirement that the bureau's editors report annually precluded their adopting that format. Arrangement by subject may sometimes obscure chronology, a distortion I attempt to reduce by providing introductory notes. In any case, the absence of chronological precision does not invalidate an undated description of the furnishings in the apartment of a working family, for example, or remarks about the influence of unions, saloons, or churches.

The agency, its publications, and the dislocation it studied endured well after 1900. But a mature government office, staffed by officials trained by their predecessors, examining apparently intractable problems, did not display the zeal and imagination of the bureau's innovative early years. Approaches that had once been fresh evolved into routine surveys and updated evidence; what had once been scholarly objectivity began to seem diminished concern. Annual volumes from 1870 to 1900 capture a sense of the immediacy of industrial change that is less apparent in subsequent years.

The first reports the bureau issued found an audience eager for official, ostensibly objective, information about the intertwined issues referred to in public discussion as "the labor question." Demand soon exhausted the stock of printed volumes, but newspapers regularly reported results of the bureau's investigations, sometimes adding local illustrations in order to make a partisan point.

The topics the bureau studied, which included most of the contentious socioeconomic problems of the time, invited partisanship. Tables, however accurate and detailed, could not entirely resolve disagreement about wages, hours, involuntary unemployment, or the distribution of wealth. Statistics demonstrating the employment of women and children did not end debate about public health, appropriate female roles, or educational opportunity. After some initial stumbling, directors of the bureau tried to maintain a distinction between factual conclusions they believed inherent in their evidence and political judgments about conditions the evidence revealed.

But the editors were not invariably detached from the material they collected. Henry Kemble Oliver, the bureau's first director, clearly believed his task included devising and advocating reform. His successors wanted to be less identified with labor's causes, but they too could not ignore every controversy about the costs and benefits of industrial development. In documenting conditions that made change urgent, the bureau's directors also demonstrated some of the political and ideological limits would-be reformers imposed on themselves. Thus, the agency's reports exemplify gender stereotypes, for instance, and the limited response to economic injustice that sometimes characterized later middle-class progressives.

A generation's effort to cope with a phenomenon now called economic restructuring emerges from the pages of the bureau's work. Current terms such as industrialization and urbanization were not explanatory concepts for people a century ago. Instead, the events those abstractions encompass were facts of daily life with an obvious personal relevance: the necessity that a child join her mother in the factory or that a family relocate. The arena of life was local and its scale small. People lived in tenements and neighborhoods, not in a nation; they worked not in some large industry, but in a nearby factory or mill, with others whom they knew, for identifiable bosses, who lived in big houses up the hill. Research conducted by the Massachusetts Bureau of Statistics of Labor often began with such individuals and with personal experiences that were not entirely submerged in columns of numbers.

In the years since the initial release of these reports, commercial publishers have reissued a few of them—*The Working Girls of Boston*, for instance—and a microfiche edition of the nineteenth-century reports. But the detailed and absorbing portrait of a society undergoing profound change is not now widely available. And even when available, the material is not accessible to every reader. Academic statisticians at the time disparaged the collection of "unsummarized and undigested" data, which needed more informed analysis than its original editors provided; nearly nine hundred pages describing rental housing in Boston at the end of the century was only one case in point. The *Nation*, a reform journal that welcomed the bureau's work, nevertheless worried that the "extreme bulk" of its reports might "prevent many from examining" them.[2]

That intimidating "bulk" stemmed from the desire of the bureau's directors to deflect criticism that their findings were unrepresentative as well as from their need to overwhelm skeptics with evidence. Tables displayed material about cities or counties, for example, that documented a subsequent summary for the state as a whole. In most instances, I have omitted the local statistics. Surveys of industrial occupations specified wages for thousands of productive tasks, of which I have selected a few. And I have sometimes omitted the illustrations and argumentation that sustained the quoted conclusion of an investigation.

Yet if the agency sometimes seemed preoccupied with amassing numbers, and if the result was sometimes flawed or statistically naive, those tables nevertheless offer as careful and inclusive a view as we have of industrial conditions at the time. The biographer of Carroll Wright, the second and best-known chief of the bureau, concedes that Wright had no special expertise and that his career was "not important because of the profundity of his insight and understanding." Wright's work, James Leiby admits, depicts more than it explains. But what it depicts is the turbulence and tension of rapid industrialization.[3]

Thomas Geoghegan, an attorney whose practice of labor law has left him few illusions disagrees with "writers who claim . . . that the old nineteenth-century problem of the 'working class' has been solved, at least in the Western industrial countries." His professional contact with workers, their unions, and their employers at the end of the twentieth century, Geoghegan asserts, demonstrates that earlier problems persist. And although his perspective is entirely different from that of Peter Drucker, Geoghegan also believes that the kind of

2. *Nation*, June 8, 1871, 398.

3. James Leiby, *Carroll Wright and Labor Reform* (Cambridge: Harvard University Press, 1960), 5.

descriptive and quantitative data the bureau collected ought to be known beyond the company of the "very few social historians."[4]

Industrial change in the later nineteenth century sometimes seemed anticlimactic to the students in my American history classes. For them, the topic was less engrossing than the debate over slavery and racial justice we had studied previously; personal emancipation engaged them more directly than did national economic transformation. In my search for ways to shrink the industrial revolution to a comprehensible human scale, I encountered the reports of the Massachusetts Bureau of Statistics of Labor. A few excerpts, selected in haste and sloppily presented, became a solution that endured far longer than I had intended. In a sense, this edition is overdue preparation for classes completed long ago.

Richard D. Schubart, then a colleague at Phillips Exeter Academy, collaborated in that early effort, though the choice of material from the bureau's reports was mine. Jackie Thomas and Jane Boesch, of the Academy Library at Exeter, have cheerfully fulfilled my whims for more years than any of us wants to recall. The staff of the Dimond Library at the University of New Hampshire in Durham met an outsider's requests with good humor; I owe a great deal to the anonymous librarian there who years ago saved the bureau's reports when they were discarded from another collection. Any reader will appreciate the luxury of using bound volumes instead of microform.

Martin Kaufman hosted a conference on women's history at the Institute for Massachusetts Studies which provided an audience for early thoughts on material in Chapter 5. Susan Porter, who presided, forced me to clarify that paper and thus influenced the treatment here. Anyone who writes about workingwomen has consulted the scholarship of Mary Blewett; I appreciate the insightful comments she made on the draft I read at the institute's symposium.

In my search for illustrative material, I had the able assistance of Clare Sheridan at the Museum of American Textile History, of Greg Laing at the Haverhill Public Library, of Aaron Schmidt at the Boston

4. Thomas Geoghegan, *Which Side Are You On?* (New York: Farrar, Straus & Giroux, 1991), 123.

Public Library, and of Rodney Armstrong and Sally Pierce at the Boston Athenaeum. Linda Neville, of the North Adams Historical Society, wrote me of her own work on Chinese contract laborers in North Adams and found a significant photograph. I am grateful for the knowledge and guidance of these skilled custodians of the nation's visual past.

Shaun and Ellen Berry, neighbors and friends, tolerated multiple invasions of their home, sometimes at inconvenient moments, when I needed their copier. They say their decision to move fifty miles north was not an effort to wean me from dependence on their machine; in any case, I have found it in their new quarters too, and their generous hospitality endures.

My obligation to the late Howard Quint is more than intellectual, although he is an unacknowledged collaborator in anything I write about working people. The collaboration of Henry K. Oliver, Carroll D. Wright, and Horace G. Wadlin, directors of the Massachusetts Bureau of Statistics of Labor, must not go unacknowledged; they gathered the evidence that comprises most of this book. Roger Haydon and the staff and anonymous reviewers of Cornell University Press suggested important stylistic and organizational revisions. Nick Salvatore, the editor of the series in which this volume appears, is both demanding and genial, a rare combination that has made working with him a pleasure and produced improvements for which my readers will be as grateful as I.

HENRY F. BEDFORD

New Castle, New Hampshire

Their Lives and Numbers

"The Labor Question"

Change now encompassed in such historical concepts as "industrial revolution," "new immigration," and "urbanization" seemed to many nineteenth-century Americans disorienting and dangerous. Social assumptions that had once unified communities, strengthened families, and reinforced the moral lessons of Protestant preachers and Poor Richard's *Almanac* became less certain in the face of obvious class divisions, ethnic diversity, wage-earning women and children, new faiths and ideas. Factories, labor unions, company stores, and monthly paydays required revision of ideals of personal independence, self-reliance, thrift, and ambition. The textile factories of Lowell, in the 1820s a symbol of national progress that had inspired lyrical optimism, provoked passages about "dark, Satanic mills" a half-century later.

By the 1870s and 1880s, economic and social trends that might earlier have been ignored as temporary or aberrational seemed likely to persist. Some Americans had always possessed more than others, but when the frontier was distant and desolate, those disparities seemed more permanent than in the early days of the republic. Although rising population was no new phenomenon, the immigrants that crowded the nation's cities differed both in degree and in kind from previous arrivals. The relative importance of agriculture diminished, and farmers, once revered as "the chosen people of God," became stereotypically embattled instead. Machinery made irrelevant skills that artisans and craftsmen had spent a lifetime perfecting and that had once differentiated them from laborers. Proliferating factories increased the productivity of women and children, even if they were exploited, thus fulfilling Alexander Hamilton's early vision.

The phrase "the labor question" recurs in contemporary discussion of these phenomena. The expression lumped together related manifestations of industrial development, a combination that conveyed interrelationship but did not clarify conflicting emphases and interpretations. Because the question confounded ethical, legal, social, and economic considerations, it was never singular, rarely articulated precisely, and not really a question at all. For some, it was a semantic convenience that simply admitted personal uncertainty in the face of perplexing change; for partisans, it was an effort to define issues in order to secure a congenial outcome to conflicts over power and policy. "The labor question" that employers raised differed considerably from that of workers attempting to form unions.

Industrial preeminence gave "the labor question" a special relevance in Massachusetts, which within the lifetime of many of its residents had become "one of the most heavily industralized territories on the face of the earth."[1] Textile mills, which multiplied across the Commonwealth after 1820, served as models for other industries. Machinery perfected before the Civil War moved production of boots and shoes out of small shops into large factories. Wartime demand for firearms, manufactured at the federal armory in Springfield, stimulated output of metals, machinery, and machine tools elsewhere in the state. Paper, barbed wire, furniture, and dozens of other industrial products became staples of the Massachusetts economy after the Civil War, sustained thousands of families, and attracted thousands more to the state in search of employment.

A large labor population, geographically concentrated, soon found political leadership. Wendell Phillips and Ben Butler, liberal Republicans and renegade Democrats, formed local political coalitions to seek industrial legislation, including a mandatory reduction in the hours of factory workers and enforceable restrictions on the employment of children. The Knights of St. Crispin, an organization of shoeworkers

---

1. Alexander Keyssar, *Out of Work: The First Century of Unemployment in Massachusetts.* (Cambridge: Cambridge University Press, 1986), 14.

1. Palmer, Massachusetts, textile mill, c. 1875. Courtesy of the Museum of American Textile History.

whose membership in Massachusetts reportedly reached forty thousand, sought a legislative charter in 1869. Opponents feared approval might imply that the state endorsed the union's effort to maintain the skills and compensation of its members by preventing employment of nonmembers.[2]

ESTABLISHING THE MASSACHUSETTS BUREAU OF STATISTICS OF LABOR

The General Court, as the Massachusetts legislature is formally styled, denied the Knights' petition. But political expediency required,

2. In *Beyond Equality* (New York: Vintage, 1967), 141, David Montgomery writes that the reported membership of the Knights was a considerable exaggeration. Although not directly relevant to the topic here, the sketch of Wendell Phillips in Richard Hofstadter, *The American Political Tradition* (New York: Knopf, 1948), remains worth reading.

as the first chief of the Bureau of Statistics of Labor later explained, "that something . . . be done for labor." So, two days before adjournment in 1869, with a hasty voice vote, legislators established an agency to soothe an increasingly restless labor constituency and to guide them toward a less controversial answer to the labor question than the one the Knights proposed. "The duties of such Bureau," the resolution read, "shall be to collect, assort, systematize and present in annual reports . . . statistical details relating to . . . labor in the Commonwealth, especially in its relations to the commercial, industrial, social, educational, and sanitary condition of the laboring classes."[3] About a month later, Governor William Claflin appointed Henry Kemble Oliver the bureau's director; within a week Oliver selected as his deputy George E. McNeill, an advocate of labor reform closely identified with efforts to reduce the hours of factory workers and a critic of the power employers exercised over employees through control of wages.[4]

"The growing interest in the labor question, the problem of the age," Oliver wrote in retrospect, "increased the demand for all works bearing upon the question, especially when they be of an official nature."[5] In one dense sentence, he avowed his intent to investigate widely:

> It was our duty to inquire into the very important subjects of the hours of labor, the wages, the savings, the manner of life at home and from home, the recreation, the culture, moral and mental, of the laborers, and the influence of the several kinds of labor upon their health of body and brain, not ignoring the subjects of cooperation, strikes, trades-unions, and the general relations of capital and labor, with such matters relating to labor and labor legislation, here and abroad, as we might be able to gather; so that the actual status . . . of the laboring men, women, and children of Massachusetts might be ascertained and be set forth to the legislature and people of the state.[6]

3. Massachusetts Bureau of Statistics of Labor (hereafter MBLS), *Report* (1869), 5.
4. See Wendell D. MacDonald, "The Early History of Labor Statistics in the United States," *Labor History* 13:2 (1972), 267–78, and David Roediger, "Ira Steward and the Anti-Slavery Origins of American Eight-Hour Theory," *Labor History* 27:3 (1986), 410–26. George E. McNeill edited *The Labor Movement* (Boston: A. W. Bridgman, 1887) and became actively engaged in the movement himself. For a brief account of the first years of the bureau, see MBLS, *Fourth Annual Report* (1873), 7–41.
5. MBLS, *Fourth Annual Report* (1873), 5.
6. MBLS, *Report* (1869), 7.

State officials probably had a less expansive view of Oliver's responsibility; in any case, they did not endow the new agency generously. Legislators set modest salaries for Oliver and McNeill and added five thousand dollars for the office's expenses. The attorney-general told Oliver that he had no authority to compel testimony from anyone and that he could not require submission of documents. The state's manufacturers at first refused to respond to the bureau's inquiries, pleading insufficient time to prepare detailed reports; later their association dropped the pretense of cooperation and urged the General Court to cut off the bureau's funding. Dissatisfied with the substitution of study for substantive legislation, even labor reformers criticized the bureau. Members of the Knights of St. Crispin looked at his agency, Oliver noted, "perhaps as an enemy in disguise" and submitted fictitious data to discredit his research.[7]

Established amid conflicting expectations in an impulsive political compromise, the bureau had no supportive constituency. Eager to end a legislative session with a conciliatory gesture to working people, elected politicians gladly delegated the labor question to appointed bureaucrats. Manufacturers, reformers, and labor organizations already had answers, which they thought the state should adopt rather than study. At the start, the nation's first Bureau of Statistics of Labor seemed more likely to serve as a model of institutional futility than as a prototype. Indeed, four years after the agency's founding, the Massachusetts Senate voted to eliminate its appropriation, and only the refusal of the House to concur preserved an insecure mandate.

The bureau's persistence and eventual significance, in the absence of much early support, suggests both the intrinsic importance of the labor question and the public's interest in it. Newspapers popularized the bureau's reports, which went out of print soon after they were released. Lack of support in the Massachusetts Senate did not faithfully reflect a popular appetite for data, however imperfect, that might reduce widespread fear of slum-bred pestilence and disorder and inform debate about the gap between traditional egalitarian ideals and the reality that emerged in the bureau's reports. If that was no full-throated political

7. MBLS, *Fourth Annual Report* (1873), 9, 10, 14, 17.

demand, it did suffice to sustain the agency until it earned more enthusiastic backing. For students of American industralization and for people caught up in the process, the bureau's survival was, and is, a fortuitous, though not quite accidental, boon.

THE BUREAU'S DIRECTORS

Carroll D. Wright, the second and best-known director of the Massachusetts bureau and later the United States commissioner of labor, spent most of a professional career asking "the labor question" and seeking answers to it. Although he investigated topics of great concern to industrial workers, Wright had no personal experience with factories and cultivated a scholarly detachment from the data he collected. His research and the authoritative tables he compiled, he believed, would not themselves solve the riddles of industrial change. A solution would require not only the objective facts in his reports but the wisdom of classical economists, the insights of scientific socialism, and the applied ethnics of the New Testament. And any fully persuasive answer would depend on a compelling notion of social justice.[8]

Henry K. Oliver needed no philosophical help with a definition of justice, or at least he knew its opposite when he encountered it. Born when the century began, Oliver had several careers before 1869, when Governor Claflin selected him to direct the first official investigations of the life and work of "the working classes." Oliver had taught and managed schools, founded an academy for young women, and served the state as adjutant-general during the Mexican War and treasurer during the Civil War. He had also equipped and managed a profitable textile mill in Lawrence until ungrateful owners dismissed him because, according to local rumor, he coddled employees. For two years before he assumed his post at the bureau, he toured the state's factories to observe compliance—or, more frequently, noncompliance—with legislation requiring employees under the age of fourteen to meet

8. Carroll D. Wright, *Some Ethical Phases of the Labor Question* (Boston: American Unitarian Association, 1902), 17.

educational requirements. Oliver knew industrial injustice firsthand.[9]

And he had an empathy for working people that belied his station in life, and an energy that belied his seventy years. Reviewing his first *Report*, the *Nation* observed that Oliver was evidently "in warm sympathy with the workingmen, and from conviction inclined to favor them."[10] He depicted appalling conditions in factories, whose owners he named, and in tenements, whose landlords he identified. He demolished the myth that industrial workers had fortunes on deposit in the state's savings banks and disclosed extensive use of these institutions as "storehouses" where wealthy people "preserved their plenty out of the reach of taxation." His investigation irritated the Massachusetts Senate's Committee on Banking, all of whose members had associations with savings banks; it mounted its own whitewashing inquiry. Critics charged that, in this and other instances, Oliver's conclusions stemmed from partisanship rather than research and that the slanted views of McNeill and occasional unpaid contributors to the bureau's reports overshadowed the fragmentary evidence collected by the investigative staff. To calm the continuing uproar, Governor William Washburn decided in 1873 to replace Oliver with Carroll Wright. Oliver returned to Salem, where he was elected mayor and embarked on another career as a composer and conductor of sacred choral music.[11]

Born forty years after Oliver and reared in small New England towns where his father filled Universalist pastorates, Wright shared many of his predecessor's attitudes; he also brought to industrial change the outlook of another, later generation. Wright's first paid job was in a village school; his last was as president of a college. He enlisted as a private early in the Civil War; two years later, he was a colonel in the same regiment. A failed retailer after Appomattox, he went on to success as a patent attorney. Twice elected to the Massachusetts Senate, where he served from 1871 to 1873 and voted against efforts to limit the daily and weekly hours of factory workers, he was well aware of the political tempest Oliver had provoked. The new director seemed

9. See MBLS, *Seventeenth Annual Report* (1886), 3–47, for a memorial sketch of Oliver by Rev. Jesse Jones, who contributed occasional pieces to early publications of the bureau.

10. *Nation*, June 8, 1871, 398.

11. MBLS, *Seventeenth Annual Report* (1886), 28, 33, 41.

the personification of folklore about opportunity and unsympathetic to the aspirations of industrial labor.[12]

Yet if Wright had unquestionably done well, like Oliver he also intended to do good. His personal view was that the golden rule applied to problematic economic conditions; Wright believed in a pragmatic Christianity that was more concerned with "the good to be done and the way to do it" than with doctrine. "A just distribution of profits," he wrote, depended less on "purely economical conditions" than on "habits of frugality, temperance, good morals, sanitary conditions, educational privileges, and various forces of a moral nature."[13] Economic justice, therefore, required not only responsible employers but also employees who behaved in socially approved ways. In addition, Wright's sentence seems to imply that prudent, thrifty, sober, diligent, clean laborers could somehow secure an equitable share of factory output through their own conduct. That notion, of course, did not subvert received middle-class American wisdom at the time and foreshadowed the social attitudes of reformers who, a decade or two later, would be called "progressive."

For Wright, as for those progressives, economic questions, including the labor question, had an ethical dimension. In a book published after he left Massachusetts, Wright noted that the inquiry involved "the great struggle of humanity to secure a higher standard of living, to be able to indulge in the spiritual affairs of life." Thus, possession of more consumer goods alone did not denote "a higher standard of living," which also required the opportunity to develop a "spiritual . . . life." The latter phrase encompassed participation in the uplifting activities of family and community in addition to pious thoughts and deeds. Anxious not to be misread as simply an advocate of higher wages and greater leisure, Wright kept reexplaining. He used the term "labor question" in two ways, he wrote: "in a limited sense as embracing the wants of the wage-laborer," and more generally to connote a "just and equitable distribution of profits, or the products of capital and labor."

---

12. See the biographical sketches of Wright by Horace G. Wadlin in MBLS, *Fortieth Annual Report* (1909), 359–400, and James Leiby, *Carroll Wright and Labor Reform* (Cambridge: Harvard University Press, 1960).

13. Wright, *Ethical Phases*, 26–27.

In grappling with the problem, political economists must "not confine [themselves] to wealth alone" but consider family—"the relations of the sexes, marriage and divorce, the position of women, and the education and employment of children"—and the proper role of the state as well.

> These considerations . . . will be demanded to answer the question constantly put, how labor may be rendered more generally attractive and remunerative, without impairing the efficiency of capital, so that all the workers of society may have their proper share in the distribution of profits. This I conceive to be the true labor question of today.[14]

To remark Wright's difficulty articulating concisely the inquiry that was at the core of his professional career is not to belittle him or demean his work. Instead, Wright's continuing effort to find the right words reflects the pace of change in the late nineteenth century and the perplexed reaction to that change among able, informed, sympathetic people, who believed that, with enough facts, the problem was susceptible of solution. The reports Wright produced in Massachusetts from 1874 to 1887 show both his fuzzy formulation of the labor question and his refusal to answer it with simplistic clichés from either end of the ideological spectrum.

Those reports also reveal Wright's progressive faith that an enlightened public would act responsibly when provided reliable documentation of industrial conditions. Wright consciously differentiated himself from his predecessor's partisanship. "It is not our business," he wrote in 1889, "to seek or offer solutions" but "to collect information and present it impartially and fearlessly to the public." He saw himself as a judicious scholar—not isolated from society, since the evidence he compiled had immediate relevance, but not an engaged advocate either.[15] Although he did not ordinarily exhort his readers, he did seek more of them than the usual audience for government documents. He presented his research in lectures, recycled those talks in articles, and collected his articles in books, including the *Outline of Practical Soci-*

---

14. *Ibid.*, 25, 26, 38, 29.
15. MBLS, *Fortieth Annual Report* (1909), 369, 388–90.

ology, a title that named his intellectual discipline and affirmed its relevance.[16] In 1902, scholarship became his profession when Wright left his post as U.S. commissioner of labor to return to Massachusetts as president of Clark College in Worcester.

Progressive reformers in the early twentieth century might have used Wright's work as a model. It furnished facts, which a receptive audience then relied on to require factory inspection, to change the system of convict labor, and to begin defining employers' liability for industrial accidents.[17] None of this legislation conformed precisely to the program of those who claimed to represent working people. But Wright thought he spoke for a broad public, rather than some fraction of it, and he attempted to avoid identification with any interest group. Early in his career, Wright probably thought that the demands of unions contravened the general interest. Although Oliver had chronicled the expansion of the Knights of St. Crispin and noted early efforts of other workers' organizations, Wright subordinated unions to the point of near invisibility. The twenty-year index for 1889, which covered the period of greatest notoriety of the Knights of Labor, contains no entry for that body.[18] The founding pangs of the American Federation of Labor in the 1880s and 1890s also went essentially unrecorded. Sensitive to Wright's apparent indifference, organized labor did not promote his nomination in 1885 as the first U.S. commissioner of labor.

Wright thought of the numbers he collected as only "imperfect evidence of the facts," wrote Horace Wadlin, Wright's long-time deputy and successor. Until new and better data were available, however, both Wright and Wadlin believed their tables provided the best approximation of "the facts" that impartial researchers could provide.[19]

That tentativeness may have been partly a function of scholarly temperament; it may also have been responsive to the critiques of other

16. Carroll D. Wright, *Outline of Practical Sociology* (New York: Longmans, Green, 1890).

17. MBLS, *Fortieth Annual Report* (1909), 375.

18. The Bureau of Statistics of Labor and Industry in New Jersey, by contrast, demonstrated considerable interest in the development of the Knights of Labor. See Kim Voss, *The Making of American Exceptionalism* (Ithaca: Cornell University Press, 1993), 129.

19. MBLS, *Fortieth Annual Report* (1909), 375.

scholars. Whereas Oliver's detractors focused on his deductions and recommendations, Wright's tended to challenge his statistical method. Of course, Wright provided fewer conclusions than had Oliver to which critics might take exception, so methodological objections may simply have seemed the best tactic for deflecting unwelcome interference with matters employers believed were their prerogatives. But reputable social scientists such as Francis Walker, an economist from whom Wright himself sometimes sought guidance, once remarked that appropriations for collections of labor statistics would have been better spent to train shrewder analysts, who could correct "great errors of judgement and sometimes monstrous errors in conclusions."[20]

However statistically naive, Wright's discussion of the labor question was more congenial to a generation attuned to practical speech than Oliver's moral outrage. Born in 1800, at the end of John Adams's presidency, Oliver had written with the conviction and urgency of early New England divines, certain of premises, disdaining dissent, impatient to accomplish what was perceived to be duty. Wright's sense of duty was no less acute, but it developed in another time and had another emphasis. Still a federal official during Theodore Roosevelt's administration, Wright saw duty as procedural—the efficient collection of verified facts to serve as a basis for substantive reform. Horace Wadlin's later, unfair, characterization revealed the generational gulf between his two predecessors. For labor partisans such as Oliver, Wadlin wrote, "the thing to do was to choose your side, and then bring forward such figures as were needed to give verisimilitude to a bald and unconvincing narrative, leaving out or carefully obscuring all others."[21]

But the contrast between individuals and generations ought not to be that sharply drawn. Wright and Oliver had the same legislative charter and confronted similar professional problems. Neither limited his inquiry to the conditions of employment; both investigated other dimensions in the lives of working people. Shifting economic and political circumstances, and differing personalities and interpretive perspectives, sometimes obscured the continuity in the bureau's work. Where Oliver tended to blame landlords for the condition of tenements,

20. Leiby, *Wright*, 85.
21. MBLS, *Fortieth Annual Report* (1909), 368.

for instance, Wright suggested ways that tenants might improve their rented surroundings. Yet the two directors clearly agreed that working families deserved better quarters. Differences of means and of style are not differences of ends.

And whatever their disparity in age, Oliver, Wright, and Wadlin all believed that an informed American public shared their hope for and would act to advance the democratic society they idealized. If, as they toured the strange urban and industrial landscape in their own land, the bureau chiefs did not tote identical cultural baggage, they all did carry the moral aphorisms of the preindustrial republic and the ideals associated with the Civil War; all knew the uncertainty and dislocation that followed. Older and more impatient, Oliver felt called to urge and persuade. Younger and more detached, Wright and Wadlin tried to document conditions they believed society would want to correct through changed behavior or, occasionally, through law.[22]

TENSION IN THREE TEXTILE CITIES: AN EXAMPLE OF THE BUREAU'S RESEARCH

In a memorial written after Wright's death in 1909, Wadlin packed into a single sentence sixteen topics of his mentor's research:

> The education of working children, the condition of working men's families, the social life of working men, illiteracy, the growth of manufactures in the Commonwealth, profits and wages, the relation of intemperance to pauperism and crime, the question of divorce, cooperation and profit-sharing, prices and cost of living, employers' liability, early factory labor in New England, the condition of working girls in Boston, Sunday labor, factory legislation, strikes and lockouts—these and other subjects were treated in elaborate investigations. . . .

Wadlin's list had interesting omissions: immigration, urban congestion, class-based politics, and the development of unions, for example, some of which Wright had examined at least obliquely. With these

22. Leiby, *Wright*, 20, 100–101, 145; Wright, *Outline*, 423; Wright, *Ethical Phases*, chap. 3, passim.

additions, the inventory would serve as a satisfactory guide to the work of labor historians in the twentieth century. In the same sentence, Wadlin also described Wright's investigative technique, "which began with careful preparation of schedules of inquiry, followed by intelligent agency work in the field, the final tabulation of results, and their presentation in lucid statistical tables accompanied by sufficient textual analysis."[23]

An essay Wright wrote for the bureau's 1882 report illustrates Wadlin's expansive claim. A comparative study of labor unrest in Fall River, Lowell, and Lawrence reveals Wright's meticulous preparation and some of the defects of his research design, shows his reluctance to generalize from the broad range of data he believed pertinent to this rather specific inquiry, and demonstrates the relevance of his work for later historical analysis. He began at the request of a lawmaker who wanted to know why Fall River was "in constant turmoil" while the other two textile centers were "quiet." Wright's response, which required more than two hundred published pages, affords an instructive example of his treatment of the labor question and of the varied statistics he believed would help answer it.

His evidence came from replies to detailed questionnaires Wright prepared for the bureau's interviewers. What sort of individuals, Wright asked, worked in the mills of each city and what were their tasks? How old were they? Male or female? What were their family circumstances? Where were they and their parents born? How long had they worked in factories and what had their experiences been? Could they read and write? In what condition were their homes, and how did they use the leisure their jobs afforded? How well did they live, and how had their standard of living changed over time? What were their relationships with employers, supervisors, fellow workers, labor unions, neighbors?

Wright suspected that the surrounding environment—the uniqueness of each city and the distinctive features of particular factories—as well as the characteristics of the labor force, might differentiate Fall River from Lowell and Lawrence. He asked for information about

23. MBLS, *Fortieth Annual Report* (1909), 374.

2. Lawrence tenements, c. 1900. Courtesy of the Museum of American Textile History.

schools and libraries and parks and clubs, about the credit arrangements of retailers, the sanitation of streets, and the enforcement of laws. Was, for instance, the state law observed that limited to ten the number of hours of mill work for women and children? Were there elevators in factories, and fire escapes, and decent light and ventilation? Would managers discuss the speed and safety of machinery, or the hours of operation, with employees or their representatives? What were the owners' profits, insofar as they could be gauged?

Finally, Wright told his investigators to ask "leading citizens" in all three cities to explain strife in Fall River and its relative absence in Lowell and Lawrence. These dignitaries included city officials, physicians, lawyers, bankers, merchants, several dozen clergymen, and a few individuals Wright could categorize only as "well-informed parties." Apparently, teachers, policemen, saloon keepers, newspaper reporters, union officers, and almost all women failed to qualify as either "leading" or "well-informed."

Wright's choice of informants, and his questions as well, betrayed little challenge to economic and social orthodoxy. Like muckraking journalists later, Wright documented specific situations and abuses, not systemic failures. The comparative nature of his investigation implied that Fall River ought to imitate Lowell and Lawrence and that local reform would suffice.

Nor did he give the General Court the prescriptive guidance Henry K. Oliver might have offered. Less concerned than Oliver that his work have a legislative outcome, Wright listed, without much editorial elaboration, the "direct" and "indirect" causes of contrasting labor relations in the three cities. He thought industry in Fall River had developed too quickly and that shoddy tenements, unassimilated immigrants, inept management, and insecure capitalization could be traced to rapid growth. The city's factories also produced less expensive cloth than was the case in Lowell and Lawrence. "We manufacture cheap goods," one mill owner remarked, and we hire "cheap help to make them." Varied production in the other two cities probably provided workers more opportunity to develop skills and earn higher wages, thereby reducing labor's discontent. Wright did not emphasize wages, however, and used the word only once, almost incidentally, in his treatment of causation.

He did discuss class conflict, though he avoided the term and clearly found the phenomenon distasteful. Rivalry was probably endemic and easily explained: "The mills are run to make money; the operatives work for money."

Each class wishes to get as much as it can. The manufacturers are often served by unscrupulous superintendents and overseers; the operatives are often deceived by false teachers. Both sides are prone to look upon antagonism as a natural and healthful state.

"This spirit," Wright continued, "has been shown more in Fall River than in the other cities under consideration." A strike in 1871, for instance, probably stemmed from the unwillingness of either party to focus on anything other than "money"—"profits on the one hand and existence on the other." Although Wright did not hesitate to draw what he called "ethical" distinctions in his later work, in this instance he apparently saw no important difference between "profits" and "existence."[24]

Wright offered his legislative correspondent no statutory remedy for social conflict. Indeed, he thought, the facts he collected might lead to "an awakening of honest public sentiment" that could accomplish more than law. Enlightened individuals, Wright hoped, might inspire a moral revolution through examples of progressive industrial behavior that proved infectious. Owners should take first steps voluntarily; workers would reciprocate. Until the moral millennium arrived, if he had to suggest one legislative response to his research, Wright thought public health officials needed more power: "Let the state declare by its Board of Health that families shall not live in filth."[25]

That anticlimactic recommendation did not mollify an angry Fall River Board of Trade, which dismissed the bureau's study as "worthless rubbish." The assessment was defensive hyperbole, but the comparative question that precipitated Wright's inquiry was indeed flawed. Economic hard times in the next few years did not invalidate the premise that industrial tension in Fall River exceeded that in Lowell and Lawrence. The incidence of strikes was greater in Fall River from 1881 through 1886 than in the other two cities combined, and the total number of Fall River employees involved was also larger. But the cost to strikers in lost wages in Lawrence was nearly double the total for Fall River, and the postulated contrast that had precipitated Wright's work was transient.[26]

24. MBLS, *Thirteenth Annual Report* (1882), 412.
25. *Ibid.*, 413–14.
26. Philip T. Silvia, Jr., "The Position of Workers in a Textile Community : Fall River

The sources Wright relied on could also have been improved. His staff talked to almost as many clergymen as workers and their families—each group constituted about a fifth of his informants. In spite of that sampling bias and his own emphasis on ethical Christianity, he did not find that organized religion promoted harmonious communities and social justice. Clerics seemed sure that churches could advance those goals, but those statements owed more to conventional New England piety than to the reality in their parishes. The bureau's published reports made a more convincing case for the irrelevance of churches than for their influence; working people were said to be too exhausted to attend religious service or to lack appropriate clothing or funds for pew rent. Those explanations, or excuses, may have applied more directly to Protestant than to Roman Catholic parishioners; French Canadian and Irish Catholics were often excepted from observations that working people were not regular in their religious observance. The questions of the bureau's interviewers may have disclosed the suspicion of Catholics that pervaded Protestant New England in the nineteenth century; cautious replies to loaded queries perhaps interfered with a more accurate estimate of religious influence.[27]

The influence of the nation's secular creed, on the other hand, was not in doubt. Wright's text rarely displayed dissent from conventional notions of appropriate behavior, prevailing assumptions about property rights and gender roles, and enduring myths of economic individualism. Descriptions of workers' housing, for example, illustrated the popularly assumed link between cleanliness and virtue. Differing standards for men and women, and class conflicts, were facts of life, rather than conditions to be deplored and altered. Employers, not workers or the public or politicians, regulated wages and profits. The economic orthodoxy of Wright's sources shaped both their analytical comments and their suggested reforms: some thought improved environment— cleaner, safer, with more "healthy" diversions and fewer tempting dissipations—would increase the number of public-spirited individuals

---

in the Early 1880s," *Labor History* 16:2 (1975), 240; MBLS, *Twentieth Annual Report* (1889), 102–3.

27. MBLS, *Thirteenth Annual Report* (1882), 266–67.

and promote civic peace; others believed individuals had to change first and then improve their surroundings.

Temperance was the first reform to come to the minds of most of the bureau's respondents. The usual view was that workers ought simply to stop using alcohol, an obvious step toward more constructive use of leisure, enhanced family life, and less wasteful expenditure. Only occasionally did the realization surface that the prospect of relaxed companionship and a need to escape dreary housing might enhance the attraction of neighborly taverns. Established Americans also worried that foreign languages, ethnic organizations, and Roman Catholic churches and schools signified unwillingness on the part of immigrants to adopt conventional ways. Since most Massachusetts factory workers were immigrants or the children of immigrants, civic reformers proposed broadly conceived campaigns of public education to be conducted through churches, lodges, and libraries, to lead newcomers to traditional values and customs. Whether the topic was drink, ritual, or belief, the behavior to be modified was that of working people, rather than that of their employers.

Yet the most articulate attacks on the "wage system," the thoroughly traditional method of regulating employer-employee relations, came from middle-class critics. Wages, the indictment ran, converted independent artisans and entrepreneurs to animate machines, and it was a Lowell clergyman, not an immigrant spinner, who protested that employers regarded workers as "a wheel or a pin to a machine," or "a mule or a spindle . . . , and no more." He did not deny, the minister continued, "frequent or general kindness and fairness on the part of officials personally: it is the fault of the system, not of any man or set of men."[28]

Mill hands had a narrower view. They tended to complain of unyielding, arrogant men, not economic or legal systems, of personal power rather than larger principles. Nearly every worker interviewed resented the prevailing attitude that leaving a job was the best remedy for discontent. "There is no redress here, no appeal," said a Fall River operative: "The by-word is, 'if you don't like it, get out!'" A local

28. *Ibid.*, 378.

physician concurred: "There is intimidation, cruelty, and dishonesty practised [*sic*] and winked at here, that should call for the execration of all just men." The treasurer of a Fall River corporation affirmed that management would never consider arbitration or conciliation. Occasional paternalistic exceptions, which seemed to occur most frequently in Lawrence, simply emphasized the usually rigid managerial stance.[29] Although David Montgomery and other historians have written of workers elsewhere who enjoyed considerable autonomy, the Massachusetts workers who talked with the bureau's investigators felt they had little control over industrial processes or even over their own jobs.[30]

Directors of the Massachusetts Bureau of Statistics of Labor evidently shared that view. Most of Oliver's research concluded that somebody in authority ought to do something for working people, who apparently could not put things right for themselves. More clinical (they would have said "objective"), Wright and Wadlin presented immigrants and the hardworking poor as subjects for the enlightened concern of high-minded Americans who shunned slums, sweatshops, saloons, and immigrant churches. Whereas Oliver explicitly pleaded for change, the work of his successors implied that a sensitized public would impose it, as progressives did early in the twentieth century. In either case, workers did not themselves control the remedial agenda, and the bureau betrayed the unintentional condescension that often taints American reform.

That defect does not invalidate the volumes of data the bureau collected. As the example of Wright's work on Lowell, Lawrence, and Fall River reveals, those data are an extraordinary resource for contemporary students of nineteenth-century American workers. Although Wright, in particular, had little interest in trade unions, he shared unions' concerns about wages, hours, working conditions, strikes, lockouts, and violence. Curious not only about the work people did and

---

29. *Ibid.*, 338, 396, 399, 343–44.
30. See, e.g., David Montgomery, *Workers' Control in America* (Cambridge: Cambridge University Press, 1979), and *The Fall of the House of Labor* (Cambridge: Cambridge University Press, 1987); but see also Isaac Cohen, "Workers' Control in the Cotton Industry: A Comparative Study of British and American Mule Spinning," *Labor History* 26:1 (1986), 53–85.

3. Industrial Boston, c. 1900. Courtesy of the Boston Public Library, Print Department.

the products they made, he also probed their private lives: family, leisure, reading, worship, ethnic associations, and bad habits. Whatever the methodological myopia of Oliver, Wright, and Wadlin, they viewed the labor question broadly, gave industrial workers an attentive ear, and published what they learned.

The Old Labor History and the New

The result has great relevance for twentieth-century labor historians of both the "old" and the "new" schools. Distinctions between these two interpretive emphases can be exaggerated, and to assign all scholarship on industrial labor one label or the other is to oversimplify. In general, those who wrote labor history in the first half of the century—the "old" labor history—emphasized skilled workers, their leaders, and their unions. The "new" labor history concentrates less on institutional arrangements in unions and factories than on the personal accommodations that working people achieved in their families and communities.[31]

John R. Commons, usually acknowledged as the dean of American labor studies, outlined the reserach field for the "old" labor history in his scholarship and in his teaching at the University of Wisconsin. Selig Perlman, Philip Taft, and others of the Wisconsin school argued that labor accepted the basic tenets of American free enterprise and aspired simply to enlarge the workers' share of the products of industrial capitalism. Strikes and labor politics, in this view, were not examples of class warfare as Marxists use the term, or even efforts to make major changes in the nation's economic system. Rather, they were attempts to raise wages, reduce hours, improve conditions in the

---

31. This historical debate may be sampled in almost any issue of *Labor History*. Relatively recent historiographical articles in that quarterly include Robert H. Zieger, "Workers and Scholars: Recent Trends in American Labor Historiography," 13:2 (1972), 245–66, David Brody, "The Old Labor History and the New," 20:1 (1979), 111–26; David Montgomery, "To Study the People: The American Working Class," 21:4 (1980), 485–512; Robert Ozanne, "Trends in American Labor History," 21:4 (1980), 513–21; Melvyn S. Dubofsky, "Give Us That Old Time Labor History: Philip S. Foner and the American Worker," 26:1 (1986), 118–37; Howard Kimeldorf, "Bringing Unions Back In (Or Why We Need a New Old Labor History)," 32:1 (1991), 91–103; and the symposium on David Montgomery's *Fall of the House of Labor*, 30:1 (1989), 93–137. Other important articles include Leon Fink, "The New Labor History and the Powers of Historical Pessimism," *Journal of American History* 75:1 (1988), 115–36, and the subsequent remarks of several commentators; T. J. Jackson Lears, "The Concept of Cultural Hegemony: Problems and Possibilities," *American Historical Review* 90:3 (1985), 567–93; John Patrick Diggins, "Comrades and Citizens: New Mythologies in American Historiography," *American Historical Review* 90:3 (1985), 614–49; and Ira Berlin's "Introduction" to *Power and Culture: Essays on the American Working Class* (New York: Pantheon, 1987). Michael Kammen has edited *The Past Before Us* (Ithaca: Cornell University Press, 1980), which includes articles on social history by Peter N. Stearns and on labor history by David Brody. Michael H. Frisch and Daniel J. Walkowitz have edited examples of the new labor history in *Working Class America* (Urbana: University of Illinois Press, 1983), and J. Carroll Moody and Alice Kessler-Harris have edited efforts to reach a synthesis in *Perspectives on American Labor History* (DeKalb: Northern Illinois University Press, 1989); on the latter volume, see Melvyn S. Dubofsky, "Lost in a Fog: Labor Historians' Unrequited Search for a Synthesis," *Labor History* 32:2 (1991), 295–300.

shop, and pierce the perceived indifference or hostility of the nation's political elite.[32]

Philip S. Foner, who began his multivolume *History of the Labor Movement in the United States* in 1947, thought that interpretation too tepid. Like the bureau's Henry K. Oliver decades before, Foner did not disguise his sympathy with workers, among whom he discovered more women and racial minorities than had most of his predecessors. If Foner's research was more inclusive, however, it seemed still to emphasize conflicts, contracts, and conditions in the factories. Those topics, of course, had preoccupied the "old" labor historians as well, but Foner provided a new more class-conscious, interpretive slant.[33]

Influenced by and participating in the recent explosion of social history, "new" labor historians have concentrated on finite geographical areas, limited chronological periods, and specific factories or industries. These sharply focused inquiries reach the experiences of ordinary working people in their homes and jobs. Such scholarship, writes one of its most important practitioners, examines the "social relations peculiar to industrial production," the "social consciousness created by people to cope with those relationships," and the "impact of workers' consciousness and activities on the rest of society." David Montgomery then summarizes his own list: "work, culture, and the working class presence," a phrase that echoes the title of a collection of Herbert Gutman's essays: *Work, Culture, and Society in Industrializing America.*[34] Gutman

32. See John R. Commons, *A Documentary History of American Industrial Society* (Cleveland: A. H. Clark, 1910–11), and his *History of Labour in the United States* (New York: Macmillan, 1918); Selig Perlman, *A History of Trade Unionism in the United States* (New York: Macmillan, 1922), and *A Theory of the Labor Movement* (New York: Macmillan, 1928); and Philip Taft's two-volume history of the American Federation of Labor (New York: Harper, 1957–59). Leon Fink examines the work of early labor historians in "'Intellectuals' versus 'Workers,'" *American Historical Review* 96:2 (1991), 395–421; see also Ellen Fitzpatrick's comment (pp. 422–28), which points out that the "old" labor historians were not of one mind and that the group included scholars not mentioned here.

33. Philip S. Foner, *History of the Labor Movement in the United States* (New York: International Publishers, 1947). Sally Miller, in "Philip Foner and 'Integrating' Women into Labor History and African-American History," *Labor History* 33:4 (1992), 456–69, argues that Foner's consideration of women, especially African American women, is not entirely adequate.

34. Montgomery, "To Study the People," 485; Herbert G. Gutman, *Work, Culture, and Society in Industrializing America* (New York: Knopf, 1976).

believed workers were "actors, not just . . . victims—creative beings, not statistics— . . . bearers of their own resilient 'cultural baggage,' which enabled them to survive and resist the impositions of nineteenth century capitalism."[35]

The careful studies reflecting this enlarged view of the past of American workers still lack a persuasive synthesis comparable to E. P. Thompson's *Making of the English Working Class*.[36] The absence of a unifying thesis is due in part to the bewildering variety of the American industrial experience; the contrasts Carroll Wright documented in three textile cities make generalizations about just one industry in only one state difficult. Interpretive differences also persist, though few deny the central importance of such topics as family, ethnicity, community, gender, and religious tradition, which Gutman and others have explored. John Patrick Diggins, for instance, admits that those social institutions shaped the behavior and values of nineteenth-century American workers. But as did earlier labor historians, Diggins insists that traditional social and economic individualism was at the core of what working people learned. Occasional class-conscious talk, he says, had almost no behavioral consequence. Nineteenth-century workers, in Diggins's view, were poor people with a middle-class outlook on life.[37]

A sampling of the nineteenth-century reports of the Massachusetts Bureau of Statistics of Labor cannot illustrate every nuance of this historiographical controversy and will not resolve it. Although Henry K. Oliver, Carroll D. Wright, Horace Wadlin, and their successors were conscious of the historical importance of their work, they could not imagine the interpretive lenses through which it might be glimpsed. Conventional nineteenth-century social and economic vertities limited their view; they had only primitive statistical tools and none of the analytical insights of modern social science. But the numbers and the oral testimony the bureau gathered, the material on gender and

35. Montgomery, "To Study the People," 501; see also his "Gutman's Agenda for Future Historical Research," *Labor History* 29:3 (1988), 300–301.

36. E. P. Thompson, *The Making of the English Working Class* (London: Gollancz, 1963). For one effort to achieve an American synthesis, see the volume edited by Moody and Kessler-Harris and the essay by Dubofsky cited in note 31 above.

37. John P. Diggins, "The Misuses of Gramsci," *Journal of American History* 75:1 (1988), 141–45.

ethnicity, and the investigation of the industrial context foreshadow many of the interests of new labor historians and furnish an evidential base for their scholarship. In addition, the bureau's directors were sympathetically disposed toward the conditions and people they studied and were extraordinarily diligent. They followed a policy of "judicious investigation and fearless publication." Their work provides a substantial body of evidence for those interested in trying to recreate and understand the circumstances in which people lived and worked at a time of staggering social and economic change.[38]

38. MacDonald, "Early History of Labor Statistics," 274.

CHAPTER ONE

In Their Own Words

Henry K. Oliver wanted to rely on employers for much of the data he began to gather in 1869. Payroll records, for instance, could provide otherwise unavailable statistics about wages, hours, and income. Accounts at company-owned stores and rental records of company-owned housing would reveal much about the cost and standard of living of captive consumers. Supervisors could describe the skills, schooling, ethnic backgrounds, and family circumstances of workers whom they directed. The cooperation of employers would make the initial studies of the Bureau of Statistics of Labor more inclusive and reliable, enhance the agency's efficiency, and help stretch its small budget.

But the first responses the bureau elicited from owners and managers, if they responded at all, were dilatory and grudging. The agency had no authority to subpoena records or testimony, and proprietors declined to disclose voluntarily information that might assist competitors or document illegal personnel practices. Their suspicion moderated and they provided somewhat more information after Carroll Wright replaced Oliver in 1873, but even those later submissions were, as Wright himself observed, only one version of a story that had at least two. To achieve a balanced basis for public policy, the bureau actively sought written and oral contact with workers themselves.

The experience of individuals and their opinions about industrial change gave a personal dimension to the more comprehensive statistical information employers were asked to supply. The bureau did not quite claim that employees' remarks were valid for taciturn comrades, but it did imply that they were somehow representative. In 1879, for instance, Wright doubted that "more 'different' opinions would have been advanced" had the bureau received thousands of additional returns. Even if they expressed only idiosyncratic reactions, Oliver noted in his 1871 introduction to reports of scores of conversations, the material warranted "careful perusal."[1]

Oliver's assertion was uncharacteristically modest and undeniably correct. Leading questions and the encouragement of sympathetic interviewers may have prompted some answers, and the editors may have corrected syntax and spelling. But the bureau offered skeptics the opportunity to review the conversations it reproduced, a policy that probably minimized editorial intervention. Diaries, correspondence, or contemporary oral reminiscence, to be sure, might furnish more direct, firsthand evidence of industrial conditions than did the bureau's publications, though such material is scarce and no more assuredly typical. The bureau located literate and articulate factory workers, gave them a forum, and allowed readers—then and later—a rare glimpse of industrial change from an employee's point of view.

The first selections here come from Oliver's report for 1871. Appropriately, several of the narratives derive from interviews with shoeworkers, among whom resistance to factory regimentation was fierce and widespread. Machinery introduced before the Civil War had eroded the skill and independence of entrepreneurs, who had once controlled the design, manufacture, and marketing of footgear. They attempted to protect their income and status and to avoid becoming interchangeable human parts of an industrial process by forming the Knights of St. Crispin, a secret union that tried to limit entry to the trade. The shoemakers' fear that their most prosperous days might be behind them probably colored their descriptions of the Commonwealth's shoe factories.[2]

1. MBLS, *Second Annual Report* (1871), 570; *Tenth Annual Report* (1879), 104.
2. Scholarship about the shoe industry in Massachusetts includes Mary H. Blewett, *Men, Women, and Work* (Urbana: University of Illinois Press, 1988); John T. Cumbler, *Working-Class Community in Industrial America* (Westport, Conn.: Greenwood, 1979); and Alan Dawley, *Class and Community: The Industrial Revolution in Lynn* (Cambridge: Harvard University Press, 1976).

The final selection in this section, by a journeyman mechanic, is less personal than the other accounts. Instead of describing his own home and job, he reflected on the maldistribution of wealth that seemed to him characteristic of American society.

G., boot cutter, 40 years old. ... About all the working people around him are in debt, and many have been reduced to a condition of want and absolute dependence. Cause, low wages. They don't go to church very much, though their children attend Sunday school. Reason, the church is composed of moneyed men, and it is no place for a day laborer to show himself. There is no suitable place in the neighborhood for instruction or innocent recreation. ... Has lived in twenty different factory towns, and has observed that young women who work in the factories are many of them ruined in morals and nearly all in health. A rosy-cheeked girl put in a mill will begin to fade in three months. They make poor housekeepers.

Laborers are told by their employers that they must elevate themselves and lay up money; that nobody's wages are so small but that something can be saved. This is sheer nonsense, for it is impossible for day laborers to elevate themselves under the present wage system. If one of them does step up one round in the ladder of the social scale, he is pointed out to use as a sample of what *all* might do. Opportunity makes a man quite as often as brains. My hand-work has taken the second premium at a State Fair, yet I have been obliged to work for 40 cents per day and support my family, which consisted of four. I have been so poor that I have borrowed a pair of pants in order to make a decent appearance on the street. Fifteen years ago an opportunity was offered by which I could better myself. I accepted it, and by prudence have saved the great amount of $600, while my employers have got rich in the same time. There are many men who have worked the same lenght of time, and have not been able to save one dime,—all because capital is powerful and dictates its own terms.

S., a shoemaker, 50 years of age, has worked at the trade 40 years. Has a family of six; wife covers bat or base balls, besides doing her housework, and the children work in the shop also, besides going to school three months in the year. Wife works from 5½ A.M. to 10 A.M., and himself and three children work fifty-nine hours a week, besides chores. Rented last year five rooms for $132, but this year will have seven rooms and pay $200, and be more comfortable. House three-quarters of a mile away. Keeps but one store account, which is settled monthly; is paid once a month for his work. Takes a daily, two weeklies, and two monthlies. Spends two evenings in the lodge-room from 7½ to 10 o'clock, and other evenings, after sawing and splitting wood, spends the time in reading and writing. Shoemakers in the place generally dance on Saturday nights; Saturday afternoons in the right season many play base ball; while six evenings in the week many of the young and middle-aged roll ten-pins and play billiards. Works in a shop where there are 153 men, women and boys, and in a room with 31 others. The building is heated by steam through iron pipes, and ventilated by windows and doors. A common wash-sink, with water at hand, gives opportunities for cleanliness, and the men find their own towels, soap, combs and glass. Each man finds his own lamp, for winter use, the company supplying oil. The stairs and windows give the only escape in case of fire. . . . Since the introduction of machinery it is difficult for a man to teach his son the trade, as only a single part is carried on in a given room. Does not desire his sons to follow the business, but necessity compels it. Three men working with machinery can do what required six men before, in making and finishing shoes. Skilled labor is of less value than formerly. A man of small means, moreover, cannot go into business and compete with the large establishments. The cost of production is lessened, as the amount is increased, taking it on the basis of a single pair. But for the Crispin order, shoemakers would to-day have been virtually beggars. Its money cost has been $2 a year; while its effects have been increased earnings, and increased soberness, temperance and industry. By restricting apprenticeship for a certain length of time, wages have been kept up, which is a virtual increase. Works now ten hours on five days, and nine on Saturday. Until last winter had worked from twelve to sixteen hours a day. . . . Very few shoemakers in the place are out of debt and able to keep out. On their small wages they cannot save enough to carry them through the four or five months when there is no work, and many have sickness to contend with also. Friends help them in such cases; and they are also aided by the Young Men's Christian Association. Wages are about the same as before the war, while the cost of living has advanced 40 per cent. . . . The employer knows just how much it costs to keep the breath of life in his employés, and if he finds they are getting ahead, he cuts wages down just low enough to prevent it. The working-people of the place are noted for their observance of the Sabbath and its privileges. The reading-room of the Young Men's Christian Association is open to all every evening, and a manufacturer of hats provides for the use of his own hands a good room, well lighted and heated; furnishes it with stands, seats, tables and reading matter, hires a janitor to attend, supplies checkers, dominoes and chess, and keeps it open from the middle of the afternoon till bed-time, the year round, wholly at his own expense, for the instruction and amusement of his help. . . . There is a cooperative store in town; its shares, in less than four years, have increased in value from $10 to $36. Few children are employed in the manufactories of the town, parents thinking more of educating their sons and daughters than of killing them with work. Concerning factory work, speaking from observation in Lowell, he thinks children would be 500 per cent better off by working on a farm, and that factory work by young people is resulting throughout New England in effeminate offspring. . . .

. . . It is hard to see why it is not better to make the consumer pay two or three cents more a pair for his shoes, than to cut lower down a man who cannot, by hard toil at the wages given, make a comfortable living. We have it constantly dinned in our ears that supply and demand govern prices; but we have found out to a certainty that this is not so. To test the thing, notice these facts: without the aid of machinery, six men will make a case of 60 pairs in a day, for which they will get $12, less the cost of findings, which would give each man about $1.70 cents a day; on the other hand, with the machinery, three men will do the same amount of work in the same time, and get about the same pay each, as the men on hand work. The goods sell as high in the market, in proportion to cost, in 1870 as in 1871. . . . Query: Who gets the difference in money saved by machinery? and how far does supply and demand govern in these things?

A journeyman mechanic gives his views upon the causes of the present condition of labor as follows:—

It is said that the rapid increase of wealth in our country, during the last eight years, is without anything approaching a parallel in the history of nations. Now the question arises, into whose hands has this wealth fallen? Has it fallen into the possession of the few, or into that of the many? Evidently the former. And I think that, could the disparity between the possessions of the two classes to-day be shown in round figures, in contrast with what it was in years gone by, we should not only be astonished, but alarmed,—alarmed because we know the greater the capital the greater the facilities for adding to that capital; or, in plain Saxon, the stronger the moneyed power becomes the stronger it may be.

And when we come to reflect upon the increasing numbers of the

4. Machinists, c. 1880. Courtesy of the Museum of American Textile History.

wealthy here at the North, and consider how natural it is for them to desire
the weakening of the working classes, we cannot fail to see the unavoidable
necessity of earnest and united action on the part of the people in order to
withstand their aggressions.

Coming more to the practical, in answering the question how can we
help ourselves, our most natural reply is: Our power lies in the government, certainly. But is the government made for us, as I have said, or are
we made for the government? We might suppose the latter, to hear some
people talk, or more especially to read some of the laws upon our statute
books. . . .

In pressing our claims upon the government there is one thing concerning which it is not easy to see how working-men can disagree, and that is,
the benefits which they would derive from a complete revolutionizing of
the present banking system, if not its total destruction. . . . Banking
corporations are the very soul of speculation. Abolish them and you would

see such a fluttering among speculators as no financial panic ever began to produce. It seems to be a scheme of robbery, the most cunningly devised and successfully carried out of anything that was ever foisted upon the American people. (MBLS, *Second Annual Report*,1871, 606, 612–17)

In an effort to look beyond factories, families, and individual tenements to communities, the bureau in 1873 asked for descriptions of the economic and social context in which people in Massachusetts worked. Based on personal observation, these responses certainly included, and probably generalized from, anecdotal experience. They also furnished a rough guide to the stages of industrialization that existed simultaneously in the state. The description of Medfield, for example, evokes a bucolic, preindustrial Eden, where agriculture was the predominant pursuit and factories were only beginning to displace scattered homes as sites for the manufacture of the straw hats the village produced. Workers in Lynn, the major center of the shoe industry, deplored the regimentation of factories and fondly recalled a situation like that in Medfield, when artisans had made shoes in workshops in or near their own homes. Workers in Taunton, by contrast, who made heavy machinery, had few nostalgic memories of a preindustrial past.

MEDFIELD

This is one of the oldest and most beautiful villages in the State, distant only one hour's ride, by rail, from Boston. It is traversed by two railroads, crossing at right angles and affording ample accommodation for public travel. It embraces nine thousand acres of varied surface and fertile soil, and is watered by two rivers.

The chief industrial occupation of the inhabitants is Agriculture; besides which, the manufacture of straw bonnets and hats, and of carriages, of different sorts, is extensively pursued, and gives employment to a great number of persons of both sexes. The general aspect of the place is that of quiet industry and thrift, with almost entire exemption from the worst evils of more populous towns and large cities, and possessing all the religious, educational, and social advantages to be found in other like villages.

The population of the village is about twelve hundred; of which four-fifths are Americans and one-fifth of foreign nativity. The number of farms exceeds one hundred; and their occupants embrace more than half the population. The value of the farms may be estimated at about $400,000, and their annual produce at $75,000. The average wages of farm laborers are $25 and board per month for eight months, or $20 for the whole year; and, without board, $35, for eight months, and $25 for the whole year. Ten hours' labor, per day, in the field and at the barn, is the average requirement, during eight months, and eight hours during the rest of the year. Day-laborers receive, on an average, $2 per day, for all common work, and $2.50 for haying. Laborers hired by the month or year, if boarded, are provided for with like care as are other members of the family.

Probably, no better specimens can be found of physical health, of good moral character, and of fidelity in all the relations of good citizenship, than are to be seen among the farmers, and, in general, among their employés. Some of the latter, however, who are almost exclusively of foreign nativity, indulge propensities and habits which render their labor less valuable, and occasion much loss to their employers. But efforts are being made for their improvement and elevation, the effect of which encourages the hope of their reform in habits and character. Occupants of farms are, in nearly every instance, owners of them; and among hired laborers, are many owners of the houses they occupy. The homes of farmers and their general style of living are fully equal to those of other citizens, in all that contributes to health and comfort. In regard to social life and privileges, citizens all stand upon equal footing. Class distinctions are nowhere to be observed, except among persons of foreign nativity, who, here as elsewhere, are inclined to separate themselves from the rest of the community, on account of social and religious preferences and customs. In educational privileges, the children of all citizens share alike, and upon equal terms.

The two large straw manufactories in the village, give employment to one hundred and twenty females, and nearly one hundred males. Both are models, in their class, of good order, industry and thrift. . . . A great part of the work is done, away from the manufactories, by females residing in this and the adjacent towns. Probably, more than a thousand persons are so employed. Materials are carried to them, and their work is returned by agents from the different firms. The work of males requires more active exercise, and, with ordinary care, there is no liability to accidents, or any injury to health. The hours of labor, for both classes, are ten, daily. Wages of females average $1.50 per day; of males, $2.50 per day. Most of the work is done by the piece, and the compensation for it varies according to the capability, skill and ambition of the worker. In many cases, it is much greater than the earnings of labor by the day.

The effect of this branch of industry is favorable to the welfare of the individuals pursuing it, and to the community at large. A similar conclusion, in relation to the carriage manufacture, is justified by the whole condition and character of those who are engaged in it. Thirty persons are employed in this branch of industry, and their wages average about $2.25 per day. In both branches, wages are paid in cash, and from the earnings in both, deposits in the Savings Banks are doubtless made. While no extremes of wealth or poverty exist, in either class, a good living is usually earned by both; and in both are bright examples of good citizens and good men and women.

The village presents, almost without exception, neat and comfortable, and, in some instances, capacious and elegant dwellings. A large public library has recently been established. Concerts, dramatic and other entertainments are frequent, open to, and attended by the laboring classes. Attendance at school, by all children, under fifteen years of age, is in accordance with requirements of the law. Public worship is, in general, observed by all classes. The principle of co-operation in manufacturing establishments and stores, trades unions and labor associations, has never obtained, nor have any strikes been put in operation here. Laborers, in all the various industries of the place, occupy nearly the same relative position in their social and pecuniary condition.

As an example of a most attractive place of residence, and of a population presenting, in their whole character and condition, the effect of industry, temperance and frugality, and of a love of peace, good order, and good citizenship, the village may justly be ranked among the most conspicuous in this section of the State,—a proof that a scattered population, away from large cities or towns, under the old system of working at home, has vastly better moral influences, and yields more comfort and happiness than the modern system of congregated labor in large towns which have been the growth of modern inventions and appliances of machinery.

Lynn

The complete and final revolution of the shoe trade, brought about by the introduction of steam power and labor-saving machinery, has changed the methods of shoe-making, which, whatever the results, are fixed and absolute. Small shops are crushed out of the business, and the factory system has been adopted. Sub-division of labor is being carried to its utmost profitable limits. There are two busy seasons and two dull seasons, and every year the busy seasons are becoming shorter, and the dull seasons longer; and, as a consequence, employés are more than ever at the mercy of employers, and subject to their dictation. During the last year the working season did not exceed six months; . . . now that the busy season has to some extent begun, the pay of the operatives in the various departments is stated as being from 25 to 41 per cent less than last season. Several large manufacturers, on the invitation of small country towns, have started shops there, the inducements being freedom from rent and taxation for a term of years and the probability of cheap labor. Some half dozen do most of their work in Pittsfield, N. H. It is a settled conviction with many, that the whole business of shoemaking will finally settle down, so that there will be in Lynn an employing class and an operative class, as distinctly marked as those in [the textile cities].

One thing is certain, the working people in Lynn are full of discontent and dissatisfaction with the present, and look forward to the future with gloomy apprehension. Ten years ago the shoe trade of Lynn was carried on in small shops; and in the houses all over the city the inmates might daily be seen, stitching and binding the uppers. Then, as the advantages of steam power applied to the sewing machine began to be comprehended, stitching shops were gradually established all over the city wherever it was convenient to obtain power, the proprietors of the shops furnishing the machines and hiring girls to do the work, many of whom could earn, in those days, from $15 to $18 a week. Now the stitching-shop is unknown, except as a part of a large concern, the manufacturers having found it more profitable to have the stitching and all other branches done under one roof, and the average earnings of good stitchers will not to-day reach more than $4 or $5 for six days' work, of ten hours each.

One fact in this connection is worthy of note. The sewing machine, when run by steam power and the constant and close application necessary by this method, seems to act very injuriously upon the sight of the operators, whose eyes are kept on a continual strain, and particularly when working on black in the evening; and the writer has personal knowledge of many cases where it is to be feared quite young girls have permanently injured their sight from daily straining their eyes while stitching boots: at all events, they have been obliged to discontinue it, and with impaired vision, take some other means of earning a living.

The city is clean, healthy, and orderly. Its public buildings, churches, and principal streets show thrift and enterprise, and its leading citizens are proud of it as a home, and jealous of its good name. Very many of the working people own their homes, and are in the main industrious, temperate, and frugal. It has a public library, Young Men's Christian Association, etc., and during the winter months the city established free evening schools, which were well attended, and its day schools are as good as any in the State. Two very large and handsome new school-houses have just been built, at a cost of about seventy or eighty thousand dollars each.

Within the last twenty years its population has more than doubled, and its valuation increased from four millions to twenty millions of dollars.

Yet with all this material prosperity and apparent advancement, those who look beneath the surface of things, with unprejudiced eyes, are painfully conscious that wealth, though year by year still on the increase, goes now into fewer hands; that the results of industry are very unequally divided; that the advantages which machinery and division of labor bring, have been altogether in favor of capital and against labor, and that these evils are dangerously increasing from year to year.

Within five years real estate has enormously increased in value, and it is largely held by a few rich men. No longer is there opportunity for an operative in a shoe shop to save his earnings, and finally purchase a home. Very few indeed of the working people of Lynn have been able to save anything or even to keep out of debt, the last two or three years; and it is only too evident that the causes now at work in Lynn may render it rich and prosperous as a city, but with a population of over-worked, under-paid hirelings, hopelessly dependent upon employers who act upon the good old rule, the simple plan,—that they may take who have the power, and they may keep who can.

TAUNTON

Locomotive and cotton machine manufactory, is one of the most extensive occupations in the city. A third of the workmen are foreigners. No women are employed in these shops. Effect of occupation upon health, not generally unfavorable, except in departments where emery dust, chemicals, and extreme heat infect the atmosphere.

Work, 60 hours per week, commences at 6.40 in the morning, and closes

5. Haverhill Shoe Factory, c. 1880. Courtesy of the Trustees of the Haverhill Public Library, Special Collections Department.

at 6 P.M., except Saturdays, when it closes at 4 P.M. If a man does not work he gets no pay, whether he be absent 15 minutes, or as many days.

Shops usually run the year round, but in case of dull season all unnecessary help is discharged. These either seek employment in other places, or hang about the city, working at anything that brings a penny. The old and favorite help is generally employed upon some kind of work calculated to retain their services.

Shops are usually well protected against accident in their construction. The common wage-laborers, must work hard to make both ends meet, but many have extra jobs, and can save money.

Apprentices, and unskilled laborers are deprived of the actual necessities of life, if they have no income from some other source. The opportunities of becoming employers are decidedly few; some may attain situations as overseers, but even these positions are difficult of access. The homes are mostly in tenement houses, and I describe the house I occupy as a fair sample of tenement houses in Taunton. There are many better, with rents beyond the reach of day laborers, and many much poorer. I have two rooms with fire, four sleeping rooms, a pantry and sink-room. It is an up-stairs tenement. Two families in the house. Rent $180 per year. Sleeping rooms miserably small, about 9 feet square. One window in each sleeping room: ventilation of these rooms is impossible, without exposing the occupant. The fire rooms are about 12 + 12. Pantry and sink-room very small. When the tenement was engaged, was informed that the water was brought up, but its impurities were carefully concealed from my knowledge. I soon found that the drainage of privy affected the water badly, and that it could not be passed through the pump, without filling the house with a disagreeable odor. No smell from the pump when it is not in operation. Have no cistern, and am obliged to bring all the water for family use from a well across the street, up a hard flight of winding stairs, except what we catch in tubs when it storms. In winter the sink-pipes freeze, and all slops have to be removed in a pail. The coal and wood must be brought from the cellar up two flights of stairs. Have said I would not live here another winter, but am obliged to remain, because unsuccessful in getting a better tenement. Tenements I have looked at are no improvement. . . .

A happy home is the whole basis of a man's life, and the desolation and sickness in hundreds of our city homes, is chargeable directly to the miserly landlord. I know some of these last remarks are strong assertions, but they will bear a rigid investigation. The Irish and foreign tenement houses are in bad condition. A while ago, city officials visited a tenement block, and in one of the upper tenements, found a live hog, weighing three or four hundred pounds. On inquiry, how he was got up there, the reply was, that he was never down; he was born there. . . .

. . . In the foreigner's home, much is the fault of the tenant's neglect; but the tenements are, in most cases, damp dreary, unhealthy resorts, more suitable for stables than homes.

The social divisions of this city, are Churches, Freemasons, Grand Army of the Republic, Odd Fellows, Good Templars, Knights of Pythias, while a large class of people have no other social head-quarters than dram-shops and eating saloons. Boarding-house life is cold, hard, and uncogenial in its associations to those that love the comforts and attractions of home, while those that possess none of the finer feelings for home, tend to conversations and influences which lower and debase their character and inclinations, indirectly excluding them from wholesome society, and leading to dissipation. . . . Most boarding-houses here will not take lady boarders, because it is not profitable. Their wages, as a class, are smaller, and they cannot pay as much as men. Therefore they are not wanted, and the result must be injurious to the social habits of our boarding-houses, for, in every feature of society, women of respectability elevate and refine all associations. Our educational advantages are good. We have one library, containing nearly 11,000 volumes, and a small reading-room connected. Think the law requiring the attendance at school, of children under 15 years, is generally observed.

The population of the city in 1870 was 18,630. It has 15 Protestant churches within the city limits, average number attending them is carefully estimated at 400, making about 6,000 persons who attend Protestant public worship regularly. Have about 3,500 Catholics, making in all about 9,500 church-going people; which deducted from a population of 18,630 leaves 9,130 men, women, and children who do not attend any kind of divine service. There are many causes for this neglect. The churches charge too much rent for their pews, and indulge in too many expenses which discourage the poor man from attending public worship. Of course, outside influences are great,—they present themselves in every possible way, and take advantage of any discouragements the church throws upon its own progress. Style, fashion, and select or aristocratic circles are the great hinderances of the church, and exclude many a laboring man from an active religious life.

We have a course of scientific lectures here this winter; admittance 25 cents, well attended. The city furnishes an evening drawing-school free to all citizens who provide their instruments. (MBLS, *Fourth Annual Report*, 1873, 288–90, 305–9)

In the past, Carroll Wright noted in 1879, much of what had passed for labor's response to industrial change had been instead the view of "reformers with some special theory to advance."[3] To correct such misconceptions, which Wright tactfully did not directly associate with his predecessor's editorial slant, he explicitly invited the Commonwealth's workers to submit their own answer to aspects of the labor question. The bureau received a disappointingly small number of replies, but they demonstrated that working people were often articulate and not of one mind. They wrote of specific and systemic abuses, about company stores, capitalism, diminished opportunity, and the

3. MBLS, *Tenth Annual Report* (1879), 116.

distribution of wealth. Some suggested a larger role for government and others no role at all. They discussed tariffs, technology, management, and medical expenses, as well as wages, hours, and unions. In their diversity of opinion, they may well have represented the larger population, though that was a question Carroll Wright did not pursue.

FROM A SHOEMAKER

I think there ought to be an eight-hour law all over the country. There is not enough work to last the year round, and work over eight hours a day, or forty-eight hours a week. There can be only about so much work to do any way: and, when that is done, business has got to stop, or keep dragging the year round, so that a man has to work for almost any price offered; when, if there was an eight-hour law, things would be more even, and a man could get what his labor was worth, according to the price of living, and there would be plenty of work for all, and business would be good the year round. I think every State ought to submit to the United States to decide how many hours people should work all over the country. Just so long as there is an over-production, business will drag the year round: and the only way to stop over-production is to work less hours; for business never will be good when we work more hours than the demand calls for.

FROM A CARPENTER

Less hours of labor will enable the man to procure more days of labor, stop the ruinous competition in the labor market, enable the producers to purchase more, give them time to study the great problems of this life without infringing upon the necessary hours of rest; in fine, make more intelligent the masses who must rule this and other countries. Under the present system of distribution of the products of labor, we are fast drifting to that condition of society which has preceded the downfall of Sparta, Macedonia, Athens, and Rome, where a few were very rich, and the many very poor. If the institutions of this country are to be preserved, it must be by an intelligent, well-to-do yeomanry, not by a moneyed aristocracy, composed of the few, while the masses are in abject poverty.

From a Wool-Sorter

As the State has admitted the principle that it can legislate for hours of labor for women and children, we think they ought also to arrange the hours per day, so that Saturday should be a half day, as there are numbers of married women and widows engaged in the mills from sheer necessity to support themselves and families. It would give them time to get their household work done on Saturday, so that Sunday can be a day of rest, or give them an opportunity to attend a place of worship.

From a Carpenter

In regard to the number of hours a day's work should consist of, I think ten hours is a fair day's work, and do not think an eight-hour law would be any help to the laboring class. There are some who would make good use of their spare time; and there are others who would not. This same class would want pay for ten hours, and would strike if they could not get it. I for one never could see where the laboring class gains any lasting good by a strike. I think a man should make the best terms possible with his boss; and, if he cannot get as much as he wants, he should try other places. He cannot expect to have every thing as he did in good times. If he gets enough to eat, and plain clothes to wear, he should be content for the present. Better times will come soon. I believe that hard money is the money for all, the poor as well as the rich. I believe in the poor making friends with the rich; and, in so doing, they will be gainers.

From a Shoe-Cutter

There is no way I think I could be paid more fairly than I now am. I do not consider that my employers profit unfairly by my labor. My labor is in the market for sale. My employers buy it just as they buy a side of leather, and expect, and I think are willing to pay, a fair market price for it. The miller who makes a grade of flour up to the very highest point in excellence will command the highest price for it in the market. The workingman who makes his labor of the most value will generally command the highest market price for it, and sharp business men are quick to discover its value.

I consider all legislation in regard to any thing connected with labor as injurious. All trades-unions and combinations I also consider as injurious to the mass of working-people. A few profit by these associations, and the many pay the bills. If working-people would drop the use of beer, tobacco, and every thing else that is not of real benefit, . . . they would have far more money for the general expenses of a family than they now have. I live in a village of about two thousand inhabitants; and I do not know of a family in destitute circumstances which has let alone vicious expenditures, and been industrious. It is the idle, unthrifty, beer-drinking, don't-care sort of people, who are out at the elbows, and waiting for some sort of legislation to help them. The sooner working-people get rid of the idea that somebody or something is going to help them, the better it will be for them. In this country, as a general thing, every man has an equal chance to rise. In our village there are a number of successful business men, and all began in the world without any thing but their hands and a will to succeed. The best way for working-people to get help is to help themselves.

From a Custom Shoemaker

The best thing the government (national) can do for workingmen is to let them alone. The wise and the prudent need no help; for the unwise and imprudent nothing effectual can be done. Forethought and economy, carefully practised in early life as well as age, would banish poverty; and nothing else ever will.

From a Quarryman

There are eight companies in the stone business here. . . . All their employés must trade in their stores; if not, "get work where you trade. We keep as good articles here as you can get elsewhere, and sell as cheap, too." And that is all the satisfaction you will get for your complaint. I have had to pay $1.35 for a pair of children's shoes that I could buy outside for 50 cents, and so on with every thing else, to $2 on a barrel of flour; and everybody else must do likewise, i.e., those who work on stone. And that is not all either: some of them have tenement houses, and they must be kept full; and those who live in them are in a complete state of vassalage. And that is not all: no matter how frugally you live, you never can get anything ahead; and those having helpless families scarcely ever receive a dollar. They are closely watched on the books, lest they might overrun their wages; and consequently they will get nothing, only as they earn it. Such is the atrocious system here; and this is a part of free, enlightened Massachusetts! I suppose, if the workingmen protested against this state of affairs, they'd be dubbed "communists;" but no: their manhood is completely gone. They dare not murmur at it even; and is it any wonder? They have no means to better their condition; and it is, to say the least, deplorable. A workingman has a boy; and that child is on the quarry, lugging tools, or, with himself, pounding on granite, at the age of ten years. He cannot afford to send him to school only a few months in winter. All summer the child must work hard for his living. Consequently, before he is twenty years old, in seven out of ten cases, he is broken down, and a sorry-looking specimen of manhood, without education or any thing else, and totally unfit to work at any other kind of laboring work. . . . All should be paid in cash at least once a fortnight, and abolish the supply stores. Anybody doing that will be blessed by the quarrymen and stone-workers in this part of the State.

FROM A PAVING-STONE CUTTER

Remedy, in my opinion, must come from Congress; and it is a very simple matter. Pass a bill aiding the industrious idle poor to a home on the public lands, thereby making them producers instead of consumers,—take them from the squalor and filth, and consequent debasement, in the crowded centres of the East, to the broad acres of the West, all of which a patriotic Congress could do,—also adjust the tariff, so as to be tantamount to prohibition, on all imported articles that can be produced and manufactured here, the raw material which we possess (this measure would stimulate labor and all the industries of the nation), and no tax on articles, necessaries in particular, such as tea, coffee, spices, etc., which we do not and cannot produce here, to which may be added a government currency in substitution for the bank notes, etc., making the same legal tender, absolute money for all debts, public and private, in the United States. But a great deal could and should be done by the Massachusetts legislature for this locality in particular. The chief employers of labor here are stone-contractors. All others allow their employés to buy where they can the cheapest; but your stone-contractor must have you body and soul. This supply-store system should be abolished. You can, if you give the subject earnest consideration for one hour, see the iniquity of the whole thing; and I hope you will call especial attention to it in your next Report. If you don't nobody here will: indeed none of the victims dare whisper it, much less say any thing publicly in reference to it.

FROM AN OVERSEER IN A PRINT-WORKS

There are a few things to which I wish to call the attention of the Labor Bureau, which are of great interest to the laboring man, and are very often a source of great hardship to him. Two of these are doctors' bills and apothecaries' charges. The doctors here charge from $1.50 to $2.00 per visit; and the apothecaries' charges for medicine are exorbitant. As a fair sample of what occurs daily, I will cite one case of late occurrence. I had occasion to purchase two ounces of a certain medicine, and was charged 20 cents per ounce. I thought the price too high: so, when I needed to purchase a second time, I sent to Boston by express for one pound, and obtained a pound, or sixteen ounces, for 75 cents. Allowing the apothecary to pay as much for it as I did, which is not probable, it gives him almost $2.50 profit. Comment is unnecessary.... Many worthy poor people, knowing they cannot meet the charges of doctors and apothecaries, delay calling a doctor until disease has advanced too far; and thus many are constantly being sacrificed to their own honesty and these exorbitant charges. There is one other matter that I will just mention; i.e. church expenses. If a poor man wishes to bring his family up religiously, he has to pay nearly, or quite as much, for pew-rent, as he would . . . for house-rent. I myself am paying as much for pew- rent as I ever knew my father to pay for house-rent; and, when I left home in 1846, he had eight children at home, and had a very good tenement on the very best street in the borough.

FROM A MACHINIST

. . . In my own case, I have been at work for a company managed in a reckless way; one of the company using money on unworthy objects, he having a wife and children. For the last five years things have been going on from bad to worse, and last week the firm went into bankruptcy. In the mean time we received our pay by driblets,—five, ten, fifteen, or twenty dollars, anyway we could get it; take orders; make one rent offset another, until eight or ten of us are out from a hundred and fifty dollars to two hundred and fifty dollars apiece,—in all, some two thousand dollars,—all because of reckless calculation. In the mean time we were cut down and cut down. We got mad, and left. Some of us, who staid it out, are out as above. I find I am coming short of paper; so I make this statement: First, pay help a living price when business is good; encourage honest labor instead of travelling dead beats, who are willing to work twenty-five or fifty cents less, because hard up. Second, the office expenses, in times past, have eaten up the profits; the help, in the mean time, take what they can get: I know it is so here in this place. When they cut help down, they simply cut off their own business; or, in other words, if the laboring class has no money, it soon shows itself in trade, and we soon get into the gloomy condition we are now in. Do corporations cut themselves down, or deny themselves any luxuries? No; but the help must suffer for reckless management. Pay help a living price, use them humanely, and, my word for it, you never will hear any complaints about capital *versus* labor.

FROM A STEAM AND GAS FITTER

The war created a class of money aristocrats, who, with old manufacturing men, are bound to keep the poorer class and laboring men down, not giving them any encouragement or help. If they start for themselves, they do all in their power to make their efforts a failure. Fifteen years ago a man could start a successful business with from one hundred to three hundred dollars; while it now requires one to three or more thousands, thereby making a poor man's chances poorer every year. In fifteen years this country will be worse off than the old countries of Europe and Asia. The rich will be very rich, the poor very poor, and the government will be controlled by the moneyed class; and the cause is, in my opinion, due wholly to the fact,—minor offices with large salaries and little work. Commissions and committees are allowed to settle government business, which should be settled directly by the State legislature, or the national Senate and House of Representatives. . . . Continual change is all that will make American office-holders honest. A party in power more than eight continuous years, will, of necessity, be corrupt.

FROM A SHOE-FINISHER

The employer unfairly profits in this way: he keeps a nice establishment; has his servants in doors and out; keeps his span of horses and family carriage; lives well; goes to Saratoga or some other place for a summer vacation; brings up his children without work; then, if his income does not pay these items of expense, with interest on money invested in business, and a profit besides, his employés must have their wages cut down whether they are earning their living or not. There are some exceptions to the above; but it is generally true.

FROM A CARPENTER

I should like to make a few remarks for your consideration. First, when we find a thing in our system of government that is a curse to the masses, it is the duty of those who are in power to shut down on it at once. I allude to the system of employing men in order to get their votes, and paying their poll taxes. . . . And another thing is, that the votes so gained are from new arrivals, who know nothing of our laws; and such people are given the preference to natives, as regards labor. When a man is voted in through fraud and ignorance, he will govern through the same means, and is at heart corrupt and dishonest: for like begets like; and it is his nature and he cannot do otherwise than be true to himself. It is the duty of every man, native and adopted, to stop the importing of laborers until we can set to work what unemployed laborers we have here with us now.

FROM A CLERK IN A COUNTRY STORE

Business is not very brisk, and there is not a large amount of money circulating in this vicinity; yet I do believe that, if a person enjoys good health, and is willing to work, he may earn an honest living, and perhaps lay aside a few dollars for future wants. A large portion of our poor people have poor ways: they will sit around the corner groceries and saloons, chew and smoke tobacco, swear and curse those who seem to be prospering, complain of the hard times and their hard luck,—nothing to do, nothing to do,—when it is a fact that their overworked wives are holding a child in one arm, and trying to cut firewood with the other to cook a scanty meal for their lazy husband's dinner.

FROM A WOOL-HAT MAKER

The key to the greater part of the difficulties under which the working-men of our State labor is because legalized and unlegalized temptation meets them at every corner, and indulgence is made respectable by the law that should shield and protect them. The workingmen of our State learn to love the grog-shop better than their homes, better than their families; and hence their poverty, hence the misery of their wives, the ignorance of their children, and oftentimes the prostitution of their daughters to fill the houses of ill fame in our large cities, all of these spreading death, disease, and ruin throughout our Commonwealth. I do not speak from any guess-work in regard to this matter. Twenty-five years' experience amid the grog-shops of our State enables me to speak in no uncertain manner. I know what I testify to, to be true. Two and a half years of labor among the reformed men in this part of the State enables me to know that rum is the most relentless enemy, the most unmitigated curse, of the laboring class. I can take you to homes that, three years ago, were the abodes of misery, where the father could not procure even a day's work (no one would employ him); and yet those homes are homes of peace and plenty to-day. Why? Because those homes are temperance homes now. Total abstinence has solved for them the problem of labor. I say that I can take you to just such homes; and mine is one of them. I know what I am speaking of; and any attempt to lift up degraded labor, without first closing the grog-shop doors, will, I fear, be time thrown away. Yours for labor reform and temperance reform, which must go hand in hand if they would win.

FROM A DRESSER-TENDER

I have worked twenty-four years in this country. My pay has averaged $2 per day. During that time I have saved, with the help of my family, $4,500. The most of it is in savings banks,—some in the——, and some in the—— Bank, in Boston. My only trouble is, that they will not come out all right; and my opinion on the labor question is, that co-operation among the working class is their only cure for their trouble. I think the most of working people might have saved something out of their pay from the year 1866 to 1874, as they received more pay then. I think ten hours a day is long enough, and short enough. Four years ago the workingmen here started a co-operative store in groceries. We have paid $3,400 to members in dividends on their purchases, and pay besides seven per cent on stock.

FROM A SHOEMAKER

I do not believe that the laboring man will be any better paid for his labor until his employer can see him as the producer and consumer: then he will see better days and more pay and labor. The manufacturer may put his goods into market, made by cheap labor, and they will stay there; for the consumer, the laboring man, and his family have not the means to purchase those goods. The children are barefooted, poorly clad, live cheaply, and do not consume. It is under-consumption which is the cause of idleness, and not over-production. (MBLS, *Tenth Annual Report*, 1879, 118–19, 121, 124, 126–28, 130, 132, 135–37)

Income and Expense

Labor reformers in the later nineteenth century used the phrase "wage system" to describe the relationship between employers and employees. Those with a more radical bent substituted "wage slavery" to denote the dominance of bosses and the dependence of workers. In his last report for the Massachusetts Bureau of Statistics of Labor, Henry K. Oliver included an essay that mingled both terms and traced the evolution of management's control over employees' compensation from postulated origins in chattel slavery.[1] Perhaps written by Oliver's deputy, George E. McNeill, an outspoken critic of the wage system, the article cited impressive authorities, including Adam Smith and J. S. Mill, but lacked the numerical evidence that would characterize Carroll Wright's later research. Demographic change over centuries because of wars, plagues, and migration, the bureau explained, had somewhat lessened the arbitrary control of employers and modestly raised wages. Remuneration early in the 1870s, however, did not approach a level the bureau believed adequate or just.

Giving those adjectives quantitative precision was no simple assignment for the bureau's statisticians. Dividing the total payroll of a textile manufacturer by the number of employees, for example, might

---

1. A more subtle statement of this argument is in Karen Orren, *Belated Feudalism* (Cambridge: Cambridge University Press, 1991), which traces the legal relationship between employers and employees to medieval common law governing masters and servants.

appear to yield an average wage. But a result that failed to distinguish between men and women, adults and children, the skilled and the unskilled, spinners, weavers, and other artisans, revealed little. To reflect industrial reality, the bureau had to mirror in its tables the complexity of industrial organization.

By 1873, even statistical objectivity might not have quieted Oliver's critics in the General Court. He and McNeill had disclosed unsanitary conditions in urban tenements, documented evasion of school-attendance requirements, and annoyed legislative defenders of savings banks. Another study, which appeared to conclude that wages in the Commonwealth were inferior to those of factory workers in Europe, irritated politicians who claimed the protective tariff kept American workers prosperous. As the financial panic of 1873 deepened, those who found fault with the bureau moved to close it, a decisive step that would prevent bad news from becoming official.

The appointment of Carroll Wright to succeed Oliver was a compromise intended to pacify the bureau's opponents without surrendering to them. While a state senator, the new director had opposed labor legislation, though he had an innate sense of social and economic justice that blended liberal Christianity, egalitarianism, and individual responsibility in an imprecise creed he shared with much of the American middle class. Yet Wright tried to separate those personal convictions from his professional duties. He believed his task at the bureau was to secure dependable data about contemporary conditions, not to buttress convictions about wages with quotations from political economists of the past. Sufficient evidence, he thought, would allay political controversy and, incidentally, provide a factual basis for the programmatic expression of his own decent instincts. So in 1874, which was not a good year for the state's economy, he dispatched investigators to thirty-six communities across the state to find out how working families lived.

Wright's elaborate questionnaires asked about income, expense, housing, diet, recreation, savings, health, and family circumstance. He tabulated the resulting information from 397 households to show the influence of ethnicity, occupation, and surroundings, and he specified the contributions made by working women and children (Tables 1 and 2).

He conceded that "no one family could be taken as representative" of others in the state, but he thought the bureau's sample sufficiently comprehensive to be reliable.[2] He published in full the responses of all 397 families so that skeptics could verify his composite calculations. Then he drew conclusions that seemed inherent in the evidence he presented.

Wright divided the families in his survey according to the skill and ethnic heritage of the male parent, who in every case was the principal wage earner. The case number was the bureau's way of identifying a particular family while fulfilling a promise of confidentiality.

With such an extensive evidential base, Wright's conclusions did not have the partisan ring that had previously irritated legislators. He summarized his findings about income, living expenses, and savings.

Table 1. Income and expense of five working families, 1875.

	No. 93 *Shoemaker*	French
EARNINGS OF FATHER		$540
DAUGHTER, AGED 13½		116
SON, AGED 15		308
SON, AGED 12		212
		$1,176

CONDITION

Family numbers 8, parents and 6 children from three to fifteen years of age; two go to school. Occupy a good tenement of 6 rooms, with neat and healthy surroundings. The bed-rooms and parlor are carpeted. Own a piano, sewing and other labor-saving machines. Family dresses well and attends church. The father worked 8 months and earned from $12 to $18 per week. The family has done well since the children commenced to work; before then they incurred many debts, and it was two years before they were able to liquidate them. Had to live in a poor neighborhood then, with few comforts, and the consequences were that sickness prevailed in the family. The present home has better sanitary arrangement, food and clothing. The children who work attend school three months in the year. Has money in savings bank, but declines to tell how much.

FOOD

Breakfast. Bread, butter, eggs, ham or fish and potatoes, pie and cake, coffee.
Dinner. Bread, butter, meat, potatoes, vegetables, sometimes fish, pickles, pudding and tea.
Supper. Bread, butter, cold meat, salad, cheese, sauce, cake, tea. Sometimes soup for dinner, occasionally baked beans, or anything for a change.

COST OF LIVING $1,053.80

Rent	$218.00	Fish	$32.90	Dry goods	$41.00
Fuel	54.50	Clothing	76.00	Religion	25.00
Groceries	428.80	Boots and shoes	26.00	Sundries	39.00
Meat	84.00	Milk	28.60		

2. MBLS, *Sixth Annual Report* (1875), 200.

Table 1. Continued

No. 80 *Shoemaker*		American
EARNINGS OF FATHER		$552

CONDITION

Family numbers 6, parents and 4 children from two to sixteen years of age; the two elder go to school. Have a tenement of 6 rooms situated in a pleasant neighborhood. Two rooms are well furnished and carpeted, and the house kept clean and orderly. Family dresses respectably and well, and attends church. On account of the shoe business being very dull for the past two years, the family has had a hard struggle to pay bills, and during the last year has run behind some $70, as there was work only eight months and a half. Had a little money in the savings bank, but was obliged to use it. The oldest child will begin work at the close of the present school term. This family is very economical. Had no sickness; bought a few clothes.

FOOD

Breakfast. Bread, butter, hash or potatoes warmed from the day before, doughnuts or cake, coffee.
Dinner. Meat, potatoes, pie or pudding, and tea.
Supper. Bread, butter, sauce or cheese, cake and tea. Buckwheat or griddle-cakes occasionally for breakfast. Baked beans on Saturday night and Sunday morning.

COST OF LIVING $622

Rent	$200.00	Meat	$52.00	Clothing and dry goods	$28.50
Fuel	36.50	Milk	18.00	Sundries, taxes, etc.	11.00
Groceries	260.00	Boots and shoes	16.00		

No. 106 *Iron-moulder*	American
EARNINGS OF FATHER	$695
SON, AGED 15½	254
	$949

CONDITION

Family numbers 5, parents and 3 children from six to fifteen years of age; two go to school. Occupy a tenement of 6 rooms up stairs, in a poor locality, with unpleasant surroundings and little yard-room; there is no space in front of the house, as the door opens on the street. The parlor is carpeted and the house kept remarkably neat, considering the locality. Own a sewing-machine. Family dresses well and is healthy; have had no sickness for several years. Cannot save money, as it takes all to keep family comfortable. Subscribe for one daily and one weekly paper, also "Scientific American" and "Atlantic Monthly."

FOOD

Breakfast. Hot biscuit, brown bread, butter, graham bread, meat or eggs, cake, tea.
Dinner. Bread, (brown or white), butter, meat, potatoes, vegetables, pickles, pudding or pie, cake, tea.
Supper. Bread, butter, cold meat, sauce, pie, cake, tea. Have fish once a week, and baked beans Saturday night and Sunday morning.

Table 1. Continued

Cost of Living					$949
Rent	$192.00	Fish	$13.00	Dry goods	$29.75
Fuel	49.70	Milk	26.50	Books and papers	21.00
Groceries	329.62	Boots and shoes	37.25	Sundries	38.43
Meat	97.75	Clothing	114.00		

No. 219 *Laborer, in mill*	F. Canadian
Earnings of father	$382
son, aged 10	190
	$572

Condition

Family numbers 6, parents and 4 children from nine months to ten years of age; one goes to school. Have a tenement of 4 rooms in an eight-tenement block, with one door on the front and none on the back; the locality and surroundings unclean and disagreeable. The privy is within six feet of the building. The inside of the house is as dirty as the surroundings, and very poorly furnished. Family is poor.

Food

Breakfast. Pork or salt fish, potatoes, bread and coffee.
Dinner. Meat, potatoes, sometimes vegetables, and bread.
Supper. Bread, butter, sometimes gingerbread, and tea. Fish for dinner, instead of
          meat, two days in the week.

Cost of Living					$572
Rent	$84.00	Fish	$18.60	Dry goods	$11.50
Fuel	29.50	Milk	12.00	Sundries	53.43
Groceries	273.25	Boots and shoes	14.80		
Meat	47.92	Clothing	27.00		

No. 356 *Shoreman*	American
Earnings of father	$678

Condition

Family numbers 5, parents and 3 children from one to eight years of age; one goes to school. Occupy a tenement of 5 rooms, in a good and healthy locality. The house is well furnished, and parlor carpeted. Have a sewing-machine. Parents and children dress well and respectably, but cannot save money, as it takes all the father earns to keep the family.

Food

Breakfast. Hot biscuit, butter, cold meat or eggs, cake, tea.
Dinner. Meat or fish, potatoes, vegetables, pickles, bread, butter, pie or pudding, tea.
Supper. Bread, butter, graham bread, cheese, sauce and cake, tea.

Cost of Living					$669.45
Rent	$112.00	Fish	$13.00	Dry goods	$19.00
Fuel	42.70	Milk	15.22	Sundries	25.00
Groceries	269.73	Boots and shoes	37.95		
Meat	61.85	Clothing	73.00		

Source: MBLS, *Sixth Annual Report*, 1875, 247, 252, 256, 294, 340.

Table 2. Composite statistics, working families, 1875.

Sources of Income and Percentage supplied by Each

Classification	No. of Families	Fathers' proportion	Wives' proportion	Children's proportion	Total "assisted" proportion	Children's (under 15) proportion
PLACES						
Under 8,000 population	120	.76 +	.004 +	.23 +	.234 +	—
From 8,000 to 16,000 population	124	.75 +	.007 +	.24 +	.247 +	—
Above 16,000 population	153	.75 +	.012 +	.23 +	.242 +	—
TOTALS	397	.75 +	.008 +	.24	.248 +	—
NATIONALITIES						
American	125	.89 +	.005 +	.097 +	.10 +	.02 +
English	80	.74 +	.015 +	.24 +	.25 +	.06 +
French	2	.59 +	—	.40 +	.40 +	.20 +
French Canadian	29	.61 +	—	.38 +	.38 +	.19 +
German	26	.64 +	.02	.33 +	.35 +	.10 +
Irish	133	.66 +	.008 +	.33 +	.34 +	.18 +
Scotch	2	.86 +	—	.13 +	.13 +	—
TOTALS	397	.75 +	.008 +	.24	.248 +	.12 +
OCCUPATIONS						
Building trades, sk.	57	.89 +	.001 +	.10 +	.101 +	.01 +
Boots, shoes and leather, sk.	39	.74 +	.016 +	.24 +	.256 +	.12 +
Metal workers, sk.	61	.88 +	—	.11 +	.11 +	—
Metal workers, unsk.	17	.64 +	—	.35 +	.35 +	.16 +
Mill operatives, sk.	35	.70 +	.05 +	.24 +	.29 +	.09 +
Mill operatives, unsk.	42	.57 +	—	.42 +	.42 +	.24 +
Mill operatives, overseers	4	.82 +	—	.17 +	.17 +	—
Outdoor employments, unsk.	108	.65 +	.005 +	.34 +	.345 +	.18 +
Shop trades, sk.	24	.91 +	—	.08 +	.08 +	.01 +
Shop trades, unsk.	10	.64 +	—	.35 +	.35 +	.14 +
TOTALS	397	.75 +	.008 +	.24	.248 +	.12 +
KIND OF LABOR						
Skilled,	216	.83 +	.012 +	.15 +	.162 +	.05 +
Unskilled	177	.63 +	.003 +	.36 +	.363 +	.19 +
Overseers	4	.82 +	—	.17 +	.17 +	—
TOTALS	397	.75 +	.008 +	.24	.248 +	.12 +
SIZE OF FAMILY						
2 adults	4	.71 +	.28 +	—	.28 +	—
2 adults, 1 child	27	.96 +	.03 +	—	.03 +	—
2 adults, 2 children	92	.96 +	.005 +	.03 +	.035 +	—
2 adults, 3 children	121	.76 +	.003 +	.23 +	.233 +	—
2 adults, 4 children	102	.64 +	.002 +	.35 +	.352 +	—
2 adults, 5 children	42	.57 +	—	.42 +	.42 +	—
2 adults, 6 children	9	.49 +	—	.50 +	.50 +	—
TOTALS	397	.75 +	.008 +	.24	.248 +	—

Table 2. Continued

Children at Home, at School and at Work

Classification	No. of Families	No. of Children	At Home	At School	At Work
NATIONALITIES					
American	125	291	87	169	35
English	80	239	60	114	65
French	2	10	5	2	3
French Canadian	29	104	30	35	39
German	26	91	28	34	29
Irish	133	505	161	191	153
Scotch	2	6	1	4	1
TOTALS	397	1,246	372	549	325
OCCUPATIONS					
Building trades, sk.	57	140	46	77	17
Boots, shoes and leather, sk.	39	108	23	54	31
Metal workers, sk.	61	155	50	85	20
Metal workers, unsk.	17	61	21	21	19
Mill operatives, sk.	35	104	28	47	29
Mill operatives, unsk.	42	163	46	54	63
Mill operatives, overseers.	4	12	1	9	2
Outdoor employments, unsk.	108	395	124	144	127
Shop trades, sk.	24	69	22	41	6
Shop trades, unsk.	10	39	11	17	11
TOTALS	397	1,246	372	549	325
KIND OF LABOR					
Skilled	216	577	170	304	103
Unskilled	177	657	201	236	220
Overseers	4	12	1	9	2
TOTALS	397	1,246	372	549	325

Yearly Average Cost of Living

Classification	Number of Families	Size of Family	Average yearly Cost of Living
PLACES			
Under 8,000 population	120	5.11	$718.08
From 8,000 to 16,000 population	124	5.06	717.05
Above 16,000 population	153	5.23	770.61
TOTALS	397	5.14	$738.00
NATIONALITIES			
American	125	4.33	$770.02
English	80	4.99	789.48

Table 2. Continued

French	2	7.	768.60
French Canadian	29	5.59	686.06
German	26	5.50	752.85
Irish	133	5.80	594.16
Scotch	2	5.	831.01
TOTALS	397	5.14	$738.00
OCCUPATIONS			
Building trades, sk.	57	4.46	$785.62
Boots, shoes and leather, sk.	39	4.77	736.93
Metal workers, sk.	61	4.54	803.00
Metal workers, unsk.	17	5.59	697.46
Mill operatives, sk.	35	4.97	770.35
Mill operatives, unsk.	42	5.88	665.94
Mill operatives, overseers	4	5.25	1,027.52
Outdoor employments, unsk.	108	5.66	677.22
Shop trades, sk.	24	4.88	833.90
Shop trades, unsk.	10	5.90	643.06
TOTALS	397	5.14	$738.00
KIND OF LABOR			
Skilled	216	4.67	$784.63
Unskilled	177	5.72	674.56
Overseers	4	5.25	1,027.52
TOTALS	397	5.14	$738.00

Source: MBLS, *Sixth Annual Report*, 1875, 369–70, 366–67, 372.

AS REGARDS EARNINGS

First. That in the majority of cases, workingmen in this Commonwealth do not support their families by their individual earnings alone.

Second. That the amount of earnings contributed by wives, generally speaking, is so small, that they would save more by staying at home than they gain by outside labor.

Third. That fathers rely, or are forced to depend, upon their children for from *one-quarter* to *one-third* of the entire family earnings.

Fourth. That children under fifteen years of age supply, by their labor, from *one-eighth* to *one-sixth* of the total family earnings.

AS REGARDS EXPENSES

First. That, judging from the proportionate outlay for dress, as regards entire expenses, there is no evidence that the workingmen we visited, in obedience to fashion, indulge in an excessive or disproportionate expenditure.

Second. That, from our investigations, we find no evidence, or indication, that workingmen spend large sums of money extravagantly or for bad habits.

Third. That, as regards subsistence, rents and fuel, the workingmen's families which we visited paid therefor larger percentages of their income than do workingmen's families, with like incomes, in Prussia and other European countries.

Fourth. That, as regards clothing and sundry expenses, our workingmen's families paid therefor smaller percentages of their income than do workingmen's families, with like incomes, in the countries mentioned above.

As Regards Manner of Living

First. That, among the families visited, those containing the greatest number of child workers occupy the most crowded rooms and the inferior class of tenements.

Second. That about three-quarters of the workingmen's homes which we visited are in good condition as regards locality and needful sanitary provisions; but,—

Third. That nearly one-half of the unskilled laborers live in the inferior tenements.

Fourth. That the working classes of Massachusetts, judging from our investigations, are well fed.

Fifth. That their food, in variety and quality, is above the average of that consumed in foreign countries, and that, as regards quantity of animal food used, their "higher level" is unquestionable.

Sixth. That, as far as our investigations extended, our workingmen are, on the average, well and comfortably clothed.

Seventh. That their manner of dress is, at least, capable of most favorable comparison with that in foreign countries.

Eighth. That a large proportion of the skilled workingmen visited have sewing and other labor-saving machines in use in their families.

Ninth. That, as evidences of material prosperity to a certain extent, significant numbers of the families (the aid of child labor being fully allowed), own pianos or cabinet-organs, have carpeted rooms, and maintain pews in church.

6. Haverhill shoeworkers, c. 1880. Courtesy of the Trustees of the Haverhill Public Library, Special Collections Department.

As Regards Savings

First. That more than *one-half* of the *families* visited save money; less than one-tenth are in debt; and the remainder make both ends meet.

Second. That, without children's assistance, other things remaining equal, the majority of these families would be in poverty or debt.

Third. That savings, by families and fathers alone, are made in every branch of occupation investigated; but that in only a few cases is there evidence of the possibility of acquiring a competence, and, in those cases, it would be the result of assisted or family labor.

Fourth. That the higher the income, generally speaking, the greater the saving, actually and proportionately.

Fifth. That the average saving is about *three per cent* of the earnings.

Sixth. That while the houses of the workingmen visited compare most favorably with those in foreign countries and other states of the Union, yet, in certain of the United States, workingmen have better opportunities for acquiring homes of their own. (MBLS, *Sixth Annual Report*, 1875, 442–45)

Several years later, Wright attempted to measure changes a generation of factory workers had experienced in their standard of living. To this end, he compared weekly wages in 1860 (before the distortion of the Civil War), 1872 (before the financial panic of 1873), 1878 (when recovery had begun), and 1881 (a reasonably prosperous year). He intended his survey to be comprehensive; excerpts in Table 3 omit wage schedules he secured from dozens of other industries. To avoid the average-wage fallacy, Wright mirrored the complexity of factory organization in his tables; he considered the compensation of more than seventy categories of textile workers, for example. And to correct for currency fluctuations in the post–Civil War years, he stated both wages and prices in gold dollars, whose value he assumed to be constant. Finally, he added a table that enabled readers to convert gold into the day-to-day commodities that working families had to buy (Table 4).

These data were probably more reliable for 1878 and 1881 than for the earlier years, and Wright did not calculate percentage change for 1860 and 1872. His faith in the stability of gold was naive, if conventional at the time, and that assumption introduced some error into the year-to-year comparisons of monetary compensation. But Wright's inclusion of a table displaying the purchasing power of gold provided a useful, though clumsy, corrective. And the scope of his research, which extended to dozens of industries, hundreds of factories, and thousands of workers, provided reasonable assurance that the result was a recognizable statistical snapshot of the economic condition of factory workers about 1880, even if the comparison with earlier years was perhaps blurred.

Table 3. Average weekly wage, 1860, 1872, 1878, 1881.

Occupation	Average weekly wage, standard, gold				Increase or decrease for 1881, as compared with 1878
	1860	1872	1878	1881	
Boots and Shoes					
Cutters	12.00	14.81	11.05	14.91	3.86
Bottomers	10.50	16.00	10.71	11.71	1.00
Boot-treers	10.50	—	12.00	11.41	(.50)
Crimpers	10.50	—	10.00	11.88	1.88
Fitters	—	14.22	12.00	9.63	(2.37)
Finishers	14.50	16.00	11.75	12.18	.43
Buffers	—	—	19.50	11.21	(8.29)
Heelers	—	17.78	13.75	11.31	(2.44)
Edge-setters	12.00	17.78	13.00	11.50	(1.50)
Shoemakers	10.33	14.66	8.00	12.21	4.21
Machine hands, women	$8.25	$8.89	$7.33	$7.81	$.48
McKay operators	—	22.22	17.75	15.40	(2.35)
Beaters-out	—	16.89	15.00	11.43	(3.57)
Trimmers	18.00	17.78	12.25	11.99	(.26)
Women	5.50	—	8.00	8.48	.48
Building Trades					
Carpenters	9.92	14.66	11.33	12.64	1.31
Painters and glaziers	11.03	14.11	13.85	14.66	.81
Steam and gas fitters	10.28	19.55	12.16	15.35	3.19
Slaters	14.39	16.00	12.50	13.00	.50
Paper-hangers	12.97	14.82	16.45	14.45*	(2.00)
Plumbers	14.05	14.22	18.00	18.00	(.32)
Plasterers	10.18	21.33	12.25	13.25	1.00
Masons	11.45	21.33	13.37	14.04	.67
Carpenters' laborers	7.16	—	8.29	8.86	.57
Masons' and plasterers' laborers	7.12	12.22	8.13	8.60	.47
Paper					
Foremen	16.63	16.00	26.49	25.25	(1.24)
Millwrights	9.86	16.00	15.21	14.47	(.74)
Rag-engine tenders	7.90	14.67	10.41	10.90	.49
Paper-machine tenders	10.00	16.00	15.25	15.50	.25
Thresher-women	5.70	8.89	7.40	7.50	.10
Rag-cutters	7.50	—	8.40	6.78	(1.62)
Finishers	7.70	11.33	10.20	12.31	2.11
Finishers, girls	3.92	6.93	5.27	7.58	2.31
Finishers, boys	5.50	—	7.00	7.87	.87
Finishers' helpers	5.80	—	7.27	10.50	3.23
Cutters, girls	3.40	5.33	5.00	5.70	.70
Bleachers	6.70	8.89	7.56	6.94	(.62)
Rag-sorters	3.27	4.00	4.53	4.97	.44
Men on stock	5.88	9.33	6.57	8.14	1.57
Mechanics	9.75	—	13.20	14.62	1.42
Engineers and firemen	6.64	10.52	8.77	10.48	1.71
Laborers	5.50	8.33	6.55	7.89	1.34

Table 3. Continued

Occupation	Average weekly wage, standard, gold				Increase or decrease for 1881, as compared with 1878
	1860	1872	1878	1881	
Clothing (Ready-made)					
Overseers	19.45	24.45	24.82	28.33	3.51
Cutters	13.92	19.85	16.00	19.81	3.81
Trimmers	11.06	11.26	14.31	13.69	(.62)
Pressers	9.17	16.05	10.28	14.70	4.42
Basters, women	6.32	7.77	6.46	8.00	1.54
Machine operators, women	5.53	10.81	5.92	9.47	3.55
Finishers, at home, women	4.00	—	3.46	5.42	1.96
Finishers, in shop, women	4.56	4.74	4.58	4.95	.37
Finishers, custom, women	6.00	—	8.00	8.71	.71
Pants and vestmakers, custom work, women	5.58	—	6.90	8.54	1.64
Cotton Goods					
Openers and pickers	4.76	7.35	6.23	6.67	.44
Openers and pickers, boys	2.57	4.55	3.45	3.45	—
Strippers	4.48	7.00	5.06	6.21	1.15
Grinders	6.51	7.50	7.34	8.42	1.08
Frame-tenders	3.48	5.65	4.47	4.90	.43
Drawers	2.33	—	3.70	4.52	.82
Railway and alley boys	$2.70	—	$3.45	$4.41	$.96
Slubbers	3.50	$3.30	4.80	5.90	1.10
Overseers of carding	16.70	26.67	18.72	17.80[†]	(.92)
Section hands	12.00	—	11.40	10.62	(.78)
Second hands	8.00	16.00	10.00	10.18	.18
Overseers of spinning	17.70	26.67	19.45	18.06[†]	(1.39)
Second hands	7.00	14.67	8.00	11.71	3.71
Section hands	9.00	—	11.40	10.01	(1.39)
General hands	6.00	—	6.44	5.96	(.48)
Young persons	3.46	4.59	3.72	4.11	.39
Spare hands	3.45	4.53	4.00	3.77	(.23)
Mule-spinners	6.33	10.70	7.41	10.09	2.68
Mule-spinners, women	—	6.30	4.00	8.52	4.52
Back-boys	2.07	3.68	2.32	2.97	(.65)
Doffers	3.00	—	4.65	4.27	(.38)
Frame-spinners	3.28	—	3.96	5.38	1.42
Frame-spinners, boys and girls	2.68	4.55	3.34	2.95	(.39)
Frame-spinners, girls	2.37	—	3.52	4.38	.86
Frame-spinners, boys	—	—	2.70	3.00	.30
Ring-spinners, overseers	11.52	—	18.00	13.80	(4.20)
Ring-spinners, second hands	7.50	—	9.00	10.51	1.51
Ring-spinners, third hands	4.00	—	5.50	8.61	3.11
Ring-spinners, girls	3.60	—	4.20	4.95	.75
Doffers, boys	2.56	4.00	2.80	2.70	(.10)

Table 3. Continued

Occupation	Average weekly wage, standard, gold				Increase or decrease for 1881, as compared with 1878
	1860	1872	1878	1881	
Cotton Goods—Cont.					
Fly and jack-frame tenders	3.50	—	5.80	7.05	1.25
Reeling and warping, overseers	9.00	14.67	15.00	16.05	1.05
Reeling and warping, second hands	4.50	9.33	9.00	9.44	.44
Reeling and warping, spare hands, girls	2.40	4.48	4.20	4.33	.13
Reeling and warping, spoolers	2.62	4.85	3.96	5.21	1.25
Reeling and warping, young persons,	2.53	4.53	3.00	5.10	2.10
Beamers	7.35	—	9.25	5.57	(3.68)
Warpers	4.22	5.90	5.30	6.23	.93
Dressers	8.19	15.47	11.27	10.23	(1.04)
Dressers, overseers	21.91	21.33	20.40	18.00[†]	(2.40)
Slasher-tenders	—	10.00	9.79	7.50	(2.29)
Drawers	4.56	5.64	5.55	5.49	(.06)
Drawers, section hands	6.25	10.67	8.34	6.78	(1.56)
Drawers, third hands	6.00	8.80	6.90	6.86	(.04)
Drawers, room hands	5.00	—	6.00	8.19	2.19
Twisters, women	4.50	5.33	5.00	5.85	.85
Weavers	4.44	—	5.88	6.44	.56
Weavers, overseers	17.41	—	20.00	16.39[†]	(3.61)
Weavers, second hands	7.00	—	9.00	10.91	1.91
Weavers, section hands	7.74	10.67	9.71	9.18	(.53)
Weavers, spare hands	4.50	6.61	5.25	6.06	.81
Weavers, 4 looms	—	5.78	3.96	5.64	1.68
Weavers, 5 looms	—	7.81	4.50	5.66	1.16
Weavers, 6 looms	—	9.50	5.01	6.74	1.73
Weavers, 8 looms	—	11.33	6.30	8.23	1.93
Bobbin-boys	4.00	—	4.50	3.78	(.72)
Cloth room overseers	18.10	14.67	17.25	11.50[†]	(5.75)
Cloth room second hands	7.17	8.64	9.30	10.00	.70
Cloth room, men	5.44	8.16	6.45	7.69	1.24
Cloth room, women and boys	4.06	4.80	4.27	5.20	.93
Packing room, girls and boys	4.03	—	4.70	5.59	.89
Dyers	5.87	8.93	8.13	6.30	(1.83)
Bundlers	6.00	8.69	8.88	8.27	(.61)
Overseers of repairs	17.10	17.33	20.00	18.39	(1.61)
Mechanics	8.35	12.16	10.72	13.51	2.79
Mechanics, laborers	5.47	8.72	6.94	7.09	.15
Engineers	9.00	—	11.37	17.75	6.38
Firemen	7.09	—	8.33	9.33	1.00
Overseers of yard	11.56	—	16.05	17.37	1.32
Yard hands	5.22	8.76	6.32	7.69	1.37
Watchmen	6.83	—	8.12	9.23	1.11
Teamsters	5.40	10.67	8.01	9.31	1.30

Table 3. Continued

Occupation	Average weekly wage, standard, gold				Increase or decrease for 1881, as compared with 1878
	1860	1872	1878	1881	
Machines and Machinery					
Pattern-makers	11.50	17.60	15.24	18.10	2.86
Iron-moulders	9.50	14.67	12.30	16.40	4.10
Brass-moulders	10.00	14.67	13.25	15.75	2.50
Core-makers	5.00	—	6.00	6.28	.28
Blacksmiths	9.15	16.00	12.15	15.75	3.60
Blacksmiths' helpers	6.50	10.20	7.70	10.29	2.59
Machinists	9.64	14.40	13.05	17.09	4.04
Cleaners and chippers	6.00	—	7.50	8.64	1.14
Chuckers	6.75	—	9.75	11.33	1.58
Fitters	8.83	14.40	10.66	12.82	2.16
Polishers	8.00	—	9.75	8.59	(1.16)
Setters-up	10.00	12.80	12.00	13.38	1.38
Rivet-heaters, boys	4.00	—	5.00	5.64	.64
Riveters	9.50	14.67	12.00	13.05	1.05
Wood-workers	9.16	—	10.39	14.60	4.21
Painters	6.00	—	8.00	12.23	4.23
Laborers	6.00	8.53	7.27	9.15	1.88
Watchmen	7.00	—	9.00	12.21	3.21
Teamaters	7.50	—	10.00	11.80	1.80

Source: MBLS, *Thirteenth Annual Report*, 1882, 420–24.

Whatever its purchasing power, the average weekly wage was no sure guide to a recipient's annual income. The shoe and textile factories that employed many Massachusetts workers were particularly prone to periodic closure for lack of orders or machinery failure; during such periods, employees went unpaid. Piece workers, whose compensation depended on production, sometimes could not earn because of bottlenecks elsewhere in a factory. Workers occasionally fell ill. An average weekly wage, in short, represented what a worker who worked at full capacity for a full week might expect in Saturday's pay envelope. In many weeks, the envelope was thin, a condition beyond the control of those who did not set the speed of machinery, determine the hours of operation, or generate orders for product.[3]

3. See Alexander Keyssar, *Out of Work: The First Century of Unemployment in Massachusetts* (Cambridge: Cambridge University Press, 1986).

Table 4. Purchasing power of money, 1860, 1872, 1878, 1881.

Articles				
	1860	1872	1878	1881

Articles	What one dollar would buy in— 1860	1872	1878	1881
Groceries				
Flour, superfine, wheat	25.64 lbs.	18.18 lbs.	22.72 lbs.	19.76 lbs.
Flour, family	27.77 lbs.	15.38 lbs.	25 lbs.	22.87 lbs.
Flour, rye	33.33 lbs.	31.25 lbs.	28.57 lbs.	22.22 lbs.
Corn meal	45.45 lbs.	55.55 lbs.	47.62 lbs.	32 lbs.
Codfish, dry	18.87 lbs.	12.20 lbs.	16.67 lbs.	13.33 lbs.
Rice	13.33 lbs.	8.93 lbs.	10.87 lbs.	10.25 lbs.
Beans	12.66 qts.	10.52 qts.	12.05 qts.	7.54 lbs.
Tea, oolong	1.83 lbs.	1.45 lbs.	1.66 lbs.	1.72 lbs.
Coffee, Rio, green	4.67 lbs.	2.92 lbs.	4.22 lbs.	5.40 lbs.
Coffee, roasted	4.36 lbs.	2.35 lbs.	3.77 lbs.	3.47 lbs.
Sugar, good brown	12.19 lbs.	9.80 lbs.	11.63 lbs.	10.95 lbs.
Sugar, coffee	10.99 lbs.	9.52 lbs.	10.64 lbs.	10 lbs.
Sugar, granulated	9.70 lbs.	8.33 lbs.	10 lbs.	9.09 lbs.
Molasses, New Orleans	1.97 gals.	1.43 gals.	1.74 gals.	1.50 gals.
Molasses, Porto Rico	1.73 gals.	1.31 gals.	1.45 gals.	1.60 gals.
Syrup	1.57 gals.	1.33 gals.	1.16 gals.	1.30 gals.
Soap	11.49 lbs.	12.50 lbs.	12.34 lbs.	14.81 lbs.
Starch	9.18 lbs.	8.19 lbs.	10.64 lbs.	10.81 lbs.
Provisions				
Beef, roasting	9.18 lbs.	5.26 lbs.	6.94 lbs.	5.88 lbs.
Beef, soup	20.83 lbs.	13.33 lbs.	18.86 lbs.	18.18 lbs.
Beef, rump steak	6.85 lbs.	3.39 lbs.	4.85 lbs.	4.93 lbs.
Beef, corned	15.38 lbs.	9.52 lbs.	12.34 lbs.	9.75 lbs.
Veal, fore-quarter	13.70 lbs.	9.52 lbs.	9.80 lbs.	8.50 lbs.
Veal, hind-quarter	9.18 lbs.	5.85 lbs.	6.53 lbs.	6.34 lbs.
Veal cutlets	7.09 lbs.	3.54 lbs.	5.05 lbs.	5 lbs.
Mutton, fore-quarter	13.51 lbs.	9.80 lbs.	9.70 lbs.	8.82 lbs.
Mutton, leg	8.07 lbs.	5.26 lbs.	5.78 lbs.	5.97 lbs.
Mutton chops	7.46 lbs.	6.51 lbs.	5.40 lbs.	5.48 lbs.
Pork, fresh	9.26 lbs.	8 lbs.	10 lbs.	7.69 lbs.
Pork, salted	9.09 lbs.	9.09 lbs.	10.31 lbs.	7.54 lbs.
Hams, smoked	7.75 lbs.	7.41 lbs.	8.07 lbs.	6.55 lbs.
Shoulders, corned	11.49 lbs.	9.80 lbs.	10.75 lbs.	8.38 lbs.
Sausages	8.77 lbs.	8 lbs.	8.84 lbs.	7.47 lbs.
Lard	7.57 lbs.	7.87 lbs.	9.34 lbs.	6.77 lbs.
Mackerel, pickled	10.52 lbs.	7.57 lbs.	8 lbs.	7.59 lbs.
Butter	4.58 lbs.	2.55 lbs.	3.97 lbs.	2.88 lbs.
Cheese	7.52 lbs.	5.71 lbs.	8.13 lbs.	5.71 lbs.
Potatoes	1.67 bush.	.97 bush.	1.03 bush.	.79 bush.
Milk	21.27 qts.	12.50 qts	18.86 qts.	16.66 qts.
Eggs	4.92 doz.	3.33 doz.	4.01 doz.	3.07 doz.
Fuel				
Coal	312.5 lbs.	217.39 lbs.	310.56 lbs.	255.18 lbs.
Wood, hard	1.23 feet.	.79 feet.	1.18 feet.	.89 feet.
Wood, pine	1.90 feet.	1.14 feet.	1.58 feet.	1.12 feet.

Income and Expense

Table 4. Continued.

Articles	What one dollar would buy in—			
	1860	1872	1878	1881
Dry Goods				
Shirting, 4-4 brown	10.87 yds.	7.69 yds.	13.33 yds.	11.42 yds.
Shirting, 4-4 bleached	9.26 yds.	6.25 yds.	10.64 yds.	9.09 yds.
Sheeting, 9-8 brown	9.34 yds.	7.14 yds.	11.11 yds.	9.30 yds.
Sheeting, 9-8 bleached	7.57 yds.	5.13 yds.	8.47 yds.	7.27 yds.
Cotton flannel	6.33 yds.	3.63 yds.	6.80 yds.	6.25 yds.
Ticking	5.81 yds.	4.17 yds.	5.78 yds.	5.97 yds.
Prints	9.09 yds.	8.55 yds.	12.98 yds.	12.90 yds.
Boots				
Men's heavy	$2.75 per pr.	$3.94 per pr.	$3.24 per pr.	$3.18¾ per pr.
Rents				
Four-room tenements	6.75 days.	2.03 days.	5.40 days.	3.75 days.
Six-room tenements	3.98 days.	1.87 days.	3.18 days.	2.45 days.
Board				
Men	2.51 days.	1.24 days.	1.67 days.	1.47 days.
Women	3.92 days.	1.87 days.	2.63 days.	2.33 days.

Source: MBLS, *Thirteenth Annual Report*, 1882, 430.

Carroll Wright knew that intermittent employment and involuntary layoffs made annual income a more accurate indication of a worker's economic circumstance that the average weekly wage. To estimate annual income, he tried to determine how much time workers lost in the course of a year. Table 5 derives from the census of 1880; Tables 6–8 are based on the state census five years later.

Table 5. Estimated annual wage, by industry, 1880.

Industries	Average number of employés	Wages. Total paid during the year	Actual average working time in months and days for each establishment; short time being reduced to its equivalent in full time		Actual average day's earnings, —including men, women youth and children	Actual average yearly earnings, —including men, women youth and children
			Months	*Days*		
Boots and shoes	37,657	$14,369,284	10.60	271.18	$1.41	$381.58
Boxes	775	272,785	11.16	285.51	1.23	351.98
Building	5,645	2,684,097	10.98	280.90	1.69	475.48
Clothing	11,435	4,021,363	11.49	293.95	1.20	351.67

Table 5. Continued.

Cotton goods	59,684	15,451,347	11.95	305.72	.85	258.89
Food preparations	2,901	1,349,793	11.53	294.98	1.58	465.29
Furniture	3,133	1,445,394	11.54	295.23	1.56	461.35
Leather	6,703	3,028,610	11.76	300.86	1.50	451.83
Machines and machinery	11,580	5,655,523	11.83	302.65	1.61	488.39
Metals and metallic goods	18,249	7,768,187	11.49	293.95	1.45	425.68
Paper	6,354	2,189,883	11.54	295.23	1.17	344.65
Printing and publishing	5,227	2,775,936	11.74	300.35	1.77	531.08
Rubber and elastic goods	2,644	824,372	11.70	299.32	1.04	311.79
Stone	1,370	580,009	11.25	287.81	1.47	423.36
Tobacco	905	360,224	11.74	300.34	1.33	398.04
Wooden goods	2,534	1,007,165	11.75	300.60	1.39	393.51
Woollen goods	22,597	7,077,444	11.78	301.37	1.04	313.20
TOTALS	199,393	$70,861,416	11.52	294.70	$1.37	$401.63

Source: MBLS, *Fourteenth Annual Report*, 1883, 241.

Table 6. Distribution of the unemployed by number of months unemployed, in percentages, 1885.

Sex and Numbers of Months Unemployed	Age Periods									
	10 to 13	14 to 19	20 to 29	30 to 39	40 to 49	50 to 59	60 to 79	80 and over	Un-known	All Ages
Males	100.00	100.00	100.00	100.00	100.00	100.00	100.00	100.00	100.00	100.00
One month	8.21	6.93	8.76	8.60	6.60	5.31	3.24	2.22	5.56	7.25
Two months	14.08	17.05	20.54	20.39	18.37	16.05	11.26	6.37	11.11	18.34
Three months	14.37	14.88	17.93	18.60	17.78	15.65	12.53	7.48	33.33	16.87
Four months	15.54	18.33	20.89	21.90	22.00	22.79	21.63	18.56	33.33	21.16
Five months	7.04	6.97	6.91	7.03	7.83	7.60	7.49	4.71	5.56	7.22
Six months	22.87	20.00	16.28	16.18	18.61	20.95	27.30	33.52	5.56	18.66
Seven months	2.93	3.07	2.31	2.14	2.49	2.87	3.45	2.77	5.55	2.58
Eight months	3.52	4.23	2.35	2.20	2.53	3.69	4.76	8.86	—	2.99
Nine months	3.52	3.49	1.58	1.35	1.75	2.33	3.56	3.88	—	2.09
Ten months	4.11	2.95	1.37	0.89	1.20	1.48	2.51	4.43	—	1.59
Eleven months	3.81	1.94	0.76	0.48	0.53	0.62	0.79	2.21	—	0.83
Twelve months	—	0.16	0.32	0.24	0.31	0.66	1.48	4.99	—	0.42
Females	100.00	100.00	100.00	100.00	100.00	100.00	100.00	100.00	100.00	100.00
One month	7.31	10.85	11.50	10.38	7.20	5.88	3.85	14.82	—	10.53
Two months	19.63	22.33	25.41	24.85	23.06	19.66	14.17	7.41	50.00	23.86
Three months	15.07	16.64	19.92	19.62	19.28	16.74	14.48	—	—	18.65
Four months	14.61	13.98	15.74	15.57	16.02	16.93	17.40	22.22	—	15.28
Five months	5.94	5.88	5.34	4.99	4.38	3.73	5.52	—	50.00	5.33
Six months	16.44	15.14	13.13	15.53	18.76	23.77	27.71	25.93	—	15.05
Seven months	1.37	3.01	2.16	2.06	2.39	2.53	3.33	3.70	—	2.44
Eight months	2.74	3.54	2.37	2.56	3.28	4.26	4.48	7.41	—	2.91
Nine months	6.85	3.24	2.00	1.98	2.96	2.58	4.58	3.70	—	2.51
Ten months	3.65	3.18	1.44	1.71	1.80	2.39	2.71	3.70	—	2.08
Eleven months	6.39	2.15	0.88	0.60	0.87	1.20	1.25	3.70	—	1.25
Twelve months	—	0.06	0.11	0.15	—	0.33	0.52	7.41	—	0.11

Table 6. Continued.

Both Sexes	100.00	100.00	100.00	100.00	100.00	100.00	100.00	100.00	100.00	100.00
One month	7.86	8.56	9.72	8.95	6.68	5.36	3.27	3.09	5.00	8.10
Two months	16.25	19.24	22.25	21.28	18.98	16.39	11.44	6.44	15.00	19.78
Three months	14.64	15.61	18.63	18.80	17.98	15.76	12.65	6.96	30.00	17.33
Four months	15.18	16.52	19.09	20.65	21.22	22.24	21.37	18.81	30.00	19.63
Five months	6.61	6.52	6.36	6.63	7.38	7.24	7.37	4.38	10.00	6.73
Six months	20.36	17.98	15.17	16.05	18.63	21.21	27.32	32.99	5.00	17.72
Seven months	2.32	3.05	2.26	2.12	2.47	2.84	3.44	2.84	5.00	2.54
Eight months	3.21	3.94	2.36	2.27	2.63	3.74	4.74	8.76	—	2.97
Nine months	4.82	3.38	1.73	1.47	1.91	2.35	3.63	3.87	—	2.20
Ten months	3.93	3.05	1.39	1.05	1.28	1.56	2.53	4.38	—	1.72
Eleven months	4.82	2.03	0.80	0.50	0.57	0.68	0.82	2.32	—	0.94
Twelve months	—	0.12	0.24	0.23	0.27	0.63	1.42	5.16	—	0.34

Source: MBLS, *Eighteenth Annual Report*, 1887, 154.

Table 7. Number and percentages of unemployed persons, by occupation, 1885.

	Number and Percentages of Unemployed Persons					
	Males		Females		Both Sexes	
Classified Occupation	Number	Percentages	Number	Percentages	Number	Percentages
The State	178,628	100.00	62,961	100.00	241,580	100.00
Government and professional	2,190	1.22	5,717	9.08	7,907	3.27
Domestic service	928	0.52	3,986	6.33	4,914	2.03
Personal service	1,637	0.92	2,509	3.99	4,146	1.72
Trade	8,262	4.62	1,247	1.98	9,509	3.94
Transportation	7,014	3.93	19	0.03	7,033	2.91
Agriculture	15,130	8.47	35	0.06	15,165	6.28
Fisheries	3,533	1.98	3	—	3,536	1.46
Manufactures	117,792	65.94	49,249	78.22	167,041	69.14
Mining	694	0.39	—	—	694	0.29
Laborers	20,346	11.39	15	0.02	20,361	8.43
Apprentices	1,102	0.62	181	0.29	1,283	0.53

Source: MBLS, *Eighteenth Annual Report*, 1887, 225.

Table 8. Number and percentages of unemployed persons, by place of birth, 1885.

	Number and Percentages of Unemployed Persons					
	Number			Percentages		
Place of Birth	Males	Females	Total	Males	Females	Total
The State	178,628	62,961	241,589	100.00	100.00	100.00
NATIVE BORN	102,480	42,073	144,553	57.37	66.82	59.83
Massachusetts	78,509	32,159	110,668	43.95	51.08	45.81
New England States, Other	17,892	7,299	25,191	10.02	11.59	10.43
Other States	6,079	2,615	8,694	3.40	4.15	3.59

Table 8. Continued.

FOREIGN BORN	76,148	20,888	97,036	42.63	33.18	40.17
Ireland	38,440	8,432	46,872	21.52	13.39	19.40
Canada (English)	1,601	696	2,297	0.90	1.11	0.95
Canada (French)	11,483	4,052	15,535	6.43	6.44	6.43
England	8,193	3,206	11,399	4.59	5.09	4.72
Scotland	1,732	582	2,314	0.97	0.92	0.96
Nova Scotia	4,430	1,661	6,091	2.48	2.64	2.52
Prince Edward Island	677	238	915	0.38	0.38	0.38
New Brunawick	1,656	751	2,407	0.92	1.19	1.00
Germany	2,228	364	2,592	1.25	0.58	1.07
Sweden	1,361	194	1,555	0.76	0.31	0.65
Portugal	1,205	105	1,310	0.67	0.17	0.54
Other Foreign Coutries	3,142	607	3,749	1.76	0.96	1.55

Source: MBLS, *Eighteenth Annual Report*, 1887, 260.

An explanatory conclusion emphasized the content of these tables.

We find that of a total of 816,470 persons employed in gainful occupations the unemployed persons, 241,589 in number, represent 29.59 per cent, while 574,881 persons, or 70.41 per cent, were employed during the entire year. . . . We find, also, that the unemployed persons were unemployed at their principal occupation, on an average, 4.11 months, while for all persons employed in gainful occupations, considered as a whole, whether employed or unemployed, the average unemployment during the Census year was 1.22 months. *In other words, a little less than one-third of the persons returned as being engaged in remunerative labor were unemployed for about one-third of their working time; while on the other hand, the working population of the State, considered in their entirety, were employed at their principal occupation for a trifle less than eleven months during the Census year.*

The results just shown for 241,589 persons unemployed, on an average, 4.11 months during the year may be considered as being equivalent to 82,744 persons unemployed for an entire year. . . .

By a purely mathematical calculation based on the elements here presented, the result of this investigation would seem to indicate that all the products of manufactures could have been secured by steady work for 307 working days of 9.04 hours each, if this steady work could have been distributed equally among all the persons engaged in manufactures, while all the remunerative work of the State, of whatever kind, if it could have

been distributed equally among the entire working population, could have
been accomplished in 307 working days averaging 8.99 hours per day.
(MBLS, *Eighteenth Annual Report*, 1887, 266, 294)

Nineteenth-century factory workers expected temporary reductions
in income during "slack times," when styles and seasons changed, sales
slowed, and employers reduced production. But the economic dislocation of financial panics and industrial depressions, which seemed to
occur at roughly ten-year intervals, brought unemployment on a much
larger scale and pervasive fear that the condition might become
permanent. Five years after the panic of 1873, when demoralizing
rumors of extensive, persistent unemployment abounded, the bureau
surveyed the phenomenon and published reassuring results. The positive rhetoric of Carroll Wright's report contrasts with his customary
reliance on the weight of evidence to convey point of view.

The investigation of 1877 demonstrated the fact that the number of
hands employed in that year had actually increased, in all the leading
branches, to a considerable extent. . . .

These facts indicate a positive strength in the condition of our industrial
interest which cannot be gainsaid. That Massachusetts holds her own in
these matters, through the depression which affects all countries, is most
gratifying, and indicates a steadiness which will, in the future, produce
most excellent results. The fact that she has actually increased her
products, not only in value, but in quantity, must be taken as a guarantee
against any disaster resulting from the loss in any one industry, and as a
complete answer to any argument that her industries, or those of New
England, are on the decline, or can decline. . . .

The population of the State is 1,651,912; of which 584,690 belong to the
skilled and unskilled laborers,—447,184 males and 137,506 females. The
total unemployed [number] . . . 28,508 . . . skilled and unskilled laborers,
male and female, seeking, and in want of work, out of employment in
Massachusetts, June 1, 1878.

The public can place the utmost confidence in this statement; and we
have no fear of successful refutation. Against it can only be placed the wild
guess of some one who does not stop to consider his statement, and who

has not the slightest foundation for his figures.

It has been reported, and the report has been industriously circulated, that there are from 200,000 to 300,000 people out of employment in this State; 40,000 in the city of Boston; 3,000,000 in the United States, &c. This last figure has been quoted in papers, works on political economy, speeches in Congress, political resolutions, &c., till it has come to be believed everywhere; and yet this is the first attempt officially, or in any other way, to ascertain the facts. We say the figures reported herein are reliable. We have given the croaker the benefit of every doubt. . . .

We do not wish it to be understood for a moment that we do not think the people are poor: they are poor indeed, but they are not starving; and we venture the opinion that they are not suffering for food to the extent the popular estimate would lead us to imagine, and that the number now out of employment is not much larger than in ordinary times.

The testimony of officials in very many cases was, that a large percentage of those out of employment would not work if they could, or would not work for less than the wages of five years ago. The people are living on smaller wages, are learning to live within their means, and trying to adapt their wants to the circumstances in which they find themselves: the manufacturer is trying to keep his industry alive, is making every effort to keep his employés at work. They have been sick, both employer and employé; but they cannot be cured by constantly telling them how sick they are, certainly not by making them believe they are sicker than they really are. We have had enough of industrial hypochondria; and it is time the public recognized the facts in the case, and acted accordingly. The industrial stagnation and depression have been, and are, severe enough; but every sign indicates sure recuperation. The people are growing stronger every month; and, while this country will not jump into prosperity, it will find itself farther along during the next six or twelve months than it would have believed possible six months ago; for the assurance comes from every hand, by reports to this office from all parts of the Commonwealth, that employers of labor are starting up, or preparing to start up their works, this fall. Occasionally we still hear of works closing, but these reports grow less and less frequent. . . .

The outlook in Massachusetts and in New England is certainly much brighter, even at this writing, January, 1879, than in August last; and the same courage, patience, and faith in hard work, continued as in the near

Income and Expense

Table 9. Industrial employment and unemployment, in percentages by month, 1889–1893.

Industries and Months	Percentages of Employment During the Months Specified in—					Percentages of Unemployment During the Months Specified in—				
	1889	1890	1891	1892	1893	1889	1890	1891	1892	1893
All industries										
January	96.58	94.90	98.43	95.55	97.39	3.42	5.10	1.57	4.45	2.61
February	97.87	96.29	98.89	97.02	98.02	2.13	3.71	1.11	2.98	1.98
March	98.39	97.29	99.28	97.93	99.09	1.61	2.71	0.72	2.07	0.91
April	98.48	97.23	99.70	98.99	100.00	1.52	2.77	0.30	1.01	—
May	98.62	97.50	100.00	98.90	99.63	1.38	2.50	—	1.10	0.37
June	98.63	97.96	99.34	98.26	97.08	1.37	2.04	0.66	1.74	2.92
July	97.65	96.87	98.11	97.15	91.68	2.35	3.13	1.89	2.85	8.32
August	98.31	97.55	98.27	97.62	82.51	1.69	2.45	1.73	2.38	17.49
September	99.47	98.95	99.17	99.05	77.67	0.53	1.05	0.83	0.95	22.33
October	100.00	100.00	99.70	99.93	84.73	—	—	0.30	0.07	15.27
November	99.70	99.24	98.98	100.00	84.86	0.30	0.76	1.02	—	15.14
December	99.04	98.58	99.24	99.76	85.22	0.96	1.42	0.76	0.24	14.78

Source: MBLS, *Twenty-fourth Annual Report*, 1894, 124.

past, will reward the worker in the near future with continued occupation. (MBLS, *Tenth Annual Report*, 1879, 3–4, 6–9, 13)

The bureau responded more promptly and with a different emphasis to the depression that began in 1893 than had been the case twenty years earlier. "Enforced idleness due to lack of employment," wrote Director Horace Wadlin, "leads in importance all other topics relating to the labor question."[4] Wadlin sought not only to document unemployment but also to investigate proposals to relieve the resulting distress. In particular, Wadlin studied Boston's effort to provide "relief work" during the winter of 1893–94. Tables 9 and 10 demonstrate the rapid deterioration of economic conditions. With respect to Table 10, the bureau defined three hundred days of annual operation as full-time production.

The statistics of the number of days in operation relate only to working time, and show nothing as regards the working force, that is, do not indicate partial or extensive reductions in the number of persons employed, unless there was an entire suspension of business. If the establish-

4. MBLS, *Twenty-fourth Annual Report* (1894), xv.

Table 10. Days of operation in industrial establishments, 1889–1893.

Classification of Days in Operation	Number of Establishments					Percentages				
	1889	1890	1891	1892	1893	1889	1890	1891	1892	1893
Under 100 days	9	31	33	44	69	0.30	0.83	0.73	1.00	1.57
100 but under 150 days	28	35	50	49	80	0.92	0.93	1.11	1.11	1.82
150 but under 200 days	51	92	110	134	204	1.68	2.46	2.46	3.05	4.64
200 but under 250 days	167	221	266	228	594	5.49	5.90	5.95	5.19	13.51
250 but under 300 days	801	883	979	904	1,449	26.34	23.58	21.89	20.56	32.95
300 days and over	1,985	2,483	3,035	3,038	2,001	65.27	66.30	67.86	69.09	45.51
TOTALS	3,041	3,745	4,473	4,397	4,397	100.00	100.00	100.00	100.00	100.00

Source: MBLS, *Twenty-fourth Annual Report*, 1894, 133.

ments were not in operation, of course, all the employés would be unemployed so far as that particular establishment is concerned. . . . As a general statement, . . . it may be said that slightly more than two-thirds of the establishments, when all industries are considered in the aggregate, run on full time. This statement may be contrasted with the per cent shown in 1893, when only 45.51 per cent of the establishments were of this class. That is, to put the statement in another way, in the year 1893 less than one-half of the establishments ran on full time. (MBLS, *Twenty-fourth Annual Report*, 1894, 133–34)

To assist victims of the depression, civic groups across the Commonwealth solicited funds that, in the case of Boston, provided brief outdoor jobs for unemployed men and indoor work for women. Through the cooperation of the private agencies that administered the $136,568.70 collected in the city for this purpose, the bureau identified the beneficiaries of this "work relief." In reviewing the program's operation, a surprised Wadlin remarked that politics had not affected the distribution of funds and that many destitute recipients were not even voters. Those hired were permitted to earn an amount roughly equivalent to two weeks' predepression pay; they were then replaced in order to spread available resources to others. Two weeks' wages, of course, did not stretch far in families that had been without income for months. Boston's effort, Wadlin concluded, was inadequate though praiseworthy and no model for hard future times.

But he lacked an alternative. The problem clearly defied the resources of private charity and local government, which, Wadlin and

CHARITY IN BOSTON—THE BEDFORD STREET WORK-ROOM FOR WOMEN.
Drawn by Henry Sandham.

7. Work relief in Boston, *Harper's Weekly*, March 3, 1894. Boston Athenaeum.

most of his contemporaries believed, had neither the legal authority nor the social responsibility to devise a remedy for industrial unemployment. In effect, Wadlin argued that part of the problem might legitimately be ignored, since some of Boston's unemployed caused their own condition through lack of skill, stamina, or ambition. He seemed almost reluctant to concede that others lacked only opportunity.

Without considering the limitations which are at present placed upon the taxing power and borrowing capacity of cities, which of themselves are a sufficient bar to extensive municipal employment, it is plain that until the present industrial organization is materially changed efforts in this direction will be full of difficulty. We are not referring to direct employment on certain public works of utility or necessity, which may be undertaken in times of depression, but to the general provision of employment. The same causes which at any particular time limit production under private management will prevent economic production under municipal direction as long as the conditions controlling industrial operations in general continue as at present. Cities have no power to create work or to materially enlarge opportunities for employment, apart from the forces that control production, unless it is expected that work of no utility is to be undertaken for the sake of providing employment.

Indiscriminate relief whether of money or work harms more than it helps, and the relying upon the municipality to do those things which may be accomplished through persistent individual effort tends to become chronic, weakens character, and might easily be carried so far as to cause serious social evils.

Whatever may be the need of furnishing relief in case of emergency, or the necessity for prompt action in junctures like that of last winter, it must be frankly said that the dissemination of a temporary fund is not the way to solve the problem of unemployment. No fund that is likely to be raised is at all adequate for the purpose, and even as a source of charity-relief, is of questionable value, apart from its tendency to destroy the stamina of those who rely upon it.

The experience in Boston is sufficient to support this statement. Those who received relief were principally unskilled or of little skill, and the amount of relief afforded was no more than equal to two weeks' pay per individual on the average. This was at a time of unusual depression, but the same sort of applicants might be expected to appear in any year, although possibly in less numbers, if a fund of equal amount were provided. These remarks do not involve criticism of the committee which administered the fund, nor do they reflect upon the generosity or motives of those who subscribed to it, nor is it intended to criticise harshly those who applied, and who received work. Their condition was, in many instances, perhaps in most instances, such as to excite pity and entitle them to relief. We are merely speaking of the inadequacy of this method of removing the evil of unemployment. The meagre amount of the relief afforded through such channels must of itself discourage the skilled workman from applying, and it inevitably operated to create ill-feeling, because so little was forthcoming where much had been expected. Much ought not to have been expected, it is true, if one reflects that to have carried the 50,000 persons, who in the manufacturing industries alone were out of employment in Massachusetts during the last half of 1893, through the winter, at wages only half as large as they had previously earned upon the average, would have required a fund of nearly $6,000,000;

but this fact was neither known to, nor appreciated by, those who were most likely to complain of the small amount of work which it was possible for the relief committee to furnish.

The unemployed in general, under normal conditions, are of at least four classes:

1. Casual workers who engage for short periods and upon odd jobs; and among these may be included all without regular trades. These are relatively few in number in Massachusetts or in Boston. . . .

2. Those workers in trades which have alternating busy and dull seasons, or which are subject to weather conditions for their successful prosecution. In Massachusetts, Boots and Shoes, Building, and Straw and Palm Leaf Goods are prominent examples. But in these industries the periods of unemployment are of regular recurrence, are foreseen, and generally compensated for by the savings or foresight of the workers. In Boots and Shoes and Building, especially, earnings range much higher than in most other industries, especially, those included in the textile group, in which employment is more regular.

3. Superfluous workers in all trades. That is, workers in excess of the normal demand. This class except in times of peculiar depression has never been numerous in the United States.

4. Workers of low efficiency, untrained and relatively unskilled, who, at the recurrence of the dull season, or in times of depression, are the first to be thrown out. These are found in all trades.

The mere enumeration of these classes indicates the magnitude of the problem with which society, in certain junctures, must deal. In cases of actual want almost the sole reliance, at present, is relief . . . by private charity, and this carries with it a stigma, not always deserved, but, unfortunately, nearly always felt.

While we may say that the ordinary form of charity-relief by dole is rapidly becoming discredited, it is not yet clear what shall take its place. Just as there is great danger of chronic pauperism under the old forms of relief, so there is equal danger of absolute reliance on public aid rather than on personal effort. The problem is doubtless not insoluble, but at present we have not reached a satisfactory solution. Any panacea which is advocated for immediate adoption, no matter how strenuously, as likely to be permanently remedial, must be received with extreme caution. A warm heart without knowledge, equally with wide knowledge without sympathy, may carry one far astray on this subject as on many others.

Methods of dealing with the problem must be at once far-reaching and permanent. The subject is complicated by confusing those who are ineffic- ient, or of low morale, with those who are willing and able to work, but who are unable to obtain employment. We should recognize that besides the divisions of the unemployed which have been given, they are of two general classes which include all others: the honest and the dishonest,—the worthy and the unworthy. . . .

Any method of dealing with unemployment which is likely to succeed must rigidly discriminate between these two classes. The careful study of the various methods outlined in this report leads inevitably to this conclusion. The two classes do not readily unite, and no attempt should be made to join them in any scheme for dealing with the evil. One class should be restrained and disciplined, the other aided upon some plan which should not involve stigma nor be demoralizing in its tendency, and which should possess the following essential elements:

1. It should not be inharmonious with the present industrial organiza- tion.

2. It should aim to fit the unemployed to enter the industrial body, and should contemplate their absorption therein at the earliest possible oppor- tunity.

3. It should aim to render production more uniform, preventing, so far as possible, seasonal depressions, and it should also aim to carry produc- tion farther than at present. (MBLS, *Twenty-fourth Annual Report*, 1894, 248–51)

CHAPTER THREE

Money in the Bank

Perhaps working people in Massachusetts during the later nineteenth century believed that American society was open and that wealth rewarded personal effort. Students of the period have attributed the nation's apparent toleration of disrupting industrial change partly to broad popular acceptance of rags-to-riches mythology and a Darwinian view of social evolution. If laborers in the Commonwealth held such beliefs, the staff of the Bureau of Statistics of Labor did not often record their professions of faith. The absence of such statements may not be significant, since the bureau's questions were ordinarily intended to elicit factual responses rather than ideology. Still, the ability of workers to accumulate wealth was a subject of particular interest to Henry K. Oliver, and his inquiries surely permitted expressions of aspiration as well as experience, of hope as well as accomplishment.

Oliver asked, for instance, whether workers could save enough to acquire what he called a "competence." The notion was so alien to some of the bureau's informants as to require definition: a competence, Oliver explained, consisted of sufficient personal assets—real estate, savings, a profitable small business—to enable their owner to exist in some comfort if age or disability or economic conditions precluded further factory employment.[1] The most readily available statistic

---

1. Before the Civil War, the term "competence" had often denoted a skill or trade; Oliver gave the word a more inclusive connotation that perhaps confused the industrial workers he queried. See Kim Voss, *The Making of American Exceptionalism* (Ithaca:

bearing on that topic was the size of a working family's bank account.

Early in the nineteenth century, the Commonwealth had begun to charter savings banks, which offered incentives to attract small deposits from thrifty working people. Although individual accounts in these institutions were limited by law—to one thousand dollars in the 1870s—regulators became aware that the rule was regularly circumvented and the original intent subverted. In 1870 and again in 1871, Governor William Claflin noted that persons "seeking investment for very considerable sums" had discovered the state's savings banks; these funds, the governor continued, did not derive from "the savings of labor" but represented instead "the accumulation of capitalists."[2]

As Claflin's remarks suggest, a political controversy swirled around these banks in the 1870s. Their rising assets became part of the rhetorical stock in trade of defenders of industrial conditions in the Commonwealth. How could labor reformers, among whom these publicists numbered Oliver and Deputy Director George E. McNeill, argue that employers ought to pay higher wages when the balance sheets of savings banks demonstrated that ordinary folk were amassing ever larger resources? Why, indeed, should the state interfere in any way with labor relations that obviously led to mounting prosperity for all the state's inhabitants?

McNeill thought the bureau's earlier research belied the complacence of those questions. For families with annual incomes approximating six hundred dollars, saving seemed only theoretically possible; McNeill decided that the increasing wealth on deposit in the Commonwealth's savings banks must have another explanation. Although he received reluctant and incomplete cooperation from the banks themselves, he attempted to identify their depositors and to calculate the size of an average deposit.

McNeill's study disturbed the Massachusetts Senate's Committee on

---

Cornell University Press, 1993), 23–24. Two books by Stephan Thernstrom dealing with Massachusetts cities are examples of the extensive scholarship on social mobility and other elements of the ideology of American industrialization. For Newburyport, see Thernstrom's *Poverty and Progress* (Cambridge: Harvard University Press, 1964); and for Boston, see *The Other Bostonians* (Cambridge: Harvard University Press, 1973).

2. MBLS, *Third Annual Report* (1872), 299.

Banks and Banking, of which every member was a director of at least one savings bank. To contradict his report, the committee engaged counsel and solicited evidence from banks across the state. Unable a year before to respond in months to McNeill's queries, bank managers now filed detailed reports in forty-eight hours. The committee summoned Oliver and McNeill on Saturday to a hearing the following Monday morning at which a resolution deploring the bureau's work was debated and approved. The resolution charged that "inferences and conclusions" in the bureau's report for 1872 were "based upon insufficient . . . data, and . . . not properly substantiated by the facts."[3] The measure passed the Senate but died in the House. In its published account of the hearing, the bureau began with a table that the Senate committee particularly disliked (Table 11) and then reiterated offending conclusions from the year before.

Table 11. Total and average deposits of savings banks, 1872.

Deposits at 15 banks	No. of depositors	Average	Amount
Between $5 and $10	1,731	$ 7.50	$ 12,982.50
Between 10 and 20	1,406	15.00	21,090.00
Between 20 and 30	1,202	25.00	30,050.00
Between 30 and 50	1,399	40.00	55,960.00
Between $5 and $50	5,738	$ 20.92	$ 120,082.50
Between $50 and $75	1,440	$ 62.50	$ 90,000.00
Between 75 and 100	1,452	87.50	127,050.00
Between 50 and $100	2,892	$ 75.05	$ 217,050.00
Between $100 and $200	2,308	$150.00	$ 346,200.00
Between 200 and 300	1,334	250.00	333,500.00
Between $100 and $300	3,642	$186.62	$ 679,700.00
Between $300 and $500	1,259	$400.00	$ 503,600.00
Between 500 and 750	704	625.00	440,000.00
Between 750 and 1,000	470	875.00	411,250.00
Between $300 and $1,000	2,433	$556.86	$1,354,850.00
Total number of depositors			14,705
Estimated amount of deposits			$2,371,682.50
Number of depositors, under $300			12,272
Amount of same			$1,016,832.50
Number of depositors of and over $300			2,433
Amount of same			$1,354,850.00

Source: MBLS, *Third Annual Report*, 1872, 320.

3. MBLS, *Fourth Annual Report* (1873), 12.

By this it appears that six-sevenths of the depositors own less than one-half the deposits, the remaining seventh owning $338,017.50, more than the six-sevenths own.

In this calculation, we have allowed the workmen's yearly deposits to amount to $300; but this sum is *greatly in excess of the possibility of ninety-nine per cent. of the working classes.*

The attempt last year to suppress our Report, or so much of it as related to this question, is sufficient evidence that suppression was the only possible answer to our statements. . . .

In order the better to understand the general subject-matter of this hearing, it will be necessary to state what were the points made by the Bureau in that part of its Third Report . . . relating to Savings Banks. They were these:-

1st. That large sums of money are deposited in Savings Banks by other persons than wage-laborers. . . .

2d. That according to the returns made to the Bureau by the *fourteen* banks, which alone gave the *occupations* of depositors, twenty-five per cent only of the *sums deposited in said banks*, in 1870, belonged to wage-laborers; though sixty-five per cent of the *persons depositing* were wage-laborers.

3d. That $\frac{13}{14}$ of the whole *number of deposits* in the State for 1870, according to the Bank Commissioner's Report for that year, amounted to but little more (compared with the whole amount deposited) than the remaining $\frac{1}{14}$, as a simple arithmetical computation will show. . . .

5th. That a wage-laborer could not save *out of the annual average earnings of a single year* so large a sum as the average deposit above $300 of the year 1870, that average being $573.65, and the annual average earnings according to our tables being but a little over $600 (and by the tables of the U.S. Census for the same year, but about $540), the conclusion being that the general opinion that all the accumulations in these Banks belong to wage-laborers *is not correct.* (MBLS, *Third Annual Report*, 1872, 320)

A year later, with more complete cooperation from the banks, the bureau attempted to identify thousands of depositors by occupation. The totals, divided into four broad categories—wage earners, salaried employees, professionals, and investors—are reported in Table 12, which was the bureau's last word on the subject.

Several years later, when he studied conditions in Lowell, Lawrence, and Fall River, Carroll Wright looked again at the savings of working

Money in the Bank

Table 12. Savings bank depositors, by occupation, 1873.

Totals and Classes	Average amount of each deposit	Per cent. of number of deposits	Per cent. of amount of deposits	Number of deposits, $300 and under	Am s
Aggregate of all deposits, 24,663.	$152.91	—	—	20,901	$1,4
Aggregate amount of same, $3,870,227,					
Class I—Day Wage,	121.72	57.7	44.8	12,770	8
Class II—Salary,	129.50	11.0	9.1	2,397	1
Class III—Professional,	225.85	2.9	4.2	565	
Class IV—Use or Interest of Money,	232.27	28.3	41.8	5,169	4

Source: MBLS, *Fifth Annual Report*, 1874, 244–45.

people, though he did not stir old controversies by probing practices of the banks themselves. Wright relied on anecdotes, rather than tables, a variation from his usual pattern that may be attributable in part to his memory of the squabble that had almost caused the legislature to close his agency. The absence of more comprehensive statistical data also confirms hints elsewhere in the bureau's research that workers discussed the assets of unnamed others more freely than the extent of their own, about which they were often tight-lipped.

The operatives of Fall River, according to their own statement, do not save any money, though many said that they could if they left off drinking; that a family composed entirely of workers may be able to save, but others cannot. One operative said, "The mill people of Fall River spend as they go. . . . It will be simply a stroke of good fortune if many of them succeed in catching up with their indebtedness." Another operative said, "Seven or eight years ago there was a considerable amount of saving done, I believe; but, owing to the many strikes the assessments have eaten up the savings, and put many of the operatives in debt. If a man has a family, and they are all at work, he may be able to save something. But when a man or woman gets but one dollar a day, and has two or three dependent on him or her, the chances for saving money are slim. I do not know of one mill operative that owns his own home. Rents are very high here, higher than anywhere else in the State."

It seemed impossible to believe that there were no operatives who owned their own homes, and inquiry among the city officials brought to light a few that did; one case being mentioned that was so characteristic of thrift, that

cent. of mber of sits, $300 d under	Per cent. of amounts of deposits, $300 and under	Number of deposits above $300	Amount of same	Per cent. of number of deposits above $300	Per cent. of amounts of deposits above $300
—	—	3,762	$2,373,953	—	—
51.1	58.0	1,472	865,341	39.1	36.4
11.5	9.5	319	209,292	8.5	8.8
2.7	3.3	164	114,213	4.3	4.8
24.7	29.1	1,807	1,185,107	48.0	49.9

it was thoroughly investigated, and the following, which was told to the agent by a former operative, was proven to be true: A man who had resided in Fall River for many years was living in his own house, which he had built from his own and his family's savings, and has built another one as a wedding present to one of his daughters. Another of his daughters owns a house and lot around the corner from where her father lives. The story, as it was told the agent of the Bureau, of how the family secured the corner lot, is worth relating, to show the spirit of thriftiness maintained by the wife of the head of the family, with whom all funds were deposited: In the fall of 1880 they laid in ten tons of coal, bought enough flour, potatoes, and other household necessaries, that could be bought in large quantities, and would keep; and the wife said, "Now we will save all we can until spring." As all of the family were employed, and as all of the money was carefully laid aside, and nothing wasted, the savings of the fall and winter (six months) amounted to five hundred dollars, and the good wife said, "Let us buy the corner lot, for fear some one else may get it." It was accordingly done, and the foundation for a new house was immediately laid. There were six members of this family working in the mill until the past summer, when one left to enter another business. The agent was assured that this was really an exceptional case, as there were very few operatives now in the mills that owned their own houses, and bought them of the money made in the mills.

The operatives visited in Lowell had very little to say regarding the savings of any mill people, two or three being of the opinion that there was very little done, although acknowledging that they were not in a position to say positively. Others thought that, as a rule, the operatives were thrifty and did save, many of them owning their own homes, which had been

purchased from the money they had saved while in the mills. The single
female operatives were credited with saving large sums.

There was a feeling among the operatives of Lawrence that saving
money was as much a duty as eating, and the statement was made that
Lawrence operatives save the most, and Lowell and Fall River the least.
One operative said, "There is a large amount of money deposited in our
savings banks every month by those who are paid monthly. I cannot say
how much saving is done by those who are paid weekly, but those who are
determined to save will save, no matter how often they are paid. Those
who keep house probably save the most, as the single boarders spend about
all they earn. On holidays and Sundays our girls on the street are
sometimes more handsomely dressed than the higher class of Boston shop
girls. They dress well, and I think save money besides, for the hard times
taught us all a lesson." . . . Another operative said, "We do not spend all of
our money in drink; we save it and buy our own homes. I own my house (a
neat two-story and basement frame cottage, on a lot about 30 × 125 feet),
and on the right of my house is that of an operative, and on the left
another, both spinners; and all around you can see comfortable little
cottages that are owned and occupied by operatives. That certainly speaks
well for our thrift and hard work, as well as for our content. I have been in
the mills for twenty-three years, and in the present one for sixteen."

The following statement made by an intelligent and enterprising young
operative is well worth reproducing as showing the general spirit of
contentment and comfort that the agent found among the Lawrence mill
operatives: ". . . I bought my land for cash, and had my house built on
instalments, paying a certain sum each month, and in July I made the last
payment and received the bill receipted. I think if our young operatives
would do as I did they would be much better off than idling away their time
and wasting their money. I went to a sensible girl,—now my wife,—and told
her I wanted to marry her; that if she would save fifty dollars for the
coming year I would save seventy-five, and then we could get married. She
proved to be as sensible as I thought her to be, and saved seventy-five
dollars, and we started life on $150, a small sum to many, but a fortune to
us. I then bought this house, as I said before, and we have been living and
working together ever since. I am contented, and so is my wife. She will
quit working in September, and we will then begin to raise a family to take
care of us in our old age. I do not know much about the savings of others,
but I imagine that when wife stops work we will have in the bank about

THE RIVER STREET
AROUND 1890.

8. Haverhill family boardinghouse, c. 1890. Courtesy of the Trustees of the
Haverhill Public Library, Special Collections Department.

$350. I get good pay, and so does my wife, at present; my pay supplies us with all we want to eat and for clothing, and, since my last payment on my house, her wages have gone into the bank. I pay for every thing I want, cash down. It is the only way for a poor man to do, and it prevents him from being cheated." (MBLS, *Thirteenth Annual Report*, 1882, 214–17)

In an effort to document conclusions derived from the bureau's work on bank deposits, in 1873 Oliver reviewed the Commonwealth's tax records. When these data appeared to demonstrate a maldistribution of wealth, Oliver tried to explain why the agency's reports contradicted popularly held ideas about economic opportunity. The failure of working people to accumulate property, Oliver maintained, was not a function of bad habits and personal extravagance, as the conventional wisdom of the day declared. Low wages seemed a better; if more prosaic, reason for the poverty that afflicted segments of the state's employed population.

To this mass of testimony of wages, earnings, and savings, or inability to save, we have added, this year, a table of returns from the assessors of 295 towns in the Commonwealth showing that the total number of resident tax payers *in those towns* was 212,000, of whom 87,000 paid only a poll tax, 106,880 persons paid a tax under $50; and that $\frac{5}{6}$ of the tax payers own $\frac{1}{5}$ of the total amount of real and personal estate in those towns.

As a rule, those wage-laborers who own real estate would not be likely to pay over $25 taxes. Of this latter class, there are 40,000 tax payers. It must also be borne in mind that, as a rule, this property is more or less mortgaged. And if it is claimed that the tax does not represent the full value of the property, it can be said to represent, at least, the full value of the property not mortgaged. How much of the property was earned by the present owners, and how much is the result of purchase made by bounties during the war, or from property bequeathed or otherwise, we are unable to say. But in our personal examination into the cases of these wage-labor property holders, we have found some extra circumstance has aided them in the accumulation of these homes. . . .

There are many who assign as a reason for the failure to save, the prevailing extravagant style of living, specially showing itself in dress and drink. Extravagance is altogether of degree. A man whose income is twenty dollars a day, and who spends fifteen, is not said to be extravagant, while he who earns five and spends five, or even four, is so classed. So the workman who earns but $500 a year, would be called extravagant, if he paid a rent of thirty dollars a quarter, a grocer's bill of twelve dollars a month, a butcher's bill of the same amount, with fifty dollars a year for his own clothing, and forty-two more for spirit and tobacco, for he would have nothing left of his annual earnings. Yet this whole sum of earnings may be spent in the freest manner by the receiver of twenty dollars a day, without his becoming answerable to the charge of unthrift.

To "live within one's means," and to "owe no man anything," will save one from such charge, and put him in the direction of independence. But in the case of the average workman, under prevailing average wage, it will call for unyielding self-denial, and for equal denial in the rearing of his household. . . .

The drinking habits of workingmen are often referred to as the principal reason why the working classes do not save, and reference is made to the statistics of the expenditure caused by this single vice. . . .

Yet let it not be forgotten, that while the working classes are great consumers of spirits of some sort, it is a point well taken that poverty of income is a very prominent provocative to intemperance in drink, the deprivation of comfort at home and the general lack of innocent amusements adapted to the poor and poorly educated, alluring them to the well-arrayed saloon or lower tippling house whose "entrance is the gate to hell."

It is not difficult to write instructive generalities on this subject of extravagance, yet it must be hard for the working classes to enforce the rigid duties of perpetual abstinence from every sort of expense that may be adjudged unreasonable, denying selves and households in many a thing that helps to make life and living a desire and a comfort, lest they be reproached with "wandering beyond their means," which is the true meaning of the word extravagance. And here comes in the difficulty of reconciling the charge of extravagance in living alleged against the working classes, with the commonly accepted idea that, as a general rule, they are accumulating property out of their earnings, securing homes of their own, and making large deposits in Savings Banks. If extravagant, how have they saved? (MBLS, *Fourth Annual Report*, 1873, 405–6)

As the analysis of tax rolls reveals, the bureau's directors understood that money in the bank was not the only index of wealth. In 1895, Horace Wadlin released a study of probate records he had undertaken to test the persistent notion that the rich had become richer and the poor poorer during the nineteenth century. The bureau acknowledged that this evidence was not infallible; many estates, especially early in the century, were not inventoried, and only one in five or six left a record in the courts. Formidable obstacles loomed before a more comprehensive report on the distribution of wealth could be completed and definitive conclusions, which the bureau prudently avoided, could be reached.

That the rich are becoming richer and the poor poorer, is frequently asserted to be one of the results of the prevailing industrial system. The belief that the facts support this assertion finds constant expression in speeches, magazines, books, newspapers, and conversation, and while the impatience of a few inspired by this belief leads at times to violent outbreaks against the existing social order, there are many of milder nature who are dissatisfied because the ideal is not more closely attained. . . .

While much of the theorizing as to the tendency of modern industrialism with respect to wealth distribution is superficial and fallacious, there are some conspicuous facts which show that its ownership is concentrating. Indeed it is essential to the success of industrial operations, as at present conducted, that capital should be massed, controlled, and directed in few hands. How far this concentration has proceeded, what are its probable limitations, and what upon the whole are its advantages and disadvantages, are questions of vital interest, respecting which there is at present little exact knowledge, although there is much fragmentary information of more or less importance in a general consideration of the subject.

Statistics relating to the production of wealth are voluminous and easily accessible. Those relating to its distribution, especially in this country, have as yet received little attention. To determine the exact facts, we should have full information as to the property held by every individual in the community, the variations in distribution being then easily measured by mathematical processes. If this information were obtainable at different periods, comparisons would disclose the tendency of distribution, and would bring out the differences in wealth-holding on lines of sex and occupation, in different classes of property, and between different states and countries. Such comparisons would be both interesting and instructive. . . .

There is . . . through the Probate Offices, provision for the disclosure of wealth at death. The wealth of those who die, of course bears a definite relation to the wealth of the living. It may also be possible to trace this connection, and to draw fairly accurate deductions as to the wealth of the whole community at different periods, based upon exact knowledge of the wealth listed at the Probate Offices. . . .

Massachusetts is in some respects an ideal State for such an investigation as this. Within her borders are found the conditions which are distinctively recognized as belonging to modern civilization. Her development since the establishment of the factory system has been along industrial lines. Her per capita wealth is high. Her capital in industrial enterprises is exceeded in but two other States, namely, New York and Pennsylvania. In point of per capita wealth, of wealth invested in manufactures, and of density of population, the State exhibits conditions which afford an admirable basis for economic investigation, namely: a large amount of private capital, a high per capita average of capital, density of population, private ownership of manufactures and transportation, and a distinctively industrial form of civilization, under the factory and wage system. The State also has a comparatively small and compact territory, with but 14 counties, and but one Probate Office in each county. The records of these offices are preserved for many years, and extend beyond the earliest period that it is desirable to investigate.

The statistics obtained from the Probate records were transcribed for four periods of three years each, 1829–31, 1859–61, 1879–81, and 1889–91, and the average of each period is taken to represent the middle year. This method of procedure is taken for the purpose of eliminating possible fluctuations in the number of large and small estates. . . .

The dates of the three periods are important. The year 1830 practically marks the close of the era of hand production, and the beginning of the era of the machine in industry. Prior to 1830, the production of wealth rested largely upon domestic industry, unorganized labor, and primitive means of transportation. The period culminating in 1860 practically marks the establishment of modern methods, and enables us to measure the results of the momentous transition that took place during the thirty years previous. In the period extending from 1860 to 1880, the factory system being thoroughly established, extensive establishments were founded, railways

Table 13. Massachusetts probate records, by period.

Periods and Classificiation	Inventoried Probates			Amounts	Percentages of Classified Probates	Averages: Both Sexes
	Males	Females	Totals			
1829–1831	3,102	596	3,698	$ 14,494,107	100.00	$ 3,919
Under $50,000	3,066	596	3,662	9,536,245	99.03	2,604
$50,000 and over	36	—	36	4,957,862	0.97	137,718
1859–1861	5,103	1,819	6,922	53,256,794	100.00	7,694
Under $50,000	4,944	1,800	6,744	26,989,881	97.43	4,002
$50,000 and over	159	19	178	26,266,913	2.57	147,567
1879–1881	7,030	4,112	11,142	137,374,259	100.00	12,329
Under $50,000	6,673	4,042	10,715	52,432,701	96.17	4,893
$50,000 and over	357	70	427	84,941,558	3.83	198,926
1889–1891	8,349	6,259	14,608	155,558,788	100.00	10,649
Under $50,000	7,953	6,146	14,099	70,379,372	96.52	4,992
$50,000 and over	396	113	509	85,179,416	3.48	167,347

Source: MBLS, *Twenty-fifth Annual Report*, 1895, 295.

were extended and consolidated, workingmen and employers were perfecting organization, the country had passed through the civil war, and subsequent speculation, inflation of prices, and other causes, culminated in one of the greatest and most protracted industrial depressions that the country has ever seen. At the close of the period, the country was in a condition of great industrial stability, under new conditions. The period culminating in 1890 enables us to measure the results of modern industrial activity, under which production has been indefinitely extended, great wealth accumulated, and the peculiar conditions which have marked modern industrial operations have been operative. These conditions include the movement from individual to corporate ownership, and the general tendency to mass capital in a few hands.

The question naturally arises as to the relative holding of large and small estates as compared with population at each of the four periods compared. If, for example, we assume $50,000 as the dividing line between large and small estates, ... what proportion of the total holdings fall in each class at each period, what number of estates is included in each class, and what is the average holding? In answering these questions reference is made to [Table 13].

From the table we note that at the first period of comparison, 1829 to 1831, 3,662 estates are found below the $50,000 limit, representing 99.03 per cent of all the inventoried probates, the total holding in this class being

$9,536,245 and the average per capita holding being $2,604. On the other hand, at the last period of comparison, 1889 to 1891, 14,099 estates appear in this class, the percentage of small holdings of total holdings having fallen to 96.52, the total holding in this class being $70,379,372 and the average per capita holding having risen to $4,992. Again, at the period 1829 to 1831, only 36 estates appear above the $50,000 limit, or 0.97 per cent, slightly less than one per cent of the total inventoried probates, the total holdings of these 36 estates being $4,957,862, or an average per capita holding of $137,718; while in 1889 to 1891 we find 509 estates in this class, the percentage of large estates having risen to 3.48, the total holding to $85,179,416, and the average per capita holding to $167,347. . . .

Bearing in mind that the average holding in the estates below the line has nearly doubled in the 60 years, it is somewhat remarkable that the deceased owners of these estates represented one person in every 476 of the population in the period centring in 1890 while they numbered one in every 500 in the period centring in 1830. This, it will be noticed, is a comparatively slight change, and the proportion does not greatly vary at either of the four periods considered. (MBLS, *Twenty-fifth Annual Report*, 1895, 51–53, 55–57, 294–96)

CHAPTER FOUR

Race and National Origin

The race problem that established Massachusetts residents identified at the end of the nineteenth century stemmed from immigration, rather than emancipation; in the Commonwealth, the word "race" then signified roughly what "ethnicity" meant a hundred years later. Housed together in enclaves near the factories where they worked, immigrants sometimes seemed unwilling to assimilate. Many attended Roman Catholic churches, whose American identity remained suspect in some corners of New England, and sent their children to parochial schools. Neighborhood clubs and saloons appeared to encourage Old World customs, to cater to Old World appetites, and to foster Old World allegiances.

Yet the introduction to the Commonwealth's census for 1895 asserted that few states had "gained as much numerically from the flood of immigration as has Massachusetts." In presenting a "long, complicated, and very expensive tabulation" to demonstrate that observation, the Bureau of Statistics of Labor, which had conducted the survey, avoided any interpretive text that might have reinforced stereotypes or exacerbated ethnic tension.[1] This end-of-century discretion contrasted

---

1. MBLS, *Thirty-fourth Annual Report* (1904), 3. Probably the introductory prose was the work of Horace G. Wadlin, who directed the bureau when the census was taken. The summary, however, was published a year after he resigned to become librarian at the Boston Public Library. Charles F. Pidgin, who succeeded Wadlin, had been the chief deputy, a post Wadlin had earlier filled for Carroll Wright. Given that managerial continuity, a precise identification of the author is probably unnecessary.

with an earlier comment, made in a study of the state's paupers and criminals, that the ratio of productive to nonproductive immigrants was 1 to 3.5; the bureau had then added that more than one hundred thousand unproductive immigrants placed a "heavy burden" on their adopted land and "undoubtedly" were "often the cause of asking for public and private aid."[2]

Ironically, the bureau's inference that immigrants lacked an appropriate work ethic and their postulated dependence on charity provoked less criticism than a subsequent accusation that they worked too hard. In 1881, in accounting for the absence of support for legislation limiting to ten the hours of factory labor, the bureau's analyst reported that some sources blamed competition from "Canadian French" working people. Perhaps this explanation just paraphrased views of the bureau's informants; as published, however, the remark seemed to have official endorsement. In any case, representatives of the state's French Canadian population took immediate and vigorous exception. Resolutions of outrage flooded the General Court, which referred them to the offending agency and prudently declined to express any opinion about the controversy.

Director Carroll Wright claimed that the bureau had only reported, and did not subscribe to, opinions of those the staff had questioned. But he also issued a conciliating invitation to all interested to attend an open forum at the statehouse; he then printed the session's transcript in the *Annual Report* for 1882. To those in attendance, Wright acknowledged that "prejudice" against French Canadians existed, which he attributed to "the seeming disposition of the French to insist on preserving a distinct national existence within the Republic." "You cannot," Wright scolded, "be loyal Americans and loyal French Canadians at the same time." This admonition, he thought, might guide French Canadians toward better citizenship and thereby aid their progress. Unquestionably sincere, like progressive reformers twenty years later, Wright simply assumed the universal validity of his version of civic virtue and expected others to conform. Then, with no apparent embarrassment, he asserted that his mind was open and

---

2. MBLS, *Eighth Annual Report* (1877), 214–15.

asked the audience for reciprocal objectivity in judging the bureau.[3]

The first excerpt here is the portion of the *Annual Report* for 1881 that French Canadians found most offensive. The following paragraphs are the opening words of H. A. Dubuque of Fall River, who presided at the air-clearing meeting.

> With some exceptions the Canadian French are the Chinese of the Eastern States. They care nothing for our institutions, civil, political, or educational. They do not come to make a home among us, to dwell with us as citizens, and so become a part of us; but their purpose is merely to sojourn a few years as aliens, touching us only at a single point, that of work, and, when they have gathered out of us what will satisfy their ends, to get them away to whence they came, and bestow it there. They are a horde of industrial invaders, not a stream of stable settlers. Voting, with all that it implies, they care nothing about. Rarely does one of them become naturalized. They will not send their children to school if they can help it, but endeavor to crowd them into the mills at the earliest possible age. To do this they deceive about the age of their children with brazen effrontery. They deceive also about their schooling, declaring that they have been to school the legal time, when they know they have not, and do not intend that they shall. And when at length they are cornered by the school officers, and there is no other escape, often they scrabble together what few things they have, and move away to some other places where they are unknown, and where they hope by a repetition of the same deceits to escape the schools entirely, and keep the children at work right on in the mills. And when, as is indeed sometimes the case, any of them are so situated that they cannot escape at all, then the stolid indifference of the children wears out the teacher with what seems to be an idle task.
>
> These people have one good trait. They are indefatigable workers, and docile. All they ask is to be set to work, and they care little who rules them or how they are ruled. To earn all they can by no matter how many hours of toil, to live in the most beggarly way out of their earnings they may spend as little for living as possible, and to carry out of the country what they can thus save: this is the aim of the Canadian French in our factory districts. Incidentally they must have some amusements; and, so far as the males are concerned, drinking and smoking and lounging constitute the sum of these.

3. MBLS, *Thirteenth Annual Report* (1882), 12.

MR. DUBUQUE. Honored gentlemen of the Bureau of Statistics of Labor,—It devolves upon me to open this hearing on behalf of the French Canadians who have been called here to give their evidence relative to certain statements contained in the Twelfth Annual Report of this Bureau. Before, however, proceeding to present the evidence before you, gentlemen, I wish to impress upon your minds the abnormal attitude in which the French are placed before you. Accusations have been made against them in a report made by the Bureau appointed by State authority. These accusations are presumed to be true, and taken to be true, to a certain extent; and we are called upon here to refute them.

Of course, we understand, gentlemen, that this hearing is somewhat informal. We cannot proceed as we would in a court of justice. We must obtain the facts as best we may with the means at hand, and if certain parties are not obliged to come and testify we must rely upon the good will of those who are willing. We feel more keenly the sting of these accusations, for there they stand in black and white; there is material which will go to write the history either of the Republic, of the Commonwealth of Massachusetts, or of the French Canadians in this State or in the country. That is opposed to the fundamental law laid down in the Constitution, that no one shall be accused unless he has the right and the advantage of being confronted by his accuser. I do not say this, gentlemen of this Bureau, because I want to blame you. You are, as it were, a reflection of the evidence which has been presented to you. Your duty is that of a court of justice, or a master in chancery presenting his report according to the state of the facts as they have come to his knowledge, and then letting the court, or, in this instance, the legislature or public opinion, pass upon the report.

Gentlemen, I do not wish to say that you have not done your duty; but this Bureau, even with all the good will that it could have, with all the kind feelings towards the French people that it has had, has done us an injustice. You have felt it yourselves, gentlemen, because you have summoned us to come here to-day to present to you evidence to refute the facts which you have stated. (MBLS, *Thirteenth Annual Report*, 1882, 3–4, 12–13)

Ferdinand Gagnon, editor of a French-language newspaper in Worcester, made a detailed, point-by-point rebuttal of the bureau's report.

We come to refute opinions given *ex parte*, and to reform the verdict based on them. . . .

Moreover we say that malice, prejudice, and very probably individual interest, were the chief denunciators of our countrymen. And, moreover, we say that considering the circumstances under which the Canadians emigrate to this country; speaking, as they do, a language different from the idiom spoken in the United States; they can show a record within the last ten years that no other national element can exhibit. . . .

It may happen that ignorant or malicious gossips denounce, in their villages,the French Canadians, because the farmers who come to this country do not wear modern garments, and have not the "nobby" appearance of their traducers; but ignorance ought not to prevail.

Denouncing a whole national element because the families in a village do not send their children to school, wear poor clothing, eat poor victuals, is the act of a prejudiced man.

The faults of ten are not the faults of a nation of nearly two millions of individuals.

There was premeditated malice in the reports of the informants to this Bureau.

Who gave the key note to these denunciations? The manufacturers themselves, who send agents to Canada to recruit factory help. . . .

Never, at any place, have Canadian help asked an increase in the hours of labor, and never, at any place, have they been opposed, as a body, to the ten-hour law.

The Canadians are peaceful, law-abiding citizens; and they accept the wages fixed by the liberality, or sometimes the cupidity and avarice, of the manufacturers.

Unable to speak the English language when they arrive in this country, burdened with a family, poor as the generality of immigrants are, the French Canadians have but to go to the textile factories, and there accept what is offered to them.

After a few months, and the children have learned a few words of English, being not satisfied with the wages, they ask for more, and, if refused, they move to another village where they expect to get more. This perpetual moving displeases some manufacturers; but it shows that our countrymen do not try to reduce the scale of wages, but that, on the contrary, they put themselves to trouble and expense to get better wages.

Canadians do not go back to their country in a large number, as is believed by many manufacturers. Leaving their relatives in Canada, being at a short distance they go often to visit their friends, but come back to the States to their usual occupations. . . .

We have affirmed that the French Canadians have never asked for an increase, nor have they opposed a reduction of the hours of labor. Having many children, the Canadian emigrant living in factory towns cares for his family. He and his children do not generally take side with strikers when strikes occur, and for this reason the prejudices go against the law-abiding Canadian. Is it not probable that many of the informants of the Bureau were men who had already been engaged in strikes, and that Canadians did not follow them? And hence the malice. . . .

It has been said in the report that the Canadians did not send their children to school, and that they try to evade the tenure of the law. . . . Now let us examine our statistics. We find that thirty-two towns or cities send 56,883 children to the schools, and of this number 13,406, or 23+ per cent, are Canadian children. And we also find that these Canadians, called "the Chinese of the East," have religion enough, patriotism enough, to have forty French and English Catholic schools in these thirty-two cities and towns.

We acknowledge that some of the new comers, too poor, and unable to speak English,—and the wages being low,—are obliged to send children to the mills against the law of humanity, and, in Massachusetts, against the State law. But who is the most guilty? Is it not the manufacturer who gives employment to young children of eight or nine years of age for merely nominal salary? These children, belonging to poor families, are submitted to a daily task of nine or ten hours, for thirty cents a day. Why does not the manufacturer cut the evil at its root, and refuse employment to these poor little ones, pay a little more to the adult members of these families, and give the children a chance to have an education? But no! These manufacturers complain of the ignorance of the Canadian children, and they try to get them at their mills for a few cents a day. Yet, notwithstanding the opportunity offered by the cupidity of the manufacturer, few parents only evade the school law. . . .

The report says that Canadians do not care to vote,—another error. The informants had forgotten, probably, that the law requires a residence of five years in this country for an alien to become a citizen. In Massachusetts the law requires that a man to be a voter shall read the Constitution in the English language. In Rhode Island the law requires that a foreigner shall be a real estate owner to vote. In New Hampshire the Constitution says that no Catholic shall be elected to office. With such liberality—which is a real barrier to universal suffrage—it is yet surprising to see so many Canadians who are citizens of the United States. (MBLS, *Thirteenth Annual Report*, 1882, 16–21)

Edward Hérault, a constable from Fall River, testified that French Canadians were reliable employees, temperate and law-abiding members of the community, and regular in attendance at Catholic schools and churches. Although religious discrimination was only obliquely discussed in the meeting, the devotion of French Canadians to their faith was well known and may have contributed to the effort to exclude them from the Knights of St. Crispin, among other labor organizations.

I scarcely visited a place for the last five years where I have found parochial schools among the French, evening schools and day schools; and, as a rule, the children always attend the public schools when they haven't another school of their choice. . . .

French people like to cluster around the old church, and where there is not a church they generally build one, if they are strong enough: if not they will go where there are enough of their kind to help them to build a church. . . .

[Manufacturers have asked that I] do all in my power to get some French help for them. They say, first, they like them because the day after pay-day they are sure of having a Frenchman at work; whereas the others are generally getting on the way an introduction to some magistrate for having drank too much the day before. I see that in Fall River by actual observation this is true. And then they are not so apt to rebel as the others. . . . The French help are always found at work, and are not miserly of an hour if it was necessary to benefit their employer. I have always found them ready to work. They are quiet; they don't raise much disturbance around the factory village; they scarcely ever fight among themselves; whereas that is a thing which is very often the case with other help. . . .

They are quiet. During the hours of rest in the week you will find them sitting together in a circle in each other's houses, and they will there discuss one topic and another; they will gather round about those who have the most interesting newspaper, and one will read while the others will listen, and pass the time in that way. They very seldom have any great feast. They sometimes get together, and have a pretty good time; but there is scarcely ever any disturbance that would amount to any disturbance of the peace. . . .

For some eight years past I have been employed by the courts of Bristol County as French interpreter, and I have seen as much as two months without having one single Frenchman brought before the district court. I

9. Boston ethnic neighborhood, c. 1890. Courtesy of the Boston
Public Library, Print Department.

consulted the return of our chief of police for the last six years. In 1875 there were 2,441 people arrested by the police, 65 of whom were French or born in Canada. The French population of Fall River was about one-sixth of the entire population. In 1876 there were 2,301 arrested, of whom there were 63 born in Canada. The population then was about the same as the year before. It has not much increased, although it has increased somewhat. In 1877 the total number of arrests was 2,419; Canadians, 119. In 1878, 1,945; Canadians, 106. In 1879, 1,664; Canadians, 89. In 1880, 1,881; Canadians, 120. The number for the six years was 12,651, of whom 562 were of Canadian birth, or about 4.5 per cent. (MBLS, *Thirteenth Annual Report*, 1882, 63–65)

Insult was not Carroll Wright's customary idiom, and this confrontation may have stemmed from an editorial lapse. Moreover, by 1881, Wright already tended to rely where possible on quantitative data instead of interpretive text, so the incident probably reveals unconscious bias and ethnic insensitivity, rather than malice. But the memory of French Canadian rage may have lingered when the bureau prepared the Massachusetts census of 1895 for publication. The editor then, probably Horace Wadlin, did little more than put the obvious numerical message in words. He noted, for instance, that recent arrivals had participated extensively in the state's economic development, which was surely not a controversial observation at a time when more than 30 percent of the population had been born abroad and when almost 60 percent had a foreign-born father. (The bureau consistently assumed that ethnic identification descended from the male parent.) On the other hand, the bureau ignored, and may not have seen, the challenge to popular beliefs in economic opportunity and the melting pot that inhered in the tables the agency compiled (Tables 14 and 15).

Detailed tables revealed the clustering of national groups in specific occupations and industries, a phenomenon probably caused in part by the assistance that settled immigrants gave their newly arrived, job-seeking compatriots (Table 16). Work at the same trade or in the same factory reinforced a sense of national identity and perhaps of class solidarity which outsiders, including established middle-class Americans, often derided as clannish. And popular identification of immi-

Table 14. Number of persons employed of specified birth or descent, 1895.

Number and Percentages

Classification	Native Descent	Foreign Descent	Aggregates	Percentages Native Descent	Foreign Descent	Aggregates
NATIVE BORN	403,200	233,680	636,880	37.36	21.66	59.02
Born in Massachusetts	263,727	193,876	457,603	24.44	17.97	42.41
Born in other States of the Union	139,473	39,804	179,277	12.92	3.69	16.61
FOREIGN BORN	1,924	440,286	442,210	0.18	40.80	40.98
Born in foreign country specified	—	393,748	393,748	—	36.49	36.49
Born in other foreign countries	1,924	46,538	48,462	0.18	4.31	4.49
TOTALS	405,124	673,966	1,079,090	37.54	62.46	100.00
Native born	403,200	233,680	636,880	37.36	21.66	59.02
Foreign born	1,924	440,286	442,210	0.18	40.80	40.98

Countries, Provinces, and States	Native Born in Mass.	Born in other States	Foreign Born in Foreign Country Specified	Born in other Foreign Countries	Aggregates Native Born	Foreign Born	Totals
FOREIGN DESCENT	193,876	39,804	393,748	46,538	233,680	440,286	673,966
Ireland	132,498	17,135	144,711	15,352	149,633	160,063	309,696
Canada (French)	12,871	6,963	62,211	1,611	19,834	63,822	83,656
England	16,155	5,523	40,345	5,001	21,678	45,346	67,024
Canada (English)	5,092	1,885	22,788	692	6,977	23,480	30,457
Nova Scotia	3,788	581	23,760	519	4,369	24,279	28,648
Sweden	998	193	17,853	137	1,191	17,990	19,181
Italy	598	88	10,209	61	686	10,270	10,956
Russia	248	126	11,814	219	374	12,033	12,407
Scotland	5,104	1,965	12,462	5,508	7,069	17,970	25,039
Germany	8,276	2,872	16,952	807	11,148	17,759	28,907
Portugal	1,738	103	8,137	33	1,841	8,170	10,011
Poland	133	81	4,964	66	214	5,030	5,244
New Brunswick	1,333	396	7,496	262	1,729	7,758	9,487
Newfoundland	695	37	3,247	158	732	3,405	4,137
Prince Edward Island	528	61	3,935	201	589	4,136	4,725
France	956	525	2,156	554	1,481	2,710	4,191
Wales	243	132	708	140	375	848	1,223
Other foreign countries	2,622	1,138	—	15,217	3,760	15,217	18,977
NATIVE DESCENT	263,727	139,473	—	1,924	403,200	1,924	405,124
Massachusetts	200,763	11,504	—	605	212,267	605	212,872
Other states	62,964	127,969	—	1,319	190,933	1,319	192,252

Source: MBLS, *Thirty-fourth Annual Report*, 1904, 100.

Table 15. Specified birth or descent and classes of occupation, 1895.

States, Provinces, and Countries	Government Males	Government Females	Professional Males	Professional Females	Domestic Service Males	Domestic Service Females	Agriculture Males	Agriculture Females	The Fisheries Males	The Fisheries Females	Manufacturers Males	Manufacturers Females	Mining Males	Mining Females
The State	17,240	2,846	23,845	19,923	14,782	79,265	37,281	275	8,813	18	349,546	142,951	2,367	—
NATIVE DESCENT	8,860	1,379	16,085	13,864	6,029	16,756	27,106	210	2,367	3	116,078	34,113	322	—
Massachusetts	4,663	703	7,581	7,949	1,930	6,912	19,442	147	1,736	1	59,882	16,792	139	—
Other than Massachusetts	4,197	676	8,504	5,915	4,099	9,844	7,664	63	631	2	56,196	17,321	183	—
FOREIGN DESCENT	8,380	1,467	7,760	6,059	8,753	62,509	10,175	65	6,446	15	233,468	108,838	2,045	—
Ireland	5,835	607	2,722	3,177	4,362	36,768	4,945	32	605	5	88,776	53,272	584	—
Canada (French)	214	28	522	413	354	1,315	796	2	617	—	37,270	20,701	334	—
England	735	142	1,335	712	1,008	2,999	1,390	10	148	1	29,601	10,886	102	—
Canada (English)	263	147	374	300	265	3,147	289	3	1,874	2	9,646	4,043	71	—
Nova Scotia	282	200	281	243	341	4,591	454	3	280	—	8,886	3,508	26	—
Sweden	86	47	196	66	276	4,107	220	—	532	1	8,391	917	264	—
Italy	37	—	203	23	119	87	34	—	16	—	3,245	516	200	—
Russia	14	2	186	17	43	368	56	—	70	—	5,101	1,263	312	—
Scotland	269	108	386	268	320	2,532	573	5	80	2	10,229	3,264	51	—
Germany	241	37	764	330	324	1,336	608	2	63	—	13,139	3,350	10	—
Portugal	73	1	40	15	74	367	229	—	1,105	1	2,458	1,632	2	—
Poland	7	—	17	—	17	133	27	—	1	—	2,234	902	19	—
New Brunswick	92	71	122	113	83	1,018	96	1	4	—	3,101	1,471	14	—
Newfoundland	32	9	37	26	16	381	7	—	489	—	1,271	535	2	—
Prince Edward Island	38	43	31	26	49	1,187	37	1	18	—	1,506	587	2	—
France	39	4	194	122	120	239	128	2	42	—	1,470	506	13	—
Wales	13	3	26	13	19	81	21	—	1	—	514	137	2	—
Other foreign countries	110	18	324	195	963	1,853	265	4	501	3	6,630	1,348	37	—

States, Provinces, and Countries	Laborers		Appentices		Personal Service		Trade		Transportation		Children at Work		Aggregates	
	Males	Females	Males	Females	Males	Females	Males	Females	Males	Females	Males	Females	Males	Females
The State	98,758	207	5,320	567	25,724	19,762	129,875	24,142	69,680	368	3,223	2,312	786,454	292,636
NATIVE DESCENT	26,147	63	1,651	162	9,067	8,169	74,029	11,090	30,197	170	750	457	318,688	86,436
Massachusetts	15,403	31	980	106	3,665	3,514	40,486	6,003	14,084	89	417	217	170,408	42,464
Other than Massachusetts	10,744	32	671	56	5,402	4,655	33,543	5,087	16,113	81	333	240	148,280	43,972
FOREIGN DESCENT	72,611	144	3,669	405	16,657	11,593	55,846	13,052	39,483	198	2,473	1,855	467,766	206,200
Ireland	40,713	77	1,671	193	6,499	6,770	22,513	6,638	21,760	144	573	455	201,558	108,138
Canada (French)	8,541	11	283	46	1,850	339	4,172	713	3,525	–	893	717	59,371	24,285
England	3,117	12	404	28	1,646	1,047	7,064	1,265	2,912	18	267	175	49,729	17,295
Canada (English)	1,742	3	211	24	665	645	3,073	832	2,693	12	77	56	21,243	9,214
Nova Scotia	2,252	2	145	17	535	851	2,481	774	2,391	11	62	32	18,416	10,232
Sweden	1,713	3	130	8	276	241	809	141	667	–	60	30	13,620	5,561
Italy	3,766	16	45	3	811	19	1,369	135	201	–	70	41	10,116	840
Russia	1,106	1	38	5	144	32	3,136	216	201	–	52	44	10,459	1,948
Scotland	1,156	–	175	14	576	505	2,616	580	1,231	3	56	40	17,718	7,321
Germany	1,526	4	236	32	826	349	3,795	712	1,001	3	135	84	22,668	6,239
Portugal	2,219	6	30	3	432	83	435	68	554	–	91	93	7,742	2,269
Poland	1,183	–	7	2	46	18	509	43	51	–	19	9	4,137	1,107
New Brunswick	542	–	77	7	227	244	1,048	366	747	2	24	17	6,177	3,310
Newfoundland	474	1	36	6	85	64	305	115	226	1	10	9	2,990	1,147
Prince Edward Island	218	1	46	1	76	101	339	97	308	–	7	6	6,675	2,050
France	463	–	21	2	131	68	371	54	176	1	14	11	3,182	1,009
Wales	148	2	20	2	29	16	116	15	39	–	5	1	953	270
Other foreign countries	1,732	5	94	12	1,803	201	1,695	288	800	3	58	35	15,012	3,965

Source: MBLS, *Thirty-fourth Annual Report*, 1904, 96–98.

grant groups with particular economic pursuits no doubt contributed to ethnic stereotypes.

Table 16. Workers of foreign descent, by age and occupation, 1895.

Race, State, Province, or Country	Number	Percentages	Race, State Province, or Country	Number	Percentages
Children at work					
FOREIGN DESCENT	4,328	78.19	FOREIGN DESCENT—CON.		
Irish	1,028	18.57	Newfoundland	19	0.34
Canadian (French)	1,610	29.09	Prince Edward Island	13	0.23
English	442	7.99	French	25	0.45
Canadian (English)	133	2.40	Welsh	6	0.11
Nova Scotian	94	1.70	Other foreign descent	93	1.68
Swedish	90	1.63			
Italian	111	2.01	NATIVE DESCENT	1,207	21.81
Russian	96	1.73	Massachusetts	634	11.46
Scotch	96	1.73	Other native descent	573	10.35
German	219	3.96			
Portuguese	184	3.32	AGGREGATES	5,535	100.00
Polish	28	0.51	Foreign descent	4,328	78.19
New Brunswick	41	0.74	Native descent	1,207	21.81

Race, State, Province, or Country	Number	Percentages	Race, State Province, or Country	Number	Percentages
Manufactures—Boots and shoes					
FOREIGN DESCENT	38,972	53.77	FOREIGN DESCENT—CON.		
Irish	20,665	28.51	Newfoundland	210	0.29
Canadian (French)	6,852	9.45	Prince Edward Island	164	0.23
English	2,387	3.29	French	166	0.23
Canadian (English)	1,763	2.43	Welsh	43	0.06
Nova Scotian	1,652	2.28	Other foreign descent	536	0.74
Swedish	1,278	1.76			
Italian	384	0.53	NATIVE DESCENT	33,507	46.23
Russian	501	0.69	Massachusetts	19,827	27.36
Scotch	854	1.18	Other native descent	13,680	18.87
German	829	1.14			
Portuguese	105	0.15	AGGREGATES	72,479	100.00
Polish	92	0.13	Foreign descent	38,972	53.77
New Brunswick	491	0.68	Native descent	33,507	46.23

Race, State, Province, or Country	Number	Percentages	Race, State Province, or Country	Number	Percentages
Manufactures—woollen goods					
FOREIGN DESCENT	23,037	88.02	FOREIGN DESCENT—CON.		
Irish	10,972	41.93	Newfoundland	95	0.36
Canadian (French)	3,356	12.82	Prince Edward Island	24	0.09
English	3,608	13.79	French	181	0.69
Canadian (English)	315	1.20	Welsh	205	0.78
Nova Scotian	135	0.52	Other foreign descent	468	1.79
Swedish	149	0.57			

Table 16. Continued.

Manufactures—woollen goods—Cont.

Race, State, Province, or Country	Number	Percentages	Race, State Province, or Country	Number	Percentages
Italian	121	0.46	NATIVE DESCENT	3,134	11.98
Russian	206	0.79	Massachusetts	1,366	5.22
Scotch	893	3.41	Other native descent	1,768	6.76
German	1,969	7.52			
Portuguese	34	0.13	AGGREGATES	26,171	100.00
Polish	219	0.84	Foreign descent	23,037	88.02
New Brunswick	87	0.33	Native descent	3,134	11.98

Manufactures—cotton goods

Race, State, Province, or Country	Number	Percentages	Race, State Province, or Country	Number	Percentages
FOREIGN DESCENT	72,151	91.58	FOREIGN DESCENT—CON.		
Irish	23,298	29.57	Newfoundland	56	0.07
Canadian (French)	23,829	30.25	Prince Edward Island	76	0.10
English	12,656	16.06	French	300	0.38
Canadian (English)	1,237	1.57	Welsh	53	0.07
Nova Scotian	258	0.33	Other foreign descent	1,443	1.83
Swedish	232	0.29			
Italian	64	0.08	NATIVE DESCENT	6,630	8.42
Russian	388	0.49	Massachusetts	2,291	2.91
Scotch	2,167	2.75	Other native descent	4,339	5.51
German	2,204	2.80			
Portuguese	1,872	2.38	AGGREGATES	78,781	100.00
Polish	1,782	2.26	Foreign descent	72,151	91.58
New Brunswick	236	0.30	Native descent	6,630	8.42

Manufactures—paper and paper goods

Race, State, Province, or Country	Number	Percentages	Race, State Province, or Country	Number	Percentages
FOREIGN DESCENT	7,603	76.90	FOREIGN DESCENT—CON.		
Irish	4,599	46.52	Newfoundland	10	0.10
Canadian (French)	1,058	10.70	Prince Edward Island	11	0.11
English	558	5.64	French	63	0.64
Canadian (English)	157	1.59	Welsh	13	0.13
Nova Scotian	74	0.75	Other foreign descent	119	1.20
Swedish	38	0.39			
Italian	27	0.27	NATIVE DESCENT	2,284	23.10
Russian	22	0.22	Massachusetts	1,095	11.07
Scotch	447	4.52	Other native descent	1,189	12.03
German	319	3.23			
Portuguese	6	0.06	AGGREGATES	9,887	100.00
Polish	47	0.48	Foreign descent	7,603	76.90
New Brunswick	35	0.35	Native descent	2,284	23.10

Laborers—laborers (manufactures)

Race, State, Province, or Country	Number	Percentages	Race, State Province, or Country	Number	Percentages
FOREIGN DESCENT	16,035	89.36	FOREIGN DESCENT—CON.		
Irish	8,216	45.78	Newfoundland	148	0.82
Canadian (French)	2,739	15.26	Prince Edward Island	43	0.24

Table 16. Continued.

Race, State, Province, or Country	Number	Percentages	Race, State Province, or Country	Number	Percentages
		Laborers—laborers (manufactures)—Cont.			
English	775	4.32	French	63	0.35
Canadian (English)	290	1.62	Welsh	12	0.07
Nova Scotian	273	1.52	Other foreign descent	465	2.59
Swedish	629	3.51			
Italian	345	1.92	Native Descent	1,910	10.64
Russian	419	2.34	Massachusetts	961	5.35
Scotch	269	1.50	Other native descent	949	5.29
German	463	2.58			
Portuguese	539	3.00	Aggregates	17,945	100.00
Polish	254	1.42	Foreign descent	16,035	89.36
New Brunswick	93	0.52	Native descent	1,910	10.64

Source: MBLS, *Thirty-fourth Annual Report*, 1904, 105, 117, 119–21, 127.

The bureau concluded with the hope that immigrants would continue to accept, rather than alter, customs and institutions established by "Americans," who had become a minority in the Bay State.

The fact is plain that the strong industrial condition of Massachusetts has been secured and is held not by the labor of what is called the "native stock," but by that of the immigrants from all climes, who have left their native lands to seek here opportunities for financial advancement and political and religious liberty.

It is doubtful whether any other country or State in the world could absorb so many diverse nationalities and yet retain so fully old-time ideas and customs. That they heve been retained shows that the new comers have appreciated the worth and justice of our laws and customs, and have been content to conform to them rather than to use their predominant political power to change or subvert them. They came here with their old ideas, but hoping to learn better ones—and they have done so. So long as our institutions and laws commend themselves to our foreign born citizens and their descendants as the best and most just that they have known, there is no danger that our country will be un-Americanized, and foreign principles become predominant. Our task is to constantly raise the standard of our institutions and increase the justness of our laws, so that the contented may remain so, and the discontented be gradually shown that the evils of which they complain are more inherent in themselves than in our institutions or our governmental fabric. The Americanizing of the alien has been successful so far, and good judgment and foresight on the part of our elected rulers will increase rather than reduce its potentiality. (MBLS, *Thirty-fourth Annual Report*, 1904, 130)

The preceding data about immigrants, collected under the heading "Race in Industry," appeared in the same volume as a study of "The Social and Industrial Condition of the Negro in Massachusetts." That piece, the first manifestation of the bureau's interest in nonwhites, demonstrated just how small the state's black minority was. Indeed, until 1870, census takers, who routinely specified the provincial origin of Canadian-born residents of the Commonwealth, did not distinguish among the several groups in the population identified as "colored," a category that included people of Asian and Native American descent as well as blacks.

In undertaking this initial study of African Americans, the bureau was more than usually cautious. At a time when the Supreme Court of the United States was upholding southern laws requiring racial separation, and egalitarian idealism elsewhere was diminishing, the bureau attempted to avoid controversy with a "purely statistical" presentation. The text incorporated "editorial comment" only "to introduce or explain the tables" and explicitly took no position on "the social equation of the black and white races." The quantitative evidence was published not to make an ideological point but rather to assist "students of racial relations," among whom the bureau itself was apparently not numbered, "to make their own deductions." The historical introduction to the topic did not emphasize the state's abolitionist leaders but did absolve early colonists of charges that they were "common slave holders and dealers in slaves." Somehow their trading in and possession of black and Native American slaves derived from religious convictions that differentiated the founders of the Bay Colony from southern planters and ordinary slavemongers.[4] After that introductory apology, the bureau allowed the numbers to speak for themselves.

4. MBLS, *Thirty-fourth Annual Report* (1904), 217–18.

Table 17. Population of Massachusetts, 1790–1900.

| Years | Total Population | Negro Population | | | Percentages |
		Males	Females	Both Sexes	
1790	378,787	—	—	*5,463	1.44
1800	422,845	—	—	*6,452	1.52
1810	472,040	—	—	*6,737	1.43
1820	523,287	3,308	3,432	6,740	1.29
1830	610,408	3,377	3,629	7,006	1.15
1840	737,699	4,655	4,014	8,669	1.18
1850	994,514	4,424	4,640	9,064	0.91
1855	1,132,369	4,556	5,211	9,767	0.86
1860	1,231,066	4,469	5,133	9,602	0.78
1865	1,267,031	4,673	5,213	9,886	0.78
1870	1,457,351	6,702	7,245	13,947	0.96
1875	1,651,912	7,495	7,989	15,484	0.94
1880	1,783,085	9,049	9,648	18,697	1.05
1885	1,942,141	8,905	9,430	18,335	0.94
1890	2,238,943	10,879	11,265	22,144	0.99
1895	2,500,183	12,813	13,727	26,540	1.06
1900	2,805,346	15,591	16,383	31,974	1.14

Source: MBLS, *Thirty-fourth Annual Report*, 1904, 232.
* Free colored.

In fact, those numbers are quite eloquent. Tables 17 and 18, from the national census of 1900, suggest that one reason for the failure of the bureau to investigate the state's black population earlier was its tiny scope. Tables 19 and 20 may provide another explanation: less than 10 percent of the bureau's sample, which included roughly a third of the black population of working age and nearly a quarter of all the black residents of the state, was employed in manufacturing—the central focus of the bureau's work. Racism, of employers or employees or both, may account at least in part for the absence of blacks from the factories of the Commonwealth. In addition, several comparative tables demonstrated the level of educational and economic opportunity afforded Massachusetts blacks as the twentieth century opened; those on literacy and poverty are included here (Tables 21 and 22).

The actual jobs held by blacks in the two largest occupational categories are as shown in Table 20 for the bureau's sample of 8,335, or roughly 25 percent of the total black population.

10. Graduating nurses, Plymouth Hospital, c. 1900. Courtesy of the Boston Public Library, Print Department.

Table 18. Place of birth of native-born Negroes resident in Massachusetts, 1900.

Place of Birth	Number	Place of Birth	Number
THE STATE	28,499	THE STATE–CON.	
Alabama	114	Montana	1
Alaska	1	Nebraska	2
Arkansas	24	New Hampshire	117
California	14	New Jersey	255
Colorado	11	New Mexico	2
Connecticut	495	New York	882
Delaware	132	North Carolina	2,897
District of Columbia	570	Ohio	115
Florida	166	Oklahoma	1
Georgia	754	Oregon	1
Hawaii	1	Pennsylvania	569
Idaho	1	Rhode Island	257
Illinois	49	South Carolina	742
Indiana	19	South Dakota	2
Indian Territory	1	Tennessee	103
Iowa	12	Texas	25
Kansas	11	Utah	2
Kentucky	137	Vermont	159
Louisiana	96	Virginia	6,213
Maine	260	Washington	31
Maryland	987	West Virginia	67
Massachusetts	11,747	Wisconsin	6
Michigan	48	Born in U. S. (state, n. s.)	164
Minnesota	8	Born at sea under U. S. flag	7
Mississippi	51	Born in Porto Rico	3
Missouri	42	American citizens born abroad	125

Source: MBLS, *Thirty-fourth Annual Report*, 1904, 238.

Table 19. Occupations of Negroes in Massachusetts, 1900.

Classes of Occupations	Males	Females	Both Sexes	Proportions of the Sexes	
				Males	Females
Government	82	6	88	93.18	6.82
Professional	122	45	167	73.05	26.95
Domestic service	1,421	989	2,410	58.96	41.04
Personal service	660	863	1,523	43.34	56.66
Trade	559	17	576	97.05	2.95
Transportation	568	9	577	98.44	1.56
Agriculture	14	—	14	100.00	—
The Fisheries	3	—	3	100.00	—
Manufactures	459	209	668	68.71	31.29
Laborers	569	—	569	100.00	—
Apprentices	8	2	10	80.00	20.00
Children at work	11	7	18	61.11	38.89
Scholars and students	686	796	1,482	46.29	53.71
Not gainful, etc.	101	129	230	43.91	56.09
TOTALS	5,263	3,072	8,335	63.14	36.86

Source: MBLS, *Thirty-fourth Annual Report*, 1904, 244.
Note: Based on a sample of approximately 25 percent.

Table 20. Largest occupational categories for Negroes in Massachusetts, 1900.
Personal Service

Branches of Occupations	Males	Females	Both Sexes	Branches of Occupations	Males	Females	Both Sexes
Barbers	154	—	154	Janitors	233	21	254
Bar tenders	13	—	13	Laundry work	4	271	275
Bill posters	1	—	1	Matrons	—	2	2
Billiard room service	5	—	5	Nurses	1	27	28
Bootblacks	36	—	36	Personal service	6	32	38
Carpet sewers	—	8	8	Proprietors (laundry)	2	3	5
Caterers	31	—	31	Proprietors (billiard room)	3	—	3
Cleansers	24	—	24				
Clerks	6	2	8	Servants	—	5	5
Club house service	25	1	26	Stenographers	5	1	6
Copyists	2	—	2	Stewards	2	—	2
Drivers	3	—	3	Typewriters	1	—	1
Employés	6	11	17	Valets	2	—	2
Employment office service	2	—	2	Undertakers	3	—	3
				Waiters	30	3	33
Engineers	24	—	24	Washerwomen	—	183	183
Firemen	5	—	5	Watchmen	12	—	12
Hair dressers	17	13	30	TOTALS	660	863	1,523
Housecleaners	2	280	282				

Table 20. Continued.

Domestic Service

Branches of Occupations	Males	Females	Both Sexes	Branches of Occupations	Males	Females	Both Sexes
Bell boys	88	—	88	Lodging-house keepers	1	65	66
Boarding-house keepers	1	4	5	Nurse girls	—	9	9
Butlers	68	—	68	Pantry girls	1	2	3
Chambermaids	—	49	49	Parlor maids	—	9	9
Clerks (hotel)	2	—	2	Porters	51	—	51
Coachmen	101	—	101	Restaurant keepers	6	2	8
Cooks	136	170	306	Saloon keepers	1	—	1
Errand boys	7	—	7	Second girls	—	4	4
Footmen	1	—	1	Servants	27	560	587
Grooms	10	—	10	Stable employés	9	—	9
Housekeepers	—	25	25	Stewards	7	—	7
Housemaids	—	9	9	Waiters	844	29	873
Hotel keepers	2	—	2	Employés, n.s.	58	18	76
Kitchen girls	—	9	9	Totals	1,421	989	2,410
Ladies' maids	—	3	3				
Laundry work	—	22	22				

Source: MBLS, *Thirty-fourth Annual Report*, 1904, 245–46.
Note: Based on a sample of approximately 25 percent.

Table 21. Illiteracy, by race, 1890 and 1900.

Classification	1890			1900		
	Males	Females	Both Sexes	Males	Females	Both Sexes
Negro population 10 years of age and over	8,974	9,281	18,255	13,018	13,555	26,573
Illiterates	1,106	1,501	2,607	1,207	1,646	2,853
Per cent	12.32	16.17	14.28	9.27	12.14	10.74
White population 10 years of age and over	876,917	943,095	1,820,012	1,081,343	1,155,684	2,237,027
Illiterates	45,833	65,609	111,442	57,353	72,968	130,321
Per cent	5.23	6.96	6.12	5.30	6.31	5.83
Native white, native parents	385,564	409,392	794,956	411,854	435,457	847,311
Illiterates	2,273	1,955	4,228	2,206	1,706	3,912
Per cent	0.59	0.48	0.53	0.54	0.39	0.46
Native white, foreign parents	193,379	205,134	398,513	277,062	295,846	572,908
Illiterates	2,423	3,076	5,499	3,107	3,720	6,827
Per cent	1.25	1.50	1.38	1.12	1.26	1.19
Foreign white	297,974	328,569	626,543	392,427	424,381	816,808
Illiterates	41,137	60,578	101,715	52,040	67,542	119,582
Per cent	13.81	18.44	16.23	13.26	15.92	14.64

Source: MBLS, *Thirty-fourth Annual Report*, 1904, 274.

Table 22. Causes of poverty, 1900.

Classification	American	Negro	German	Irish	English	All Other	Totals
				Percentages			
1. Indicating misconduct	27.35	13.76	16.67	30.43	28.01	18.64	25.11
Drink	15.16	6.24	7.75	23.62	16.93	8.27	15.28
Immorality	0.63	0.92	0.12	0.27	0.32	0.30	0.44
Shiftlessness and inefficiency	9.19	5.69	7.39	5.78	7.12	7.52	7.52
Crime and dishonesty	0.74	0.73	0.47	0.38	1.11	1.05	0.68
Roving disposition	1.63	0.18	0.94	0.38	2.53	1.50	1.19
2. Indicating misfortune	69.58	83.31	78.64	67.55	69.46	79.11	72.03
A. Lack of normal support	6.04	4.96	5.17	7.04	6.33	8.12	6.32
Imprisonment of bread-winner	0.67	0.37	0.12	1.20	1.27	0.60	0.76
Orphans and abandoned children	0.37	0.37	—	0.38	0.63	0.30	0.35
Neglected by relatives	0.89	1.28	0.82	0.38	1.27	1.96	0.91
No male support	4.11	2.94	4.23	5.08	3.16	5.26	4.30
B. Matters of employment	33.40	27.15	38.73	26.14	30.85	34.59	31.60
Lack of employment	24.57	17.43	28.40	18.88	24.68	25.87	23.17
Insufficient employment	6.64	8.62	7.51	6.38	4.75	5.11	6.52
Poorly paid employment	2.08	0.92	2.58	0.82	1.42	3.61	1.81
Unhealthy and dangerous employment	0.11	0.18	0.24	0.06	—	—	0.10
C. Matters of personal incapacity	30.14	51.20	34.74	34.37	32.28	36.40	34.11
Ignorance of English	—	—	0.47	0.06	—	3.76	0.42
Accident	2.67	1.47	3.52	3.11	2.69	3.46	2.86
Sickness or death in family	20.31	39.63	22.65	19.80	22.94	21.66	22.27
Physical defects	3.41	5.51	4.70	3.49	1.74	4.51	3.70
Insanity	0.93	—	0.70	0.93	1.27	0.90	0.86
Old age	2.82	4.59	2.70	6.98	3.64	2.11	4.00
3. Miscellaneous	3.07	2.93	4.69	2.02	2.53	2.25	2.86
Large family	0.52	0.55	1.17	0.87	0.79	0.75	0.73
Nature of abode	0.07	0.18	0.12	0.06	0.47	0.15	0.12
Other, or unknown	2.48	2.20	3.40	1.09	1.27	1.35	2.01

Source: MBLS, *Thirty-fourth Annual Report*, 1904, 292.

CHAPTER FIVE

Women at Work

In the years immediately after the Civil War, Henry K. Oliver noted in 1871, a "large . . . majority" of Massachusetts residents were female, a demographic fact that made study of women's work and wages "highly important."[1] Although they were not proportionately represented in the industrial labor force the bureau had been chartered to investigate, women did constitute a substantial fraction of those engaged in the production of textiles and shoes, for example. As a matter of course, the agency included female employees in industry-wide surveys of wages, hours, working conditions, and intermittent employment; other research focused on occupations, such as retail sales, in which women had become predominant. And the men who directed the bureau were also concerned about those who toiled in kitchens, laundries, and nurseries, whether or not they appeared on the formal payrolls of the Commonwealth.[2]

1. MBLS, *Second Annual Report* (1871), 197.
2. Scholarly literature about workingwomen has multiplied in recent years. An expansion of editorial notes for this chapter is Henry F. Bedford, "Good Men and 'Working Girls': The Bureau of Statistics of Labor, 1870–1900," in Susan L. Porter, ed., *The History of Women in Massachusetts: New Perspectives on Work and Social Change* (Amherst: University of Massachusetts Press, 1995). A limited and somewhat arbitrary sampling of recent scholarship that focuses on Massachusetts includes Mary H. Blewett, *The Last Generation* (Amherst: University of Massachusetts Press, 1990), and her *Men, Women, and Work* (Urbana: University of Illinois Press, 1988). See also Blewett's "We Are Freeborn American Women," in Kenneth Fones-Wolf and Martin Kaufman, eds., *Labor in Massachusetts: Selected Essays* (Westfield: Institute for Massachusetts Studies, 1990); and Marjorie R. Abel, "Women's Work in the Western Massachusetts Rural

11. Boston cooking school, c. 1880. Boston Athenaeum.

Acknowledgement of the economic importance of those who prepared their own meals and tended their own children, as well as hired
cooks and nannies, betokened a progressive outlook by the standards of
the nineteenth century. That reform perspective, to be sure, was
sometimes tainted by Victorian condescension—the chivalric obligation of good men to protect weaker women—and never challenged the
traditional marital hierarchy. But Oliver, in particular, did use his
research to buttress recommendations that the legislature increase the
minimum age of first employment and provide more schooling for girls
as well as boys. He urged the General Court to reduce and limit the

Economy," in the same collection. Renée Toback, "Protective Labor Legislation for
Women: The Massachusetts Ten-Hour Law," (Ph.D. dissertation, University of Massa-
chusetts, 1986), and Carol Lasser, " 'The World's Dread Laugh': Singlehood and Service in
Nineteenth-Century Boston," in Herbert G. Gutman and Donald H. Bell, eds., *The New
England Working Class and the New Labor History* (Urbana: University of Illinois Press,
1987), are also relevant.

hours of daily and weekly labor of women as well as children, to require equal pay when men and women performed the same jobs, and to include female citizens in the political process. He asked employers to improve the factory environment and to modify work rules in order to ensure the health of future generations. And he hoped that municipalities, social agencies, and civic-minded individuals would open boarding houses to provide dignified lodging and healthy diets for single workingwomen.

Oliver's sympathetic, programmatic response to what he obviously believed to be injustice stemmed from conviction as much as from analysis. He concluded a survey in 1872, for instance, with an enumeration of the "disabilities" of working women, an unfortunate word that appeared to blame them for their own victimization. In fact, the "disabilities" Oliver mentioned were social attitudes and expectations that resulted in wages he thought indefensible. He identified the notion that work for women was only an interlude before marriage, not a career, as one cause of female exploitation, and the self-serving assumption among employers that parents would provide room and board for badly paid daughters as another. Reforms Oliver proposed would have corrected neither of those conditions.

Oliver thought about half the women who worked for wages in the 1870s served as domestics; he knew that an even larger number did household tasks without formal remuneration. A population of that size made it essential for the bureau to begin identifying and quantifying the several categories of "housework" (Table 23). Oliver published his first tentative tables of weekly wages for several groups of live-in employees in 1871. Transients who were hired for "scrubbing and washing" were omitted; these women tended to be widows or the wives of underpaid men, and earned, according to the bureau's figures, about fifteen cents per hour for very irregular employment. The paragraphs and tables reproduced here exclude this group of domestic workers.

HOUSE WORK

This class of workers live, as a rule, in greater comfort than any other;

Table 23. Domestic labor, house work, 1872.

Totals and Averages, with board			
Total number employed	1,220	General average wages per week	$4.76
Total number Cooks	75	Average wages	7.53
Total number Chambermaids	119	Average wages	4.27
Total number General Housework	414	Average wages	3.48
Total number Nurseries	165	Average wages	4.09
Total number Parlor Girls	90	Average wages	4.33
Total number Table Girls	128	Average wages	4.43
Total number Seamstresses	229	Average wages	5.22
General Average Earnings per year			247.52

Source: MBLS, *Third Annual Report*, 1872, 66.

that is, their food is better, lodgings more comfortable, and their wages enable them to dress neatly and comfortably and to save something.

The kind and amount of labor which they are expected to perform as an equivalent for this, depends entirely upon the family in which they work. Where two or more servants are employed, the work is not often arduous compared with other avocations, though always confining. But in most cases, where the girl is hired for general housework, she needs good health and strength to enable her to do what is required. It is therefore not unusual for her, so situated, to break down, although, when the labor is not excessive, it is one of the most healthful employments in which women are engaged. There are places for general housework where the family is small, the mistress reasonable and considerate, and where the work is not beyond a woman's ordinary strength. In such places it is not uncommon for a good and capable girl to stay for years, with comfort and advantage to herself and her employer. But there are many others where the work is never done, where the servant is regarded only as a machine for the turning off of every kind of work, and where the idea of saving her trouble or lightening her work, is one which apparently never enters the mind of her mistress. Of course, such mistresses are not ladies in the true sense of that word. The higher the culture of the woman, the more true the gentility of the mistress, the more will she look upon her servants as human beings, with natures like her own, with like needs and desires, and the less likely will she be to treat them with injustice or selfishness. Families are known where servants have all the privileges of the books of the library, of the parlor, or of any room in the house, when not occupied in their work. They are also allowed to receive their friends and companions in their own part of the house when it does not interfere with their work, besides being allowed one afternoon and every other Sunday for themselves. These families, as a rule, employ only trained domestics. They pay the highest prices and demand the best skilled labor. Instances are known where the faithful domestic received, during sickness, or injury by accident, kind attention and all needed nursing, not being required to go away from the family. An inexperienced girl must expect, during the time of her inexpertness, to put up with an inferior place and low wages.

Many who try this kind of labor become discouraged, and prefer the greater freedom and independence of the shop-girl, even if accompanied with her discomforts and privations. Especially is this true of the American girl, whose inherited love of freedom leads her to suffer much before placing herself in a position where she readily perceives tyranny to be possible. She does not always avoid it by the change.

We are convinced that all that is necessary to good relations between mistress and maid, is a more enlightened understanding on both sides, and a little of the philanthropy of "putting ourselves in others' places." This would quickly do away with much of the antagonism between employer and employed, and the feeling that makes one person look upon another as a natural enemy, instead of recognizing the bond of a common sisterhood and a mutual dependence. (MBLS, *Second Annual Report*, 1871, 198–99)

As part of a general investigation of wages and hours in 1871, Oliver attempted to identify "every branch of labor" performed by women in Boston; a year later, he extended the inquiry outside the city (Table 24). In both instances, the staff visited individual workers at home and at

Table 24. Wages of women, by occupation, 1872.

Retail Workers			
Total number employed	1,270	Gen'l average wages per week	$5.27
Total number Book-keepers	151	Gen'l average wages per week	7.69
Total number Cash Girls	265	Gen'l average wages per week	2.78
Total number Saleswomen	680	Gen'l average wages per week	6.28
Total number Saloon	174	With board wages per week	4.33
Average hours of labor per week			62⅓
Average number of weeks per year			44½
Average price of board			$4.35
General average earnings per year			234.51

Table 24. Continued.

Dresses and Cloaks

<small>TOTALS AND AVERAGES—(WHOLESALE AND CUSTOM)</small>

Total No. employed—Wholesale	1,945	Average wages per week	$7.77
Total No. employed—Custom	1,257	Average wages per week	9.93
Average hours of labor per week			60
Average number of weeks of busy season			24
Average price of board			$4.50
Average earnings per year—Wholesale			186.48
Average earnings per year—Custom			238.82

Men's Clothing

<small>TOTALS AND AVERAGES—(WHOLESALE)</small>

Total No. employed	12,507	Gen'l average wages per week	$6.53
Total No. Coat Basters	2,387	Gen'l average wages per week	5.84
Total No. Coat Finishers	2,447	Gen'l average wages per week	5.80
Total No. Pant Basters	1,665	Gen'l average wages per week	5.31
Total No. Pant Finishers	1,777	Gen'l average wages per week	5.53
Total No. Vest Basters	1,783	Gen'l average wages per week	5.44
Total No. Vest Finishers	1,571	Gen'l average wages per week	5.50
Total No. Forewomen	70	Gen'l average wages per week	8.72
Total No. Machine Operators	629	Gen'l average wages per week	8.27
Total No. Button-hole Makers	125	Gen'l average wages per week	7.68
Total No. Presswomen	62	Gen'l average wages per week	7.35
Average hours of labor per week			60
Average number of weeks of busy season			34
Average price of board per week			$4.50
General average earnings per year			222.02

Professional women

Occupation	Weeks	Wages		Salaries	
		Highest	Lowest	Highest	Lowest
Costumers	24	$10.00	$8.00	$240.00	$172.00
Designers	48	19.23	13.47	1,000.00	700.00
Dramatic	—	15.48	7.80	800.00	500.00
Engraver	—	12.58	—	—	800.00
Telegraphers	43	12.00	8.00	516.00	344.00
Organists	52	19.23	12.50	1,000.00	650.00
Music Teachers	52	13.47	8.68	700.00	450.00
Teachers	52	13.47	4.16	700.00	216.00

Boots and Shoes

Total number employed	1,867
Average wages per week	$10.38
Average hours of labor	—
Average number of weeks in busy season	34
Average price of board	$4.50
Average earnings per year	352.92

Source: MBLS, *Third Annual Report*, 1872, 72, 80, 86, 101, 104.

work and talked with employers, a practice that added a personal dimension to the tables. Three individual accounts amplify the tabulated results from the 1872 statewide survey.

TESTIMONY OF A FACTORY OPERATIVE

I have been a working-woman in the mill about twenty-five years, or more, and have never seen the time that I could save money enough from my wages to enable me to obtain books, or avail myself of the advantages of lectures, or pleasure trips. I now am growing old and wearing out. Poverty is and has been, the price of my laborious life. There seem to have been many improvements, reducing the cost of manufactures by the invention of machinery. Yet the wages of the work-women have not advanced thereby. Larger dividends have blessed capital, while labor remains the same.

TESTIMONY OF A WEAVER

In our rooms the girls tend but one loom. Principally, natives in our room. In the mill, Irish and Scotch predominate, less than one-fourth being Americans. More than one-half married women. A great many of them have children. Some of them take their children to work with them. Average age of women is 28 years, some as old as 50, others as young as 20, and some younger. No children except warp boys about 14 years old, two of them say they are 16. It does not seem as though they were twelve they are so small. Accidents occur very often. It seems to be of no account to have a finger taken off. One girl had 2 fingers off during the past year. A girl has been hurt on each successive Saturday for three weeks. I know 5 girls so hurt. A man was nearly killed by falling down from the harness frame on to the loom frame.

When girls are hurt the corporation does not continue their wages, though I have known of one girl having her wages continued.

There are 263 women employed in our room. Some of the girls say they can weave one yard more in the forenoon than in the afternoon. There is a good deal of dust, but it settles down. Some cannot work on account of the *high colors and poison dye.* The girls complain of lung diseases, sore throat, and general debility. They all have a haggard appearance, they look better than the girls in the Cotton mills. In our rooms there are windows at the side and overhead. Those overhead are painted to keep out the sunlight. We cannot open the windows on a damp day, it affects the warp, so that we could not weave. Gas is lighted at 4.40 P.M. at this time (Jan.)

The air is bad Monday mornings and after lighting up time. Have a good deal of headache in the afternoon. Have to talk with motion of the lips. Cannot hear however loud we talk. The more we keep our mouths shut the better.

A great many children are employed in the mills in the spinning room, not in our mill, but on the corporation. *Some as young as 7 or 8 years.* They have talked about enforcing a rule to have the children go to school, but I don't think they have done it. The little things look *care-worn and old*, and *are very small.*

I have hea[r]d them tell of children of 7 and 8 years of age at work in the mill. In our room four or five had the small-pox. We were all vaccinated by a Doctor whom the Corporation sent in. Many of the Irish girls would not be vaccinated by an American doctor. The Overseer stood over each girl and compelled her to be vaccinated.

I know that in the Cotton Mills the girls do not fare as well as we do. The girls would like the ten hour system, though some of them would work 24 hours a day if they could.

TESTIMONY OF A SEAMSTRESS

Miss B— C—. Am a New Hampshire girl, came to Boston March, 1865, to live with Mrs. — on Beacon Street, in capacity of seamstress, and to take some care of the children three and five years old; lived there until October, 1869, receiving $3 per week. Was allowed Thursday evening of each week, and one Sabbath per month. Became tired of the service, for as the children grew older they became restive oftentimes, using their small violence against me. The mother said she should not correct them for it unless they confessed it to her. As the boys grew older and heavier, found it impossible to carry them up and down stairs from kitchen to attic, as had to be done several times during the day. Finding my health failing, I resolved to seek employment in some shop, not thinking I should find any difficulty in obtaining work which would afford me a living. In this I was sorrowfully disappointed; procured board in Tyler Street at $4 per week, sharing a room with three others. This was unlike the living and accommodations I had been having, but I preferred to submit to it rather than to return to service. Indeed I could not easily procure another situation, for my former mistress had notified all the respectable intelligence offices that I was unworthy, having left her without just cause. This influence I felt would prevent my obtaining a situation in a good family, as I should be required to give recommendations from my former mistress, and she had warned the intelligence offices to beware of me. With these obstacles I resolved not to attempt a return to service until I had given something else a trial. I obtained work in a clothing shop at finishing pants; earned $3.85 the first week, the next a little more, and so on for thirteen weeks, paying $4 per week for board. I was then again taken sick and unable to work for two weeks; drew some of the money I had earned while in service from the savings bank; cold weather came on and I was obliged to draw more to procure clothing for the winter; dull times coming, was discharged, or rather told there would be no more work for two months. Day after day I went in pursuit of work, but having no trade was refused many times where I might have obtained it had I been qualified to make a garment entire, or to do nice embroidery. My inability was the bar to my obtaining work in dull times, so I was refused at every place. I went to my lodgings discouraged and sick; had no home to flee to, no work and was using my little savings faster than I had earned them. Was taken sick, stayed in my boarding-place until I had drawn my last dollar from the bank; growing still worse my physician advised me to go to the hospital; this I had great dread of doing, but was growing worse so fast I went, and stayed four weeks; was then able to work a little; returned to my boarding-house and was refused board without payment in advance; was obliged to accept the hospitality of two former shopmates and sleep three in one bed; next day obtained work, finishing pants; soon we were cut down ten and fifteen cents every payment. Workwomen are constantly discharged and new girls hired so often that I am now in constant dread of a discharge. (MBLS, *Third Annual Report*, 1872, 109–10; *Second Annual Report*, 1871, 223–24)

Oliver's conclusions from this research were based on the data but were not entirely the result of logical deduction. The numbered explanations that begin his essay below now seem inadequate, although at least they helped draw public attention to the inequities he found. And if his reform agenda seems incomplete, it was nevertheless more advanced than that of most of his contemporaries. The attempt to achieve political rights for women, postponed during Reconstruction, waned in the 1870s; the movement to protect women from industrial abuse had barely begun.

The first and most important, is the fact that thousands of women, the wives and daughters of farmers and mechanics, are . . . [willing to work part-time, thereby] cheapening the wage of the constant, regular work-woman.

The second is the fact that thousands of girls in our large cities, daughters of small traders and salaried men, can afford to work for wages that will only clothe them, the father willingly giving them their board. These two classes come into direct competition with the poor girl or woman, who has no other source of income but her labor.

Thirdly the short season of work in almost all her employments, is one of the bad features connected with the subject. When the season is over, those who have homes with parents or relatives, with perhaps sufficient clothing to last until the next season, are comparatively safe; while those who have no homes, . . . are often driven to desperate means for a liveli-hood. For what must be the fate of many whose wages in the busy season are not more than $6.00 or even $3.00 per week, and sometimes even less[?] What can become of them, but to lead a life of feverish anxiety, living, as so many do, in miserable houses in dirty neighborhoods, amid demoralizing surroundings, where neither physical nor moral health is sure[?] Is it any wonder that vice, holding out promises of better shelter, food and clothing, tempts so many from the path of virtue? Is it not clear that these low wages diminish the army of honest industry, and increase the army of guilty crime? Is it not clear that the cry for "cheap labor" brings dear cost elsewhere, leading to results that demand missionary work and Magdalen asylums, and charitable Institutions, and the ceaseless efforts of philanthropic hearts and hands, and all the costly outlay of charity and of crime? . . .

The hours of labor are too long. Not too long to earn a living in, for they barely suffice, as things now stand, for the purpose, but too long for the proper physical good, mental culture and moral growth of those in-volved. . . .

A great obstacle in the way of woman's success as a wage-laborer, is found in the lack of motive consequent upon her expectation of being married.

The girl of 15 or 16, looks to but 3 to 5 years of wage service, and the earnings of those years are only expected to add to the attractions that shall shorten that period.

The subdivision of labor, through its destruction of the need of skill, is rendering her more profitable as an employé; but the motive to advancement and success will only come to the majority of women, when the hours of labor are reduced to a minimum, and perfected machinery has rendered labor attractive and entertaining. . . .

Another disadvantage growing out of the same cause as those already enumerated, is the small chance of promotion or advancement in any calling she may choose, . . . the principal impediment being the force of custom, that in this, as in other matters, amounts to prejudice. But even were the prejudice removed, the poor working woman would find her poverty of means a sufficient barrier to any advancement beyond that of fore-woman or superintendent; for in the employments in which the most women are engaged, very large capital is required to make the business successful and profitable.

So she has prejudice, as well as poverty, to contend with. . . .

The slightest examination into the comparative wages of men and women, shows a very great inequality,—the excess being very largely in favor of the stronger sex, so that the suggestion is not wanting that perhaps here, "might makes right." To estimate these wages relatively is, in many cases, quite difficult, because of the wide difference in the several employments of the two parties, and the brief time out of an entire year during which women have employment. But taking certain branches in which each sex is more steadily employed, as in some departments of sewing, of clerkage and attendance in stores, and specially in teaching, it is easy to institute a comparison, though not easy to assign a satisfactory reason therefor.

The determination of wage by sex, is defended on the general ground that being women, they really live at less cost than men. This is doubtless true in application to single women. It cannot be of entire force in its application to those who have dependent families, nor should it receive aid from the thought that because they are of the weaker sex they are less able to protect themselves against depression of wage. This obstacle of sex is also fortified in the case of married women, by the generally accepted idea that the man is the supporter of the household. As a general rule he is, but there are frequent exceptions, and even if normal, it is not amenable to the laws of proportion; for no man at wage receives wages in the ratio of the number of his children, nor does anybody ever think of paying a widow at wage any more, whether she has ten or two fatherless children to provide for. . . .

An examination of our tables of women's wages will show that as a general rule, these wages are not enough to keep off want, seldom anything more, so that she can neither provide for contingent sickness, nor make savings for contingent marriage. Yet every woman desires, on this latter event, to contribute something towards setting out in the new life. Now the impossibility of this being done by the majority of working women, and the low wages of those with whom they would probably marry, and the increasing cost of living, are all operating against marriage, and tending therefore to immorality. . . .

Statistics prove, beyond doubt, that most fallen women have been compelled to their fall by poverty. The evident remedy is therefore the prevention of the impelling cause. Efforts in other directions, though eminently laudable, are but occasional, and can never eradicate the root of the wrong. We may build Magdalen asylums without number, we may strive to allure the hapless and almost hopeless victims from the fearful sin that enfolds them, . . . but all that will be effected will be partial and transitory. . . .

When woman shall be justly recompensed for her labor, with new avenues opening and new and quickening inducements to enterprise, she will become the mistress, and not continue the slave of her situation, and then confidently wait the issue, whether it be that of the associated life for which she was created, or that of singly blessing her generation by the good words and good deeds of a pure and holy life.

We add this one thought more, that she should be at once endowed with her rightful political equality. These helps will do more towards purifying the social state and correcting the great social evils under which she suffers, than years of legislation, or volumes of statutes. The vilest man can further his villainy at the ballot-box; the purest and noblest woman cannot protect her smallest right thereby. The tyranny that oppresses her is strengthened by her own disfranchisement, and makes her impotent to defend her own prerogatives. . . .

Well meant as are the efforts of good people to furnish remedies for these difficulties, they do not reach the root of the evil. That lies a good deal deeper down than has yet been sounded. Nor will it ever be eradicated and permanently cured, till the present methods of labor and of wage shall be replaced by others, which shall more justly distribute the wealth created by the producers of wealth—just wage coming out of just work by just means, and generating a feeling of self-respect and a spirit of manly and womanly independence.

Not charity, but justice is what the workwoman wants, and a just share of the world's money for her share of the world's work. We have the testimony of hard-working, respectable and rightly ambitious girls, whose lives are so utterly bare of all the innocent pleasures and opportunities of life, that it makes the heart ache to think theirs are not exceptional cases. For no fault of theirs, but because they are homeless and friendless, left out of the account in the happy things of life, with nothing but its bitterness remaining, they are compelled to take up with inferior and even repulsive accommodations, and in houses where the society is wholly undesirable. Keepers of boarding-houses are unwilling to take women boarders, especially shop-girls. They make a marked difference between shop-girls and shop-boys. Male clerks have no difficulty in procuring board, where female clerks are refused. This combination of hard labor with poor fare and shelter, and insufficient clothing, is sure to induce disease in the healthiest, and yet many of this class are living in homes wholly unfit in almost all respects, deprived of the gift of God's pure air, and in proximity to uncleanliness which it is impossible for them to avoid. Is it to be wondered at, then, that many of them are feeble, consumptive and suffering, and that when married, they impart to their children a weak and sickly organization? (MBLS, *Third Annual Report*, 1872, 114–15, 117; *Second Annual Report*, 1872, 224–27, 229)

In 1875, Carroll Wright offered uncharacteristically prescriptive "suggestions" to correct "the evils that attend the several forms of employ, and that operate against the health, happiness and usefulness of women." Perhaps Wright overcame his aversion to advocacy because the workers involved were female; most Americans in the later nineteenth century would not have questioned public policy that differentiated on the basis of sex. Later reformers took advantage of greater public acceptance of regulation of female employment than was the case for male workers. Although early in the twentieth century the Supreme Court of the United States rarely permitted states to interfere with the terms and conditions of men's work, Oregon was allowed to limit the working hours of women. Louis D. Brandeis, the Boston attorney who argued the case in 1908, emphasized facts of the sort collected by the bureau, rather than legal precedent. Before taking the case, Brandeis had corresponded with the Massachusetts agency and read its reports, which may have contributed to the evidence collected in his brief in *Muller v. Oregon.*[3]

We believe that the grave mistakes of our labor system, as affecting the class of females considered, are—

First. That we employ those therein whose years absolutely prohibit their being employed at labor *at all.*

Second. That their hours of labor are too long; and—

Third. That we sadly neglect the measures that are adaptable to ensure a correct sanitary condition of our operatives during their labor....

No child, or young person, of *either sex*, under the age of fifteen years, should ever be engaged in any form of industrial employ necessitating absence from school or a draft on vital energy. The normal position of those of that age is in the work of education, and until this is recognized, the nation and individuals must suffer present and future loss,—loss of bodily vigor, without which a nation must die,—loss of knowledge, which is power, ... loss in the higher values that belong to the nobler parts of our being, and that cannot expand in a soul or body, dwarfed and exhausted by the gross demands of purely animal existence.

But it is objected, it can be clearly shown in this Commonwealth that, while it is true that the money in savings banks, to a considerable extent, belongs to laboring people, little of it would be there if it were not for the labor of children, the wives and offspring of laboring men; indeed, that without their assisting labor, it is proved, that the average laborer could not make the ends of the year meet. Granted, and yet our proposition is nevertheless of full force, and for two reasons: *First.* Because it is plain that there is an error in that price and form of labor that will not permit a man to support his family in comfort without drawing on the vital powers of those to whom we must look to make his place good, and to not only carry on, but improve upon, the work of society. *Second.* Because we can never afford to set a price upon body and soul.... An hour more in the

3. 208 US 412; see Melvin I. Urofsky and David W. Levy, eds., *Letters of Louis D. Brandeis* (Albany: State University of New York Press, 1971–78), I, 350.

morning for the young and forming female (and that is where it may be most advantageously gained, as all labor investigators agree), would save the necessity of ill-cooked, hurriedly-eaten, badly-digested breakfasts (made on hurriedly-prepared food, in which tea holds a prominent place), unwashed faces, neglect of nature's calls, hurried passage to the place of employ, and a disturbed, dissatisfied and fermenting body and mind, stomach and brain. . . .

It is hence essential, that such enactments should be made and prosecuted as shall best establish the condition of things that should be; and it is to such well considered and efficient enactments that we must look for the prevention of much that now affects, most unfavorably, the condition of working-people, and, especially, women and children. (MBLS, *Sixth Annual Report*, 1875, 107–10)

In order to "ascertain the moral, sanitary, physical, and economical conditions of the working girls of Boston" in 1883, Carroll Wright ordered comprehensive interviews with about a thousand of the twenty thousand women employed in other than domestic service. The sample, drawn from nearly eighty occupations and all sections of the city, eventually totaled 1,032, of which 83 were classified as performing personal (but not domestic) service, 123 were engaged in retail trade and accounting, and 826 in manufacturing. Researchers met each individual separately, usually in her residence, where they enjoyed a "courteous reception and ladylike treatment" from subjects who were supportive of the bureau's work.[4] The resulting data, printed in more than one hundred pages of tables and text, examined not only wages, hours, and working conditions, but residential arrangements, living expenses, marital status, age, ethnicity, morality, and health. Wright's summary of this material follows.

Results of the Investigation

Summarized, the investigation into the condition of the working girls of Boston enables us to state that in round numbers,—

4. MBLS, *Fifteenth Annual Report* (1884), 4.

There are 20,000 working girls in the city of Boston, exclusive of domestics; of these 68.7 per cent are living at home with parents or other relatives; 11.3 per cent are living in boarding houses; 15 per cent in lodging houses; and 5 per cent in private families.

The single constitute 88.9 per cent of the whole; the married, 6.7 per cent; the widowed, 4.4 per cent. In regard to nativity, 58.4 per cent were born in Massachusetts, but both parents of 73.8 per cent were foreign born, and 3.9 per cent had one parent foreign born, the purely American girls being 22.3 per cent of the whole.

The present average age of the working girls is 24.81 years, while the average age at which they began work was 16.81, and the average time actually at work, 7.49 years; the average number of occupations followed is 1.78, and the average time spent in each, 4.43 years. Of the whole average time employed, during 6.31 years they have been employed in Boston, or 84.3 per cent of the whole time; so the working girls of Boston are Boston girls.

Of the whole, 85 + per cent do their own housework and sewing, either wholly or in part.

But 22 + per cent are allowed vacations, and 3.9 per cent receive pay during vacation; the average vacation for those receiving it being 1.87 weeks. A little over 26 per cent work the full year without loss of time, while 73 + per cent of the whole lose an average of 12.32 weeks each; the average time worked by all during the year is 42.95 weeks. In personal service, 26.5 per cent work more than 10 hours per day; in trade, 19.5 per cent are so employed, and in manufactures, 5.6 per cent; in all occupations, 8.9 per cent work more than 10 hours per day, and 8.6 per cent more than 60 hours per week.

In regard to health, out of 7.49 years employed, the average time for the working girls, 5.57 years have been in good health, or in other terms during 74.4 per cent of the whole time employed they have been in good health; or referring to numbers, 76.2 per cent of the whole number employed are in good health.

The present actual weekly earnings (week of investigation, 1883) are for all employed $6.35, but the average weekly earnings for the average time employed, 42.95 weeks, was $6.01, *and the average weekly earnings of the working girls of Boston for a whole year are $4.91.*

The average weekly income, including earnings, assistance, and income from extra work, is $5.17 for the year.

12. "Working girls" in Boston, c. 1890. Courtesy of the Boston Public Library, Print Department.

The average yearly income from all sources is $269.07 and the average yearly expenses for positive needs are $261.30, leaving but $7.77 on the average as a margin for books, amusements, etc.

Those making savings are 11 + per cent of the whole, their average savings being $72.15 per year. A few run in debt, the average debt being $36.60 for the less than 3 per cent incurring debt.

Of the total average yearly expenses 63 + per cent must be expended for food and lodging and 25 + per cent for clothing, a total of 88 + per cent of total expenses for subsistence and clothing, leaving but 11 + per cent of total expense to be distributed for all the other wants of living.

The working girls of Boston, as a class, are honest, industrious and virtuous, and are making an heroic struggle against many obstacles, and in the face of peculiar temptations, to maintain reputable lives; they are entitled to the aid, sympathy, and respect of all who love good order, honest lives, and industrious habits. (MBLS, *Fifteenth Annual Report,* 1884, 127–28)

Reference to the "virtuous . . . reputable" lives of Boston's "working girls" rested on a serious effort to investigate prostitution in the city. Boardinghouse keepers and police officials alike assured the agency's staff that women who were employed at other pursuits were not among those who were corrupted by their employers or who wantonly walked the streets at night.[5] From police sources, the bureau identified and interviewed 170 prostitutes about their previous occupations and their reasons for changing careers. Wright's findings did not directly contradict Oliver's earlier assertion that economic necessity was the fundamental cause of vice, but they did suggest serious misgivings about that explanation.

It has often been said that the shop girls are an immoral class, that it is largely from their ranks that prostitution is recruited, and the vile charge has often been made that in great stores where many girls are employed, an engagement often depends upon the willingness of the saleswoman or shop girl to become the intimate friend of either the proprietor or head of a department. The assertion is often very flippantly bandied about that when a girl seeks employment and the wages offered are very low and she objects to such low wages, she is coolly informed that she must seek some gentleman to help her to support herself. In addition to our desire to ascertain the general moral condition which surrounds the working girls of Boston, we have had a very strong desire to ascertain the truth or falsity of these damaging assertions and charges. . . .

Let us now consider how far the ranks of prostitution are fed by girls from our shops. From 170 inmates of houses of ill-repute, known to the police, we have gathered some very valuable information; the causes given for their taking up the life they follow is of interest. Of these 170, 22 declined to give any cause, 17 entered their present life on account of illtreatment at home, 59 from choice, most of them on account of love of easy life and love of dress, 26 testify that they were driven into the life by poor pay and hard work, while 46 were led into the life through seduction. . . .

To summarize the previous occupation, or that immediately preceding their entry upon the life of shame, we reach the following results: 60 came directly from housework, table or hotel work; 32 from textile factories; 6 from shoe factories; 19 were dressmakers, seamstresses, or tailoresses; 5

---

5. Ibid., 120, 123.

were saleswomen; 18 had been in various occupations, while 30 had had no previous occupation.

The foregoing statements do not prove unfavorable to the working girls. These 170 women are leading lives of shame it is true, many of them leading lives of sorrow, also. Often during this investigation when considering this class of women, and the temptation to which girls are exposed, we have wished that public condemnation could fall as severely upon the seducer, and upon the tempter, as it has in the past upon his victim. This punishment would be quite severe enough.

In conclusion, so far as this part on moral condition is concerned, we can most freely and positively assert that the working girls of Boston are making an heroic, an honest, and a virtuous struggle to earn an honorable livelihood, and that it is rare that one of them can be found following a life other than one of integrity. We can also assert, to the credit of the merchants and employers of Boston, that they do not make the honor of the girls they employ the price of a position. (MBLS, *Fifteenth Annual Report*, 1884, 118, 124–26)

A few years later, the bureau broadened its inquiry and changed its terminology from the working girls of Boston to women in all branches of the state's industry. This wider focus required greater precision than in the past about the work women did at home. Previous reports had noted the importance of housework, but earlier categories did not seem sufficiently definitive for the state's census in 1885, on which the summary below was based. Census takers also disclosed the ownership stake women held in the state's industries and concluded with some general observations about the Commonwealth's workingwomen.

Housekeeper.—Use this term only for such persons as receive *wages* or *salary* for their services.

Housewife.—Use this only for the female head of a family, whether a wife or a woman keeping house for herself, who has no other gainful occupation, and who receives no stated salary or wage for her services.

Housework.—Use this for daughters, sisters, or other relatives or friends, who assist in the family without a stated salary or wage for their services, and who have no other remunerative employment. See *Servants.*

Housekeepers were properly included. They are regularly employed and receive a stated salary or wage for their services.

Housewives were excluded because, although the work they perform is absolutely necessary, and although it requires as much brain and muscle as many other occupations, it is performed in the house instead of in the mill, factory, or workshop. Strictly speaking, housewives are as much in industry as any other women wherever they may work. Conventional thought however considers the "home" and "industry" as dissimilar. . . . It would be contrary to generally entertained opinions to include the home, that is, the housewives, under industry. . . . There were 372,612 housewives in Massachusetts in 1885, and only 300,999 women engaged in all other branches of industry. If a housewife were not expected nor required to work, then for the labor of 372,612 women paid service would have to be substituted. Such a demand for labor could not be supplied by the inhabitants of the State itself. Consequently, as the labor of the housewives was absolutely necessary to allow society to exist in its present form, the housewife is certainly "in industry". As has been stated, she is excluded . . . for conventional and arbitrary reasons alone. The housewife is as much a member of the army of workers as the clerk or cotton weaver. . . . In succeeding censuses she should be lifted to her proper position and considered to be as much "in industry" as those women engaged in any other branch of labor.

The 372,612 housewives, in 1885, formed 36.92 per cent of the total female population in that year. In 1875, there were 328,188 housewives, being 38.27 per cent of the total female population in that year. This shows a decrease of 1.35 per cent in 1885. This per cent applied to the female population of 1885 indicates a falling off, as regards numbers, of 13,625 housewives.

The same reasons that excluded housewives might be given in support of the omission of those engaged in housework. Although those engaged in housework receive no stated salary or wage, their labor at home secures them a living, and they are free from the heavy responsibilities of the housewife. They are "in industry," for they displace others who could be hired to perform their duties, and their number is not so large but that the unemployed women in the State, if they wished, or immigrants from other States or countries, could be obtained, in sufficient numbers, to fill their places. There is another reason why those who reported themselves as being engaged in "housework" should be included. Many of them, how many cannot be definitely stated, are, at some time during the year, engaged in other gainful pursuits.

PARTNERS AND STOCKHOLDERS

1. In the manufacturing and mechanical industries of the Commonwealth, in 1885, the proportion of female partners was 1 in 16; that is, of the whole number of partners, one-sixteenth were women.

2. In the same industries, and at the same time, the proportion of female stockholders was 1 in 3.69; that is, of the whole number of stockholders in manufacturing corporations, more than one-fourth were women.

3. The aggregate business influence of women, on the basis of numbers, considering their presence as partners in private firms and as stockholders in corporations in our manufacturing and mechanical industries, was a little less than one-fifth.

EMPLOYÉS IN GAINFUL PURSUITS

1. In 1875, the women engaged in gainful pursuits formed 21.33 per cent of the total female population; in 1885, the percentage was 29.82, a gain, as regards total female population, of 8.49 per cent.

2. In 1875, the males formed 73.19 per cent and the females 26.81 per cent of all persons employed in gainful pursuits. In 1885, the males were 66.62 per cent and the females 33.38 per cent of the total persons employed. This shows an absolute gain of women in industry of 6.57 per cent, and an industrial displacement of an equal percentage of men. Of the total gain in number of employés from 1875 to 1885, the percentage for males was 46.19 and for females 53.81.

3. From 1875 to 1885, the male population increased 17.44 per cent; in industry, the males increased 20.30 per cent. During the same period, the female population increased 17.69 per cent; the women in industry increased 64.56 per cent. The female net excess was 0.25 per cent as regards population, and 44.26 per cent as regards representation in gainful pursuits.

4. Considering comparative increases, the males in industry increased 1.16 times as fast as the male population; women in industry increased 3.65 times as fast as the female population; and women in industry increased 3.18 times as fast as the males in industry.

5. In 1875, there were 19 branches of industry in which women were not employed; in 1885, there were but 8 branches of industry in which women

were not employed. In both 1875 and 1885, there were 15 branches of industry in which women were in a preponderance, representing 50 or more per cent of all persons employed therein. . . .

SOCIAL STATISTICS

1. Of the whole number of persons in industry, 73.97 per cent were single and 26.03 per cent were married. Of the males, 67.69 per cent were single and 32.31 per cent were married. Of the females, 88.29 per cent were single and 11.71 per cent were married. In 1885 as compared with 1875, the increase in married females was 39.64 per cent.

2. The females in industry considered were at least 10 years of age. Those from 10 to 13 years of age formed 0.13 per cent of the total; from 14 to 19 years of age, 23.19 per cent; from 20 to 29 years of age, 41.08 per cent; from 30 to 39 years of age, 15.05 per cent; 40 years of age and over, 20.55 per cent.

3. Of the total female population from 10 to 13 years of age, 0.55 per cent were engaged in gainful pursuits; from 14 to 19 years of age, 61.11 per cent; from 20 to 29 years of age, 59.77 per cent; from 30 to 39 years of age, 30.44 per cent; from 40 to 49 years of age, 22.58 per cent; from 50 to 59 years of age, 19.79 per cent; from 60 to 79 years of age, 21.80 per cent; 80 years of age and over, 15.84 per cent; those whose ages were unknown, 45 per cent.

4. Of the women employed in domestic service, 62.33 per cent were native born and 37.67 per cent were foreign born; in manufacturing and mechanical industries, 63.16 per cent were native born and 36.84 per cent were foreign born; in all other occupations, 76.80 per cent were native born and 23.20 per cent were foreign born.

5. Of the women in all branches of industry, 64.48 per cent were native born and 35.52 per cent were foreign born. Of the native born, considered as 64.48 per cent of the total, 48.56 per cent were born in Massachusetts, 11.32 per cent were born in the other New England States, and 4.60 per cent were born in other States of the Union. Considering 35.52 as the foreign born total, 17.19 per cent were born in Ireland, and 18.33 per cent were born in other foreign countries.

6. Of the whole number of native born females in the State, 10 years of age and over, 34.70 per cent were engaged in gainful pursuits. Of the whole number of foreign born females in the State, 10 years of age and over, 39.47

13. In a spinning room, c. 1890. Courtesy of the Museum of American Textile History.

per cent were engaged in gainful pursuits. Of both native and foreign born women, of the ages specified, 36.26 per cent were so engaged.

7. In 1885 as compared with 1875, the number of housewives fell off 13,625, or 1.35 per cent.

8. Of the 88,985 women engaged in housework, 12,366, or 13.90 per cent, were from 60 to 79 years of age.

9. Of the 88,985 women engaged in housework, 71,341, or 80.17 per cent, were native born.

10. More than one-fifth (20.92 per cent) of the women engaged in gainful pursuits in Massachusetts, in 1885, were unemployed for a greater or less period during that year. (MBLS, *Twentieth Annual Report*, 1889, 578–80, 598–600)

A major motive for the bureau's study of workingwomen was social concern about the impact of employment, especially in factories, on what were delicately termed "functions peculiar to the sex." Questions the bureau posed about working conditions sometimes pertained directly to the effect of long hours, constant standing, inadequate ventilation, hurried meals, and other circumstances on fertility. This preoccupation would later find expression in public discussion of "the future of the race," a phrase that betrayed the unease of established citizens about growing numbers of immigrants, especially in industrial cities. Any untraditional female activity was cause for worry: although the bureau itself did not conduct the research and only a small fraction of the sample involved Massachusetts residents, the *Annual Report* for 1885 reassured readers that achieving a college degree, for example, did not appear to endanger the health of female students, including their reproductive capacity.

Keeping a quantitative watch on patterns of family behavior became part of the bureau's regular investigative agenda. Conventional wisdom at the time tended to use the employment of women in other than domestic tasks as a partial explanation for social problems ranging from demographic change to a perceived decline in public morality. Wright and Wadlin attempted to inform this discussion with reliable data about marriage and divorce and rates of births and deaths. Table 25 was part of the state census of 1875; Table 26 comes from the federal census of 1900; the statistics on divorce in Table 27 were part of a study in the state census of 1885.

Although the number of workingwomen escalated rapidly between 1875 and 1885, rates of marriages, births, and deaths did not change proportionately. Moreover, figures for the fifty largest centers of population in the state, where industrial employment seemed most likely to affect results, differed only slightly from those elsewhere. That insignificant variation demonstrated to the bureau that "the presence of women in industry has not decreased the number of births or marriages, nor increased the number of deaths."[6] Tables 25–29 contain the numerical basis for that assurance.

6. MBLS, *Twentieth Annual Report* (1889), 601.

Table 25. Marriage and motherhood, 1875.

Conjugal condition of mothers

	Single	Married	Widowed	Divorced	Total Mothers
THE STATE	440	247,426	60,485	1,169	309,520
Native born	325	151,840	37,106	1,040	190,311
Foreign born	115	95,586	23,379	129	119,209

Married women with and without children

	Married Women	Mothers	Married Women not Mothers	Percentage Married Women with Children	Percentage Married Women without Children
THE STATE	398,759	309,520	89,239	77 +	22 +
Native born	254,531	190,311	64,220	74 +	25 +
Foreign born	144,228	119,209	25,019	82 +	17 +

Nativities and ages of mothers

Nativities	Under 18	18 to 21	22 to 30 inc	31 to 45 inc	Above 45	Total
Massachusetts	71	3,358	27,099	46,975	52,104	129,607
Other States	78	1,426	12,144	23,393	23,663	60,704
England	6	194	2,771	5.021	3,319	11,311
Ireland	4	564	15,779	35,295	24,837	76,479
Scotland	1	45	757	1,397	1,165	3,365
Wales	—	8	48	84	77	217
Canada	35	748	5,968	7,949	4,001	18,701
Other British Possessions	—	17	254	305	199	775
France	—	11	115	188	151	465
Germany	1	75	1,259	2,229	1,455	5,019
Other Foreign Countries	8	105	1,069	1,141	554	2,877
TOTALS	204	6,551	67,263	123,977	111,525	309,520

Nativities and ages of married women not mothers

Nativities	Under 18	18 to 21	22 to 30 inc	31 to 45 inc	Above 45	Total
Massachusetts	326	3,277	10,429	8,798	19,142	41,972
Other States	118	1,312	6,383	5,471	8,964	22,248
England	10	171	816	804	1,087	2,888
Ireland	10	386	3,398	4,090	6,781	14,665
Scotland	2	31	209	229	203	674
Wales	—	4	20	18	8	50
Canada	77	578	1,811	1,010	1,350	4,826
Other British Possessions	—	10	55	43	19	127
France	1	8	39	36	13	97
Germany	5	73	236	230	267	811
Other Foreign Countries	12	89	310	241	229	881
TOTALS	561	5,939	23,706	20,970	38,063	89,239

Source: MBLS, *Ninth Annual Report*, 1878, 123, 144, 158.

Table 26. Marriages, births, and deaths in Massachusetts, 1870–1901.

Years	Number of Marriages	Number of Marriages per 1,000	Number of Births	Number of Births per 1,000	Number of Deaths	Number of Deaths per 1,000
1870	14,721	20.20	38,259	26.25	27,329	18.75
1871	15,746	21.07	39,791	26.63	27,943	18.70
1872	16,142	21.06	43,235	28.21	35,019	22.85
1873	16,437	20.92	44,481	28.31	33,912	21.58
1874	15,564	19.32	45,631	28.32	31,887	18.55
1875	13,663	16.54	43,996	26.63	34,978	21.67
1876	12,749	15.20	42,149	25.12	33,186	19.79
1877	12,758	14.98	41,850	24.57	31,342	18.40
1878	12,893	14.91	41,238	23.85	31,303	18.10
1879	13,802	15.71	40,295	22.95	31,801	18.11
1880	15,538	17.43	44,217	24.80	35,292	19.79
1881	16,768	18.49	45,220	24.93	36,458	20.10
1882	17,684	19.17	45,670	24.75	36,785	19.94
1883	18,194	19.39	47,285	25.14	37,748	20.11
1884	17,333	18.15	48,615	25.46	36,990	19.04
1885	17,052	17.56	48,790	25.12	38,094	19.61
1886	18,018	18.03	50,788	25.42	37,224	18.63
1887	19,533	19.00	53,174	25.86	40,763	19.83
1888	19,739	18.19	54,893	25.95	42,097	19.90
1889	20,397	18.75	57,075	26.23	41,777	19.20
1890	20,838	18.60	57,777	25.81	43,528	19.44
1891	21,675	18.94	63,004	27.53	45,185	19.74
1892	22,507	19.24	65,824	28.13	48,762	20.86
1893	22,814	19.07	67,192	28.09	49,084	20.52
1894	20,619	16.86	66,936	27.37	46,791	19.13
1895	23,102	18.48	67,545	27.02	47,540	19.01
1896	23,651	18.09	72,343	28.27	49,381	19.30
1897	23,038	17.57	73,205	27.96	47,419	18.11
1898	22,142	16.53	73,110	27.29	46,761	17.45
1899	23,523	17.16	70,457	25.70	47,710	17.40
1900	24,342	17.35	73,386	26.16	51,156	18.23
1901	24,891	17.34	71,976	25.07	48,275	16.82

Average ages at marriage

Years	Average Age of All Bridegrooms	Average Age of All Brides	Average Age of Men Marrying for the First Time	Average Age of Women Marrying for the First Time
1872	28.6	24.7	26.3	23.4
1873	28.7	24.8	26.3	23.5
1874	28.8	25.3	26.2	23.6
1875	28.9	25.0	26.3	23.6
1876	29.2	25.3	26.5	23.7
1877	29.2	25.2	26.4	23.8
1878	29.2	25.0	26.5	23.8
1879	28.2	25.2	26.7	23.9
1880	28.9	25.1	26.5	23.8
1881	28.8	25.1	26.5	23.9
1882	29.2	25.4	26.5	23.9
1883	28.8	25.3	26.6	23.4
1884	29.1	25.1	26.6	24.1
1885	29.2	25.3	26.8	24.2
1886	28.9	25.3	26.9	24.2

Table 26. Continued.

Average ages at marriage—Cont.

Years	Average Age of All Bridegrooms	Average Age of All Brides	Average Age of Men Marrying for the First Time	Average Age of Women Marrying for the First Time
1887	29.0	25.5	26.8	24.4
1888	28.9	25.5	26.8	24.4
1889	29.1	25.8	26.9	24.5
1890	28.8	25.5	27.2	24.3
1891	28.6	25.4	26.8	24.2
1892	28.8	25.4	26.7	24.3
1893	28.8	25.5	26.9	24.4
1894	29.1	25.0	26.9	23.7
1895	28.9	23.2	26.7	24.2
1896	29.1	25.6	27.1	24.4
1897	29.1	24.8	27.1	24.5
1898	29.2	25.7	27.4	24.4
1899	29.2	25.6	27.3	24.3
1900	28.9	25.8	27.4	24.5
1901	29.2	25.8	27.3	24.6

Source: MBLS, *Thirty-third Annual Report*, 1903, 247–49.

Table 27. Divorce in Massachusetts, 1885.

Causes for Divorce, 1869–1887	Number Granted for each Specified Cause
Adultery	3,037
Desertion	4,834
Intoxication	1,242
Extreme cruelty	571
Cruel and abusive treatment	739
Neglect to provide	213
Imprisonment	63
Impotency	19
TOTALS	10,718

Source: MBLS, *Twentieth Annual Report*, 1889, 591.

Table 28. Death-rates for males and females in Massachusetts, for census years 1865–1885.

Census Years	Death-rates of Males	Death-rates of Females
1865	21.7	19.6
1870	19.5	18.6
1875	21.8	20.5
1880	20.3	19.3
1885	20.2	19.0

Source: MBLS, *Twentieth Annual Report*, 1889, 592.

Table 29. Births, marriages, and deaths, 1875 and 1885.

Classification	1875	1885
Total female population	857,529	1,009,257
Number of females employed in gainful pursuits	182,906	300,999
Percentages	21.33	29.82
Female population 20 years of age and over	528,541	645,437
Number of births	43,996	48,790
Number of marriages	13,663	17,052
Number of deaths of females 20 years of age and over	9,710	12,044
Proportion; births: one in—	12.01	13.23
Proportion; marriages: one in—	38.68	37.85
Proportion; deaths of females 20 years of age and over: one in—	54.43	53.59

Comparisons for 50 cities and towns, and for the state, 1885.

Classification	Fifty Cities and Towns	Other Cities and Towns	The State
Total female population	649,831	359,426	1,009,257
Number of females employed in gainful pursuits	204,871	96,128	300,999
Percentages	31.53	26.74	29.82
Female population 20 years of age and over	413,735	231,702	645,437
Number of births	34,150	14,640	48,790
Number of marriages	11,797	5,255	17,052
Number of deaths of females 20 years of age and over	7,652	4,392	12,044
Proportion; births: one in—	12.12	15.83	13.23
Proportion; marriages: one in—	35.07	44.09	37.85
Proportion; deaths of females 20 years of age and over one in—	54.07	52.76	53.59

Source: MBLS, *Twentieth Annual Report*, 1889, 596–97.

In commenting on the number of women employed in 1900, Wadlin pointed to the "most gratifying" fact that not quite 12 percent of married women in Massachusetts were employed outside the home.[7] Probably his satisfaction arose from a proportion thought to be small, rather than from evidence that the number of employed married women had risen. But in this respect, as in others, the bureau's opinion as the century closed had moderated after thirty years of research, as a second glance at the rhetoric at the beginning of the chapter discloses.

7. MBLS, *Thirty-third Annual Report* (1902), 254.

CHAPTER SIX

The Education and Employment of Youth

Images of forlorn, emaciated waifs, dwarfed by huge textile machines, are among the most familiar and evocative illustrations of the nation's industrialization. The plight of children, working in factories often in excess of sixty weekly hours, engaged the Massachusetts General Court before their depiction became a visual commonplace. Prodded by constituents as well as compassion, legislators tried two regulatory approaches: a maximum number of hours young employees might work and compulsory school attendance. A law in 1867, for instance, limited to sixty hours the weekly labor of children under fifteen and required the attendance at school for at least three months of those between ten and fifteen.

Before his appointment as the bureau's first director, Henry K. Oliver had monitored industrial compliance with this legislation. He recorded both the continuing failure of Massachusetts employers to observe the statutory requirements and his own mounting frustration at his inability to compel obedience. Perhaps this experience, and his long career as an educator, motivated his search for innovative ways to harmonize the conflicting needs of employers, parents, and the larger society. The half-time school, which divided a child's time between instruction and employment, seemed to him an appealing resolution, which he promoted in the bureau's publications.

Carroll Wright did not lack sympathy for youthful factory operatives, but his editorial treatment of them lacked Oliver's prescriptive urgency.

Solutions were properly the responsibility of legislatures, in Wright's view, not of appointed bureaucrats, and the General Court in 1876 had acted. With this legislation, the linked topics of education and child labor practically vanished from the bureau's research agenda. Disappearance, of course, did not signify that industrial exploitation of children ceased or that no one under fifteen was truant. The income of employed children remained essential to the survival of some families and to the economic progress of many. That reality was evident in some of the bureau's tables, even if the inquiry that produced them had another focus. And more than forty years later, the Supreme Court of the United States continued to find constitutional barriers to legislation that might keep children out of the nation's factories.

14. Class in typesetting, c. 1890. Courtesy of the Boston Public Library, Print Department.

The first excerpt below is a prose snapshot of children at work in a textile mill; the second is an employer's explanation of those circumstances; the third is the legislation passed in 1874 and 1876. Wright may have taken these laws to be the General Court's final word on the matter, thereby effectively removing the need for further investigation and perhaps even prohibiting it.

Testimony of —

An Overlooker of seventeen years' experience ... in a cotton mill. ... Now works eleven hours per day, except Saturday; thinks there are many children under fifteen years of age; according to the best of my knowledge, I believe there are 150 under that age, in the room in which I am employed; one, a girl, measuring 4 ft. 5 in. high, weighing 62 lbs; another about the same height weighing 64½ lbs; think they are about eleven years of age. These children are poor, emaciated and sickly; none of them have attended school during the past year. Six years ago I ran *night-work* from 6:45 P.M. to 6 A.M.., with forty-five minutes for meals, eating in the room. The children were drowsy and sleepy; have known them to fall asleep standing up at their work. Some of these children are now working in the mill, and appear to be under fifteen years of age. I have had to sprinkle water in their face to arouse them, after having spoken to them till hoarse; this was done gently, without any intention of hurting them.

Testimony of a Woollen Manufacturer

A Woollen Manufacturer says: We find it very difficult to comply with the law in regard to sending children to school for several reasons:—

1st. We have considerable Canadian-French help, and many families that come to the States, do so with the intention of remaining only a few years at most, and then returning to their homes in Canada, and they regard it as time thrown away to send their children to school, as they (many of them) do not understand our language, and do not want to learn it; as they will not use it when they return to Canada. Many of these will leave, and go to Rhode Island or Connecticut if compelled to attend school, and in order to supply their places we are obliged to substitute others of the same stamp.

2d. We occasionally have families that are obliged to work in order to support themselves.

3d. Many of the parents do not feel the interest they ought to in having their children obtain an education. We have had some leave and go to Connecticut and Rhode Island, that have been to school during the year they were here; and had they remained, the number that have not attended schools would be materially less. We endeavor to have all attend school that the law requires to go, and if others will go, we never object to their taking the time to do so, but encourage them in availing themselves of the provisions so bountifully provided in the Old Bay State. (MBLS, *Annual Report*, 1870, 126–27, 248–49)

CHAP. 221, ACTS OF 1874

An Act establishing the hours of labor at sixty per week for women, and children under eighteen years of age.

SECT. 1. No minor under the age of eighteen years, and no woman over that age, shall be employed in laboring by any person, firm or corporation in any manufacturing establishment in this Commonwealth more than ten hours in any one day, except when it is necessary to make repairs to prevent the stoppage or interruption of the ordinary running of the machinery: *provided, however*, that a different apportionment of the hours of labor may be made for the sole purpose of giving a shorter day's work for one day of the week; but in no case shall the hours of labor exceed sixty per week.

SECT. 2. Any such person, firm or corporation which wilfully employs any minor or woman, or which wilfully has in its employment any minor or woman contrary to the provisions of this act, and any superintendent, overseer or other agent of any such person, firm or corporation, who wilfully employs any minor or woman in laboring for any such person, firm or corporation, and any parent or guardian of such minor who permits such minor to work or be so employed contrary to the provisions of this act, shall, for each offence, be punished by a fine not exceeding fifty dollars, to be recovered on complaint in any court of competent jurisdiction, and all prosecutions for offences under this act shall be begun within one year from the commission thereof. No building or premises used solely for the purposes of a dwelling shall be deemed a manufacturing establishment within the meaning of this act.

CHAP. 52, ACTS OF 1876

AN ACT relating to the Employment of Children, and regulations respecting them.

SECT. 1. No child under the age of ten years shall be employed in any manufacturing, mechanical or mercantile establishment in this Commonwealth, and any parent or guardian who permits such employment, shall for such offence forfeit a sum of not less than twenty nor more than fifty dollars, for the use of the public schools of the city or town.

SECT. 2. No child under the age of fourteen years shall be so employed, unless during the year next preceding such employment he has attended some public or private day school, under teachers approved by the school committee of the place where such school is kept, at least twenty weeks, which time may be divided into two terms, each of ten consecutive weeks, so far as the arrangements of school terms will allow; nor shall such employment continue, unless such child shall attend school as herein provided, in each and every year; and no child shall be so employed who does not present a certificate, made by or under the direction of said school committee, of his compliance with the requirements of this act: *provided, however*, that a regular attendance during the continuance of such employment in any school known as a half-time day school, or an attendance in any public or private day school, twenty weeks, as above stated, may be accepted by said school committee as a substitute for the attendance herein required.

SECT. 3. Every owner, superintendent or overseer in any establishment above named, who employs or permits to be employed, any child in violation of the second section of this act, and every parent or guardian who permits such employment, shall for such offence forfeit a sum not less than twenty nor more than fifty dollars for the use of the public schools of such city or town.

SECT. 4. The truant officers shall, at least once in every school term, and as often as the school committee require, visit the establishments described by this act in their several cities and towns, and inquire into the situation of the children employed therein, ascertain whether the provisions of this act are duly observed, and report all violations to the school committee. (MBLS, *Seventh Annual Report*, 1876, 293, 302)

Municipal officials, parents, and employers devised several expedients to balance competing demands for the time and energy of children. Some school districts made instruction available in the evening so that education did not reduce a child's contribution to family income. A few cities established the half-time schools Director Oliver advocated. Attendance requirements varied from school to school, but these institutions generally enabled pupils to combine schooling and work in roughly equal segments; some employers encouraged education with a small proportional increase in wages. After Oliver's departure, however, the bureau's enthusiasm for half-time schools cooled, partly because they inevitably separated students by socioeconomic class. Carroll Wright preferred compulsory full-time schooling for all children in the Commonwealth under the age of fifteen.

Descriptions of school visits excerpted here illustrate Oliver's support for half-time instruction. Wright's less positive description of half-time schools follows, together with his argument for abandoning that solution and adopting a more comprehensive educational program. The case is forcefully made and based on democratic ideals rather than the statistics that Wright would later prefer; he holds, for example, that segregation by income, occupation, or class violates egalitarian principles as surely as does segregation by race, to which idealistic Massachusetts residents objected in the aftermath of the Civil War.

Is there no remedy for the wrong of depriving children of a proper education, and for the great evils that will ensue, if an ignorant class of persons is permitted to grow up to increase the unnumbered host of ignorant men and women already with us, and to perpetuate a debased class crowded upon us, and still crowding in with every year, and threatening danger; nay, already weakening the foundations of the republic? . . .

The State and the Republic is in danger of being controlled by corporations. Let early means of prevention be secured. In Massachusetts itself, spite of her law, . . . children, *under*, as well as over ten years, are employed over ten hours a day, and that too, in many cases, without the legal schooling; and yet the strong manner in which the fact has been represented to the legislature, has failed to secure an effective law preventive of the acknowledged evil. What between parents, covetous of the earnings of their children, or driven, as is true in many instances, by the unsparing necessities of positive want; or, because of idleness or dissolute habits, reckless of the moral and intellectual, or even physical growth of their own children, on the one hand,—and the inordinate pressure for gainful product, and greed of wealth of employers, on the other hand,—the poor children are subjected to a pretty effectual grinding, as between an upper and a nether mill-stone. God help them, if man's law cannot! . . .

Now we know indeed that there is a compulsory statute of the Commonwealth in relation to the schooling of its children, but like a great many other statutes on the books, it is paralytic, effete, dead—killed by sheer neglect. It was never enforced, and never supposed to be anybody's duty to enforce it. In fact we are inclined to believe that it is not generally known that such a law was ever enacted. *Nobody looks after it, neither town authorities, nor school committees, nor local police, and the large cities and many of the towns of the State are swarming with unschooled children, vagabondizing about the streets and growing up in ignorance and to a heritage of sin. The mills all over the State, the shops in city and town, are full of children deprived of their right to such education as will fit them for the possibilities of their after-life.* Nobody thinks of either enforcement or obedience in the matter, so that between those who are ignorant of the provision, and those that "care for none of these things," thousands of the poor younglings of the State, with all her educational boasting, stand precious small chance of getting even the baldest elements of education.

And this brings up thought of the successful experiment in . . . half-time schools. (MBLS, *Annual Report*, 1870, 126–27, 248–49; *Second Annual Report*, 1871, 493)

NAUMKEAG HALF-TIME SCHOOL, SALEM

December 9th, 1872. Hearing incidentally that this school was falling off and the original interest therein diminishing, the chief of the Bureau visited it at date, and reports as follows: I find the rumor that this most valuable school was diminishing in numbers and interest, wholly unfounded, and not only so, but that the contrary is the fact. The forenoon passed there, and the examination I made, demonstrated that it is of inestimable value, and that its managements and method of detail in instruction and discipline are of the very best. In fact I am prepared to say, that I have never visited a school of its grade, where better order and conduct were exhibited, nor where the instruction given was more judicious, or better adapted to the wants of its class of pupils.

The teacher originally appointed over the school, Miss C. A. Dunn, continues in the position, and it is matter of great benefit and gain to the children, as most of them are from French Canadian families, that she speaks French, and can give her instructions in either the English or the French language, as the circumstances of the children, or of any particular lesson, may demand. On the day of my visit, there were present 46 out of the 58 children enrolled, the average attendance being 48. The boys were three times as numerous as the girls. The school-room and all its furniture were in the neatest condition. A melodeon stood upon the teacher's platform, singing forming part of the school exercises. Pictures were hanging upon the walls. The desks, one for each child, were covered to protect them from soiling and wearing, and the children themselves as neat and well-behaved and respectful, as if they had come from families of higher social position. When I speak of 'children enrolled,' I mean those enrolled for the *half-day*, there being two sets, one for the forenoon and one for the afternoon; these sets alternating with each other at mill and at school. . . .

Of the Naumkeag-school pupils, at least 90 per cent are French, none of whom could speak a word of English at the time of entrance. Their early instruction is therefore necessarily given in French, but this French is likewise, at the same time, put into English, and as this sort of exercise is *viva voce*, and with the aid of the blackboard, the English speaking children are sure to acquire some little of French. Let me describe an exercise.

Teacher (standing at the blackboard, placed on the wall behind her desk, and in front of the school) writes: "*comment vous portez-vous?*—How do you do?" Telling the children that these differing marks represent the same thoughts, she utters first the one sentence and then the other; the children then repeat them after her. This phrase being made familiar to their sight and well worked into their memories, she follows it up with other ordinary sentences of frequent use, the process being one, necessarily so at first, somewhat like learning to sing by rote. The same method is applied to a general exercise in arithmetic, the figures being written on the board, and their names being uttered in both languages by all the children. In this respect the half-time scholars of this school have an advantage over those of the ordinary schools, where only one language is or could be employed. The attendance in summer is not so good as that in winter. In fact, it is more difficult to secure child-help in the mill in the warm, than in the cold months, and this affects the school attendance,—many of these younglings seeking work out of doors, rather than to endure the heated confinement of the factory. I learnt on inquiring of the French children, that in Canada, unless the parents live in or near a town or village, very little educational advantage can be had; most of those who came as laborers into the United States, lived on small farms, and far apart, and what little schooling the children got was from their priest, or from nuns.

They are taught reading, writing, spelling, grammar, something of arithmetic, and a little history. The schools are not graded. The first thing to be done with the children here, is to furnish them with sufficient English, to enable them to understand common words and phrases. After that they easily fall into the general school routine.

The French laborers in Salem are highly spoken of by their overseers. They are quiet, painstaking, industrious, respectful, sober, and easily managed. The national courtesy still continues with them, and their children, as seen at this school, have all these good qualities. (MBLS, *Fourth Annual Report*, 1873, 370–71)

LAWRENCE EVENING SCHOOL

The girls, some 300 in number, occupy the rooms of the Oliver Grammar School, on Haverhill St. They were arranged in classes, each class with its separate teacher occupying a separate room. Some five rooms were occupied. The scholars had all been at work in the mill that day, having worked there eleven hours. The studies were the ordinary studies of common schools. On asking all of those under 15 to hold up their hands, we found that a large proportion of them were under that age, and, further, *that they had not had their legal schooling, and that they had worked 64½ hours a week.* Many of these children were between 10 and 13 years of age, and, in the various rooms visited, some 15 or 20 of them were found to be employed by the Pacific Mills Corporation, *that report to us that they employ no children under 15 years of age....*

Next visited the boys' school in the basement of the City Hall building, a low, badly-ventilated room, filled with 198 persons from 10 to 25 years of age,—the majority of them under 18. Some 10 or 12 older persons occupied a separate room. The boys come into this room precisely at half-past seven, (when the doors are all locked), and remain locked into this basement one hour and a half, and are then discharged. The teachers were mostly women,—being regular teachers in the day schools, and receiving an extra compensation of $1.00 an evening, for their attendance upon the evening schools. The air was very impure and the scholars looked tired and weary, but gave fair attention to their lessons.

NEW BEDFORD SCHOOL FOR FACTORY CHILDREN

... A class ... was reciting in arithmetic. We called up a little girl, Mary A. Carroll, a very small child. She was 10 years old, that day. Had worked in the mill 5 months; she was not much larger than an ordinary child of 7 years of age. We called up all who had worked in the mill before they were 10 years old, and 38 *responded*; all *very small*. The French children were called up by a French boy, whose name is Napoleon; 3 of these children had never been at school.

We asked the scholars to vote on the question of Half-Time schools; if they would like to work *half the day*, and go to school *half the day*; and all hands went up with a will. We then asked, if they liked to work in the mill, and they hesitated, and looked at each other; some hands going up and then others following.

The children look brighter and cleaner than those of Fall River; the room a little better, but not what it should be. The teachers expressed themselves well pleased with the result of the 5 weeks' schooling. Two little French children, a boy and girl, were called up, who could not speak a word of English, 5 weeks ago. They pronounced their words well; the teacher asking object questions and the children answering. We have thus to record another school gained for Factory Children and hope there will be many more ere long. We are persuaded that the creation of Half-Time Schools all over Massachusetts will be a long step in a wise direction.—And it may be added that it is now deemed competent for any School Committee to establish them. (MBLS, *Third Annual Report*, 1872, 443–45)

THE HALF-TIME SCHOOLS OF MASSACHUSETTS

Salem

Each scholar is required to attend one hundred and thirty half-days. If but a half-dozen have been inconstant in their attendance, . . . very soon that condition is reached . . . when every week the term is expiring for some and beginning for others.

This constant accession of new scholars, coming mostly in mere driblets of one, two or three, makes the labor of the teacher doubly onerous and lessens greatly the progress of the pupils.

Added to this their great diversity of gifts and attainments makes any such thing as classification and gradation nearly or quite impossible.

Those who attend school in the forenoon, work five and one-half hours in the afternoon; and those who attend in the afternoon, work five and three-fourths hours in the forenoon.

Those who are not attending school work not over sixty hours in a week.

The wage which each receives, when not attending school, is $2.64 per week; when attending school, $1.75.

To correspond as nearly as possible with this increase, piece-workers, while attending school, receive a gratuity of fifty cents a week.

In other words, when in school, all receive for their half-day's work, two-thirds of a day's pay.

A time-table of attendance at school is kept, in the same form as of labor at the mill, and being regularly transmitted to the agent, the same deductions in wages are made for the former as for the latter. . . .

On the first of January, 1874, the whole number of different scholars during the preceding twelve months had been	288
Boys	170
Girls	118
Number coming from the mills	193
Boys	113
Girls	80
Average number belonging for each half-day	43
Boys	29
Girls	14

Average number attending for each half-day	39
Boys	26
Girls	13
Per cent of average attendance	90.7
Boys	89.6
Girls	92.8

There is no doubt but half-time schools have been of great value in England. In one sense they would be of value to us. They do there, and they would here, no doubt, furnish large numbers of children, who might otherwise grow up completely illiterate, with some rudimentary knowledge of books; but there is one other thing which they accomplish there which totally unfits them for our use. They help to perpetuate the class distinctions which England conceives necessary to the stability of her existence. They would serve here, and quickly, to introduce the same distinctions. The homogeneousness of society is of the highest importance to us; and a somewhat more general diffusion of elementary knowledge would not by any means make amends to us for its loss. As long as Massachusetts objects to other states establishing schools to which *color* is the sesame of entrance, she can hardly deny that she is likely to become, in turn, a fair subject of criticism, if she shall establish schools to which *occupation* is the criterion of admission. Class schools are class schools just the same when they are for those of a certain employment as when they are for those of a certain color.

With factory schools once in full blast, how long will it be before the tradesman's or the lawyer's child will look upon their ill-clothed and dirty-handed pupils as inferiors and aliens? . . . And will not the factory child in turn view himself in the light of one degraded? Will the little book-learning he acquires bring him up, as much as this banishment from opportunities of social culture will sink him?

Most assuredly it will not. The book-education which the children of poor parents get in our present public schools is but a tithe of all their gettings. The cultivation of the moral and social natures from association with those blessed with a better home-training; the opportunities of self-comparison with them, and for the formation of friendships on a basis the nearest to perfect equality which the world has ever seen; the stimulus to exertion for such, in all ways, toward perfect man and womanhood which exists in these schools, in the knowledge that if they but zealously continue in them and honorably graduate, there will be no shred of the badge of their uncultured origin remaining, and no barrier left to their future advancement, but poverty, the implements for whose destruction they will hold in their hands; the very surroundings of costly desks, instruments of music and pictured walls (for these do not now, nor will not exist, in any such sumptuousness for the factory child in his school),—all these, and many more, are the choice acquisitions which the child of humble parents obtains in our public schools. These are the things which cultivate him. Education which has no smack of culture about it is but an effort of the memory and of little worth. . . .

The establishment of half-time schools in England was an advance, but for Massachusetts we believe it would be a retrogression. . . .

We believe that it is the business of children to attend school and acquire an education, and that they should have no legal status as workers. . . .

We believe it is especially necessary for the perpetuity of our form of government that there should be universal intelligence among our citizens, and to have that we must first have universal education; and not only universal education, but there must be a certain homogeneousness about it. The education of the poor man must not be of a kind to specially fit him for associating with poor men, and remaining a poor man, becoming a barrier to oppose his progress except in one particular direction, and on one particular level; nor on the other hand must it happen that the education of the rich shall be of a distinct kind and quality to insure that they will be kept rigidly through life in certain grooves. And to prevent these two things, nothing more efficient can be provided than the heterogeneous assocation of all classes, as regards wealth and social position, in the common schools. There was undoubtedly a great deal of force in that word "common" in the minds of our forefathers.

We see no way to attain this universal education except by making it compulsory. Our right to do this is established by many precedents, and supported by reason and justice. On this latter point it is enough to say, that if we can compulsorily take taxes from property for the support of schools, we can with equal right compulsorily take the children to fill them; indeed we shall hardly be fair to property unless we do. . . .

Feeling thus, we cannot witness with sympathy the establishment among us of what are called half-time schools. And we perceive with regret, a popular tendency in the direction of this system. To our minds it is a system which is but a makeshift, and a dangerous and deluding makeshift,

15. Ninth-grade schoolroom, Haverhill, 1881. Courtesy of the Trustees of the Haverhill Public Library, Special Collections Department.

which "keeps the word of promise to the ear, but breaks it to the hope." Its specious appearance of merit and acceptableness has produced, in the minds of many, very favorable opinions of its usefulness; but we trust that in so important a matter as the elementary training of the young, haste to cure a great evil may not lead to the adoption of any empirical means. . . .

We believe that, generally speaking, the period of childhood and youth should be a period of free and unrestricted physical growth, that the bodily man and womanhood may be vigorous and vital.

We believe, in short, that children should have no legal status as workers, but only as pupils; and, above all, that the poverty of parents should not be allowed to foster the one condition or frustrate the other, inasmuch as it is unwise for the state to permit the future usefulness of its citizens to be jeopardized by causes within its control.

We believe that the opportunities for education should be the same for *all* the children in the state; and that a special and necessarily poorer class of schools should not be established for the children of the poor. We believe this, because it would be a direct blow at the democratic foundations on which our governmental structure rests.

And ... we would recommend that our laws be so revised as to provide compulsorily for the attendance of all children between the ages of five and fifteen (not in attendance upon any private school) in the public schools for as long a time each year as they are kept in operation. And for the general accomplishment of this, that the state or local authorities be required to investigate and relieve, to such extent as is necessary, all cases of absolute and unavoidable individual poverty, which would otherwise prevent compliance with this obligation. (MBLS, *Sixth Annual Report,* 1875, 28–30; 57–61)

Those recommendations, Wright acknowledged, did not have a firm statistical base. Indeed, his effort to quantify some aspects of education in the Commonwealth seemed only to demonstrate the unreliability of numbers published in other official documents. In 1873, for instance, the bureau had tabulated illiteracy in eight Massachusetts cities (Table 30); preceding the table was an uncharacteristic apology that the bureau could not vouch for the accuracy of the data. "We have no doubt," Wright wrote later, that at least "25,000 children" were "growing up without any, or but the slightest knowledge of the rudiments of education." But "in the absence of exact and trustworthy figures," he could only suggest that interested citizens resolve for themselves the contradicting reports of illiteracy contained in local school reports and in the national census.[1]

Table 30. Illiteracy in eight Massachusetts cities, 1873.

Cities	Population, 1870	Over Ten Years Old, who cannot Write		Total over Ten Years		Total illiterates in one or the other, or in both	Per cent of Population
		Native	Foreign	Who cannot Write	Who cannot Read		
Boston	250,526	1,427	21,993	23,420	17,487	40,907	16
Worcester	41,105	116	2,659	2,775	2,143	4,918	12
Lowell	40,928	99	2,345	2,444	2,216	4,660	11
Cambridge	39,634	141	2,267	2,408	1,888	4,296	10
Lawrence	28,921	176	3,307	3,483	2,871	6,354	22
Charlestown	28,323	44	1,304	1,348	898	2,246	8
Lynn	28,233	96	767	863	476	1,339	4
Fall River	26,766	593	4,009	4,602	2,659	7,261*	27

* A large French Canadian population probably swells these figures.
Source: MBLS, *Fourth Annual Report,* 1873, 386.

1. MBLS, *Sixth Annual Report* (1875), 5.

Table 31. Wages of male and female teachers, 1873.

Whole number of teachers in Mass., 1871–72	
Males	1,024
Females	7,419
TOTAL	8,443
Average wages of male teachers per month	$85.09
Average wages of female teachers per month	32.39
Average wages of male teachers per year	709.08
Average wages of female teachers per year	269.91

Source: MBLS, *Fifth Annual Report*, 1874, 27.

A survey of wages completed in 1873 enabled a comparison of the salaries of male and female teachers (Table 31) and sustained the conclusion that the average compensation of female teachers in the Commonwealth was somewhat smaller than the wage of men employed in the state's factories.

CHAPTER SEVEN

Rooms for Rent

During three December days in 1869, John Cluer, a Boston police officer, guided Henry K. Oliver and members of the staff of the Massachusetts Bureau of Statistics of Labor on a tour of the city's tenements. The buildings Cluer selected may not have been typical of the dwellings of Boston's poorest workers, and the visits, though numerous, were brief. But the published description of slum conditions stimulated additional investigation by newspapers and public health authorities. And the experience triggered Director Oliver's rhetorical outrage.

Oliver noted room dimensions, sanitary facilities, and furnishings; counted the number of tenants; asked their occupations; and estimated their general health. He also included landlords' names, the tax assessments of their properties, and the rents that were charged—information that demonstrated exploitation and specified culprits—and he urged the Board of Health to enforce more vigorously the existing state regulations. Then Oliver contrasted his depressing narrative with a Boston journalist's breathless account of the lavish dwelling of one of the city's "successful accumulators." The reason Oliver reprinted a descriptive inventory of carpets, chandeliers, and drawing-room splendor, he wrote, was "to illustrate . . . the marvelous inequality of the distribution of wealth, and . . . the results of a system which has engendered unnecessary riches and unnecessary poverty."[1] Although

---

1. MBLS, *Annual Report* (1870), 188. See also Henry F. Bedford, "Tenement Houses

his first essay had some effect, poor Bostonians, of course, continued to reside in quarters Oliver thought substandard, a fact he highlighted with alarm in subsequent reports.

Oliver's treatment of workers' housing was more than ordinarily impassioned and unusually empty of suggested remedies. Perhaps his angry prose was not only a sympathetic reaction to the shocking conditions he found but also a conscious tactic to shame feckless, corrupt Boston officials into enforcing measures already on the books. Those regulations rested on the state's responsibility to protect public health; more drastic ones, which probably would have restricted property rights or invaded the sanctity of a family's home, were of doubtful constitutionality and politically untenable. Oliver may well have concluded that stimulating a demand for compliance with ordinances already enacted was as much as he could achieve. His rage may have been a calculated effort to arouse that response.

TENEMENT HOUSES, OR HOMES OF LOW-PAID LABORERS IN BOSTON

We have again made a tour of inspection among the tenement houses of Boston, viewing some new localities, and reviewing some of those that we visited in December, 1869. The infamous, befouled, and disgraceful lairs in "Friend (!) Street Court" have most fortunately received their "baptism of fire" and been purified thereby. Nothing less purgative could have cleaned them out,—though it must have been a most offensive function even for fire. The ground has since been used for the erection of a stately pile of brick stores, erected by Mr. Cyrus Wakefield, the owner of the old iniquitous abominations, most happily made holocaust. There remain yet a plenty of them all about the city, quite as bad, the purification whereof would task the best energies of the same element.

Before entering upon an account of our recent visitations, we give, repeated from our last report, for those who may not be familiar with the law of tenement houses (chap. 281, 1868), a summary of what the statute requires for their regulation. It demands,—

---

in Salem: A Report for the Bureau of Statistics of Labor," in *Essex Institute Historical Collections* 128: 1 (1992), 3–16.

1. A transom window over each door for ventilation.
2. Ventilation of each hall or entry.
3. Balusters to each stairway.
4. Suitable fire-escapes
5. Water-closets or privies, connected with city sewage.
6. Cesspools, permitted only when unavoidable.
7. Cellars not to be occupied as sleeping places, except under permit.
8. Cleansing of garbage boxes.
9. Whitewashing twice a year.
10. Owner's or agent's name to be posted up on walls or doors.
11. Free access to board of health.
12. Vacating of buildings infected or out of repair.
13. Relates to dimensions of rooms, size of windows, water supply, garbage and waste boxes, etc.
14. Supervision by city board of health.

On page 182 of former report will be found a letter to the city Board of Health, relating to the premises we visited in 1869, and a reply thereto. In the latter occurs this passage:—

"We (the board), rely principally upon the police for information, *and such is very limited*, yet we live in hope that a united effort of the two departments during the year 1870, will accomplish more than has been done during the whole time since the passage of the Act. In the early spring (of 1870) steps will be taken to cause the owners of such buildings to conform *to certain requirements* of the Building Act. . . .

How effectually these steps were taken, and what thoroughness of official action followed them, may be learned by a perusal . . . of that most instructive and valuable Report . . . made by the Massachusetts State Board of Health for 1870. It will there be seen that these same beastly abominations, these pestilent stench-holes, reeking with frowzy fluids, and bestenching the atmosphere with their malarious effluvia, these fertile nurseries of disease and death, and skulking haunts of villainy and crime, are still permitted to remain in their unmitigated defilement, although after the exposure made by this Bureau in its report for 1870, the public press confirmed all we then said, and added still more proof of the neglected shames. The authorities of Boston have made no efficient movement to check this scandalous violation of law, winking at the wrong,

and letting the owners go "unwhipt of justice." Yes, Boston permits it
all,—Boston, the Athens of America; the home, as she is vaunted to be, of
culture and refinement, of high art and pure morals, of missionary effort
and Christian philanthropy,—Boston, that feeds the hungry, clothes the
naked of foreign lands, and inaugurates fairs, with the receipts of which to
soothe the horrors of war, (blessed work it all is!),—Boston, that builds
palatial school-houses for her children, and hospitals for her sick;* that
rears statues and memorial monuments to her deserving sons, and many
she has,—Boston still indulges all this violation of sanitary statute, this
squalor of filth, this physical debasement and depravity, these unscav-
enged nurseries of strumpets, thieves, jailbirds, cut purses, burglars and
robbers! And who, we ask, are the owners of these courts of death to the
body and ruin to the soul? . . . Are they men who buy fame and town names
with rentals of 25 per cent. on their capital out of the hapless tenants of
these foul-aired pest-holes, with their dingy ceilings, their dark and grimy
windows, their murky and stenchy atmosphere, and their perilous thor-
oughfares? Does not everybody know that if one of the penniless starvel-
ings found therein, were, in the desperation of hunger, to steal a baker's
false-weighted loaf, or under impulse of poverty, to filch a dollar from the
counter of a bank, whose tricky cashier had robbed it of thousands, or,
were he shivering with nakedness and cold, to pilfer a yard of cloth from a
mill whose scot-free official had swindled it of millions,—does not every
body know that the sheriff, the court and the prison, would victimize him
with pitiless speed and certainty?—while for a miserly landlord to slay his
fleeced tenants, to poison the air they must breathe, to taint the neighborhood with the foul stench of deep stratas of filth, that breed dirt, flies, fleas,
lice, and all the verminous curses that plagued Pharaoh, to grind the face
of the poor on the roughest of grindstones, is as easy, as safe, as
unmolested, and unchastised as the frauds of the cheating baker, the
irregularities of the banking robber, or the swindling of the peculating
official! . . .

Our first visit was made to Johnson's Block, in Meander Street, between
Malden and Dedham Streets, the letting agent of which is Edward Follis,
No. 8 Shawmut Avenue. The rents are collected every week in advance.
Each tenement consists of two rooms, a living and a sleeping room, both
dark, damp, dirty and unhealthful. A police officer told us that there
seemed to be a death every week in the block, during the summer months.

*A good proportion of them come from these very dens.

No trace of whitewash was found , nor any marks of compliance with the law. The stairways are rickety and dangerous, and water only to be had from a hydrant in one corner of the yard. There were five privies, the vaults being replete with excrement, and everything about them in a condition of indescribable nastiness. There are twenty-four tenements, one only being vacant.

Visited family of Mr. E. E——, a laborer in a stone yard, consisting of himself, wife and five children, occupying two rooms, one 15 × 10, with seven foot post, the other 8 × 6, with seven foot post. The father had been sick for some time with erysipelas. A child, three weeks old, was lying sick upon the floor with its head resting upon a wooden box; three other children were tending another, a sick child, a mere baby. Mrs. E—— said that she should go out washing, but could not leave the children, they were so small, and so she grubbed along with what little work she could get to be done at home. The furniture consisted of one old table, one rocking-chair, the bottom of which was a barrel-head, four rickety chairs, some wash-tubs in one corner of the living room and the usual scant furniture in the bedroom. . . .

We could describe other tenement-house abominations of the same foulness and beastly defilement, but it would be but a repetition of nastiness and negligence, and for which neither memory or dictionary could supply words not yet used, or language adequate to the filthy picturing. You that are incredulous of the narrative, go, look, be nauseated, be convinced, be justly angered and strive for the laws and for justice, and so help the wretched dwellers in these dens. (MBLS, *Second Annual Report*, 1871, 517–21, 528)

Carroll Wright's first report disclosed the bureau's continuing concern with tenement housing, but a stern indictment of landlords was not the new director's style. Oliver had depicted tenants as helpless victims of greedy tenement owners; Wright implied that renters at least shared the responsibility for filth, disease, and the other disagreeable attributes of slums that had stretched Oliver's descriptive powers. Where Oliver sought reform from socially conscious landlords, enlightened bureaucrats, and an aroused public, Wright suggested practices that slum residents themselves might adopt to improve their circumstances.

The gap between the bureau's first two directors may seem to extend from a sympathetic response to injustice, in one case, to condescending blame for the victim, in the other. Those reactions have been associ-

16. Boston backyards (Nashua Street alley), c. 1890. Boston Athenaeum.

ated with millenarian reformers of the nineteenth century, in the first instance, and progressives of the early twentieth century, in the second. But the contrast, whether of attitude or generation, is in fact one of tactic rather than substance. Both Oliver and Wright understood that major change in housing the Commonwealth's workers, however urgent, was as a practical matter beyond the reach of the Bureau of Statistics of Labor and the General Court that had created it. They rested their hopes for future change on different agents, and they offered differing palliatives to those awaiting relief from conditions both agreed were wretched.

It is safe to say that in the homes of nearly all representatives of unskilled labor, and in those of a large percentage of the better orders of working-men, there exist numerous agencies by which the inmates of these homes are made more immoral, less healthful, and poorer than they ought to be, which can be, in whole or in part, prevented or removed.

These agencies are:

1. The character of the buildings occupied, which are often converted into tenements from other uses, old, dilapidated, ill-situated, ill-ventilated and low studded.

2. The crowded condition of these buildings, into which human beings are packed as closely as possible, without regard to decency, the supply of air or water, with little light or sun, ill-supplied with sewerage or privy accommodations, and regardless of cleanliness or order.

3. The foul and destructive state of privies, sink-drains, sewers, cesspools, cellars, garbage-tubs and yards, to say nothing of the neglected and filthy condition of stairs and passage-ways, and of the rooms themselves.

4. The modes of life of the occupants, their habits corresponding with the surroundings in which they make their homes; vice and drunkenness abounding; cleanliness of person being disregarded; their food badly prepared and poor in quality, and comfort and convenience comparatively unsought.

The influences of these agencies are,—

To create diseases of various types;

To entail enfeebled powers of life upon children;

To break down self-respect, decency and honesty;

To make the bar-room and saloon attractive;

To impose the expenses and burdens of sickness;

To throw disfavor upon the family relation and promote immorality; and

To increase crime, pauperism and misery. . . .

THE MODES OF LIFE OF THE OCCUPANTS, ETC.

That their character and habits should partake of the nature of their surroundings is not to be wondered at, and that they are so is the severest commentary on the surroundings themselves. Where every sense of decency becomes blighted, immorality can but abound; where all is suggestive of the hard fortune only of the occupant, what wonder that refuge is taken in the "drownings of the bowl"; where even the sustenance of man is bad, and badly cooked and served, is it strange that both moral and physical strength give way, and theft, violence and crime are rife? . . .

That the personal indifference of a very large proportion of the class most needing the benefits of a change of condition is a powerful agency in creating their present unfavorable circumstances, and in maintaining them, is frequently asserted and is beyond doubt. That this indifference is both a cause and effect of so much misery, seems evident, and so slow must be the process of spontaneous advance from this to higher and more hopeful ground, that outside influence and aid must be largely and steadily exerted to make progress in this behalf appreciable.

Such then are, at least, some of the evil agencies that keep the laborer on his present low plane of social standing, which make him the inmate of jails, asylums and almshouses, and which needlessly stand between him and a true, self-helpful, respected and independent manhood. . . .

. . . [Yet] no effort to improve the moral or physical condition of any individual can be availing, except he lends his own exertions to forward the endeavor. It is not enough that a man is passive under the improving movements of his helpers, and in this connection a large, indeed, the larger part by far, of the energy in the right direction must be expended by the individual himself. When the workingman shall see the unsatisfactory character of his position and shall be ready to move vigorously in his own behalf, *at home*, then shall he rightfully demand of all men their aid and encouragement. . . . [T]o advance toward a higher standing of prosperity, dignity, wealth and influence, the laborer and artisan shall commence in his immediate present surroundings the work of reform.

If he be an inmate of one of the lowest grade tenement "rookeries," he will accomplish but little until he removes to purer atmosphere and sounder influences, nor is this so much a question of ability from the smallness of wages as might at first appear; it is far more a question of finding a better tenement at a price he can pay. It has been well said by Mr. James Hold, in "Homes of the Working Classes," "that wages are very much regulated by the habits and standard of living of the workman, is one of the best established principles in political economy. *Inferior habits of living are as much a cause* as they are a result of low wages. No real saving, even pecuniarily, accrues to the workingman from living in crowded lodging-houses or in inferior back-to-back cottages. . . ."

It must be in judicious saving at home that the first steps of advance must be taken, saving not alone of expenditure, but in a preventive way. When every cause of unhealth has by care and labor been removed from the artisan's home, when the privy-vault has taken on the advantages of the earth-closet, when the sink-drain is made water-tight and flows into an ample, water-tight cesspool, when the hog-pen is kept dry and is at a proper distance, when the well has ben made secure against the contamination of slops or sewers, when garbage is taken care of and the cellar lighted and drained, when the rooms, stairs and passage-ways are ventilated, whitewashed and scrubbed, and *are kept so*, when the food purchased, though it be ever so simple or coarse, is pure and well-cooked, when personal cleanliness has been established and the poison of alcohol is not undermining,—*then*, a saving of days' works, of doctor's and apothecary's bills, of extra labor and lost time, just as truly pecuniary as any, is being made, and treasures of infinite value, health, contentment and honesty become the possession and further inspiration of the striver. These and kindred effort must be put forth by the majority of our laboring men ... before any considerable progress can be made by them in the upward scale.

Not a few of the skilled journeymen mechanics of America, the operatives of factories and laborers of various grades and employments, occupy in our large towns, single dwellings that, for want of knowledge, care or labor, are permitted to become unhealthy and poverty-pressed homes, when only a little effort is requisite to make them abodes of health and comfort. In all these much money is spent by wasting it, and much more might be *made* than is, by saving.... (MBLS, *Fifth Annual Report*, 1874, 32–33, 35–36, 40–42)

In 1891, the General Court ordered the bureau to "ascertain ... the number of families in the city of Boston residing in rented tenements."[2] The study was not to be simply a census, for the agency was also to report the size of the quarters; the rents that tenants paid; the sex, occupation, nationality, and citizenship status of residents; and the sanitary conditions in neighborhoods and dwellings.

Horace Wadlin dispatched conscientious staff members to every identifiable rental unit in the city. "None of the statistical information" in the resulting two volumes, he asserted in his preface, rested on "estimates"; it derived instead from "personal investigation and enumeration for each family."[3] But Wadlin's definition of "tenement" included facilities that might now be called "apartments," with the difference in status, appointments, and space that the latter term connotes. Wadlin's tables do not, therefore, reveal the housing arrange-

2. MBLS, *Twenty-second Annual Report* (1892), 3.
3. Ibid., 4.

ments of working-class Bostonians exclusively, and the averages he calculated reflect the inclusion of some luxurious residences.

Presentation of these data required nearly nine hundred pages of small print. "There is indeed," Wadlin wrote in justification, "no more important branch of the social problem than that which deals with the dwellings of the people in the concentrated districts of large cities,"[4] a judgment with which both his predecessors would have concurred. But Wadlin's treatment of the topic—a numbing mass of numbers unaccompanied by "theories of improvement"—represented the culmination of Wright's conception of the bureau's task, rather than Oliver's engaged advocacy. And Wadlin's tables suggested that conditions were substantially better than those Oliver had discovered in his less inclusive surveys twenty years earlier.

So far, then, as appears from an inspection of this recapitulation of the number of tenements to a house [Table 32], which is the first and most obvious classification indicating the concentration of families in the different houses, we find no very serious indications of over-crowding.... [These data] clearly show that of all the persons residing in rented tenements, without regard to class, about 49 in every hundred, or nearly one-half, are either living in independent houses or in houses containing but two tenements, many of which are so arranged that the tenements are practically independent of each other. These persons constitute nearly one-third of the entire population of the City. About seven persons in the hundred of all persons occupying rented tenements are living in houses containing seven or more tenements each, the maximum number of tenements being 47. For the most part, these persons, who number about five in the hundred of the total population of the City, are living in well arranged "flats" or high class apartment houses. A small proportion of them are undoubtedly living in strictly tenement houses containing a large number of tenements; but the comparatively small number of persons living in all the houses of this class makes it clearly apparent that the number of persons living in such large tenement houses must be very small. About 44 persons in the hundred of all persons occupying rented tenements are found in houses of three, four, five, and six tenements each. These constitute what would be popularly understood as the strictly

4. MBLS, *Twenty-third Annual Report* (1893), xvii.

Table 32. Concentration of families in tenement houses, 1891.

Number of Tenements to a House	Number of Families	Population			Whole Number of Rooms in All Tenements Considered	Average Number of Persons to a Room
		Males	Females	Total		
One tenement to a house	11,825	34,396	35,227	69,623	92,619	0.75
Two tenements to a house	19,380	40,244	41,754	81,998	92,823	0.88
Three tenements to a house	21,865	43,472	45,085	88,557	89,528	0.99
Four tenements to a house	7,214	13,507	14,512	28,019	27,830	1.01
Five tenements to a house	2,768	5,091	5,457	10,548	8,735	1.21
Six tenements to a house	2,772	5,340	5,442	10,782	9,005	1.20
Seven tenements to a house	992	1,812	1,857	3,669	2,966	1.24
Eight tenements to a house	1,777	3,360	3,598	6,958	6,680	1.04
Nine tenements to a house	480	954	928	1,882	1,612	1.17
Ten tenements to a house	679	1,299	1,367	2,666	2,733	0.98
Eleven tenements to a house	221	392	460	852	880	0.97
Twelve tenements to a house	288	460	638	1,098	1,328	0.83
Thirteen tenements to a house	169	227	335	562	711	0.79
Fourteen tenements to a house	159	243	328	571	738	0.77
Fifteen tenements to a house	178	255	323	578	789	0.73
Sixteen tenements to a house	174	264	306	570	600	0.95
Seventeen tenements to a house	87	171	194	365	414	0.88
Eighteen tenements to a house	159	257	306	563	696	0.81
Nineteen tenements to a house	35	88	83	171	81	2.11
Twenty tenements to a house	118	144	210	354	438	0.81
Twenty-one tenements to a house	21	57	45	102	52	1.96
Twenty-two tenements to a house	39	41	61	102	92	1.11
Twenty-three tenements to a house	8	8	12	20	27	0.74
Twenty-four tenements to a house	22	22	28	50	49	1.02
Twenty-five tenements to a house	20	23	42	65	131	0.50
Twenty-eight tenements to a house	51	63	73	136	217	0.63
Thirty tenements to a house	21	26	33	59	82	0.72
Thirty-one tenements to a house	22	30	41	71	132	0.54
Thirty-two tenements to a house	25	47	48	95	65	1.46
Thirty-four tenements to a house	26	26	50	76	118	0.64
Forty tenements to a house	28	31	67	98	181	0.54
Forty-seven tenements to a house	42	54	82	136	192	0.71
TOTALS	71,665	152,404	158,992	311,396	342,544	0.91

Source: MBLS, *Twenty-second Annual Report*, 1891, 350.

tenement house population of the City. They number about 30 persons in the hundred of the total population of the City. (MBLS, *Twenty-second Annual Report*, 1891, 556, 559)

Table 33 reveals the number of rooms this population occupied.

Table 33. Size of tenements, 1891.

Size of Tenements	Number of Families having Specified Number of Rooms	Males	Females	Total	Whole Number of Rooms in All Tenements Considered	Average Number of Persons to a Room	Percentage of Population
			Population				
1 room,	1,053	920	1,147	2,067	1,053	1.96	0.66
2 rooms	5,695	7,699	8,644	16,343	11,390	1.43	5.25
3 rooms	13,876	25,384	26,243	51,627	41,628	1.24	16.58
4 rooms	18,661	38,464	38,975	77,439	74,644	1.04	24.87
5 rooms	13,002	27,879	28,943	56,822	65,010	0.87	18.25
6 rooms	7,965	18,432	19,299	37,731	47,790	0.79	12.12
7 rooms	4,042	9,897	10,762	20,659	28,294	0.73	6.63
8 rooms	2,332	6,571	6,812	13,383	18,656	0.72	4.30
9 rooms	1,639	4,925	5,137	10,062	14,751	0.68	3.23
10 rooms	1,344	4,262	4,685	8,947	13,440	0.67	2.87
11 rooms	694	2,437	2,616	5,053	7,634	0.66	1.62
12 rooms	607	2,294	2,340	4,634	7,284	0.64	1.49
13 rooms	262	1,096	1,102	2,198	3,406	0.65	0.71
14 rooms	215	805	956	1,761	3,010	0.59	0.57
15 rooms	99	462	452	914	1,485	0.62	0.29
16 rooms	92	443	436	879	1,472	0.60	0.28
17 rooms	40	195	213	408	680	0.60	0.13
18 rooms	24	115	111	226	432	0.52	0.07
19 rooms	4	17	20	37	76	0.49	0.01
20 rooms	10	46	51	97	200	0.49	0.03
21 rooms	2	16	10	26	42	0.62	0.01
22 rooms	4	30	19	49	88	0.56	0.02
23 rooms	1	6	5	11	23	0.48	*—
24 rooms	1	4	10	14	24	0.58	0.01
32 rooms	1	5	4	9	32	0.28	*—
TOTALS	71,665	152,404	158,992	311,396	342,544	0.91	100.00

*Less than one one-hundredth of one per cent.
Source: MBLS, *Twenty-second Annual Report*, 1891, 359.

Let us now determine the average size of the families found in actual occupancy of tenements of different sizes. [Table 34] presents these averages for the City at large.

From [Table 34] it is seen that, as a matter of fact, when the average is taken for the entire City, the number of persons to a family occupying tenements of four rooms is less than the average number of persons to a family in all tenements. That is to say, families occupying tenements of this class average smaller than families in general. The largest number of families is found in tenements of this sort. When the size of the tenements is increased to five rooms, we find that the average number of persons to a family becomes 4.37. This is practically the same as the average number of

Table 34. Size of families occupying tenements, 1891.

Size of Tenements	Number of Families having Specified Number of Rooms	Population	Average Number of Persons to a Family
1 room	1,053	2,067	1.96
2 rooms	5,695	16,343	2.87
3 rooms	13,876	51,627	3.72
4 rooms	18,661	77,439	4.15
5 rooms	13,002	56,822	4.37
6 rooms	7,965	37,731	4.74
7 rooms	4,042	20,659	5.11
8 rooms	2,332	13,383	5.74
9 rooms	1,639	10,062	6.14
10 rooms	1,344	8,947	6.66
11 rooms	694	5,053	7.28
12 rooms	607	4,634	7.63
13 rooms	262	2,198	8.39
14 rooms	215	1,761	8.19
15 rooms	99	914	9.23
16 rooms	92	879	9.55
17 rooms	40	408	10.20
18 rooms	24	226	9.42
19 rooms	4	37	9.25
20 rooms	10	97	9.70
21 rooms	2	26	13.00
22 rooms	4	49	12.25
23 rooms	1	11	11.00
24 rooms	1	14	14.00
32 rooms	1	9	9.00
TOTALS	71,665	311,396	4.35

Source: MBLS, *Twenty-second Annual Report*, 1891, 570–71.

persons to a family in all tenements. That is, families occupying tenements of this class are about the general average size. About the same number of families is found in tenements having but three rooms each; but the average size of such families is only 3.72, or considerably less than the average for all families. When it is stated that 1,053 families are found in tenements consisting of but one room each, the impression conveyed without further analysis is that these families must necessarily be over-crowded; but when we find, as appears from this table, that the average number of persons in such families is but 1.96, that is to say, that upon the average such families do not consist of more than two persons, it is at once seen that over-crowding is not necessarily implied, for a man and his wife may occupy a single room quite comfortably if they are employed, as is frequently the case, during the working hours of the day and do not take their meals in their room. (MBLS, *Twenty-second Annual Report*, 1891, 571)

To categorize sanitary conditions in Boston's rental housing, the bureau developed a scale ranging from "excellent" to "bad" and carefully defined those terms. About 60 percent of the population lived in quarters classified as "excellent" or "good" with respect to light and air, ventilation, and cleanliness. Some of the statistics on which that assessment rested appear in Table 35.

Table 35. Sanitary conditions in Boston tenements, 1891.

Having or not having bath rooms

	Having Bath Rooms		Not Having Bath Rooms		Aggregates		Having Bath Rooms		Not Having Bath Rooms	
	Fami-lies	Popu-lation	Fami-lies	Popu-lation	Fami-lies	Popu-lation	Percentages		Percentages	
							Fami-lies	Popu-lation	Fami-lies	Popu-lation
The City of Boston	18,476	82,716	53,189	228,680	71,665	311,396	25.78	26.56	74.22	73.44

Having water closets or privies

	Having Water Closets		Having Privies		Aggregates		Having Water Closets		Having Privies	
	Fami-lies	Popu-lation	Fami-lies	Popu-lation	Fami-lies	Popu-lation	Percentages		Percentages	
							Fami-lies	Popu-lation	Fami-lies	Popu-lation
The City of Boston	65,866	285,924	5,799	25,472	71,665	311,396	91.91	91.82	8.09	8.18

Having or not having yards

	Having Yards		Not Having Yards		Aggregates		Having Yards		Note Having Yards	
	Fami-lies	Popu-lation	Fami-lies	Popu-lation	Fami-lies	Popu-lation	Percentages		Percentages	
							Fami-lies	Popu-lation	Fami-lies	Popu-lation
The City of Boston	53,831	238,252	17,834	73,144	71,665	311,396	75.11	76.51	24.89	23.49

Classified Area of Yards in Square Feet	Number of Houses Having Yards Within the Specified Area Classification	Total Area in Square Feet	Population	Average Yard Space to Each Person in Square Feet
The City of Boston	29,431	28,073,308	239,668	117
Under 50 square feet	160	5,750	1,503	4
50 but under 100	696	52,484	7,117	7
100 but under 200	3,121	446,225	28,319	16
200 but under 300	3,455	804,698	29,601	27
300 but under 400	3,125	1,041,869	26,312	40

Table 35. Continued.

Classified Area of Yards in Square Feet	Number of Houses Having Yards Within the Specified Area Classification	Total Area in Square Feet	Population	Average Yard Space to Each Person in Square Feet
400 but under 500	3,797	1,565,034	30,887	51
500 but under 600	1,830	929,599	14,681	63
600 but under 700	2,868	1,758,982	22,591	78
700 but under 800	1,006	741,500	8,219	90
800 but under 900	1,035	856,552	8,404	102
900 but under 1,000	1,315	1,186,905	10,370	114
1,000 but under 2,000	4,461	5,985,607	33,564	178
2,000 but under 3,000	1,141	2,634,294	8,334	316
3,000 but under 4,000	517	1,747,875	3,587	487
4,000 but under 5,000	121	506,500	953	531
5,000 but under 6,000	276	1,404,195	1,807	777
6,000 but under 7,000	83	508,050	515	987
7,000 but under 8,000	117	873,900	771	1,133
8,000 but under 9,000	18	146,089	277	527
9,000 but under 10,000	8	73,950	47	1,573
10,000 but under 20,000	204	2,515,250	1,327	1,895
20,000 but under 30,000	50	1,054,250	285	3,699
30,000 but under 40,000	12	383,750	90	4,264
40,000 but under 50,000	6	245,000	44	5,568
50,000 but under 60,000	2	105,000	8	13,125
60,000 but under 70,000	2	120,000	24	5,000
70,000 but under 80,000	2	140,000	7	20,000
80,000	3	240,000	24	10,000

Source: MBLS, *Twenty-third Annual Report*, 1892, 117, 120, 125, 131.

Table 36 is a calculation of the monthly rent tenement dwellers paid.

Table 36. Average monthly rents, Boston, 1891.

Size of Tenements	Average Actual Monthly Rents Paid	Size of Tenements	Average Actual Monthly Rents Paid
1 rooms	$5.73	14 rooms	$67.09
2 rooms	8.64	15 rooms	71.93
3 rooms	10.15	16 rooms	84.29
4 rooms	12.81	17 rooms	85.95
5 rooms	17.05	18 rooms	93.69
6 rooms	20.40	19 rooms	121.46
7 rooms	26.13	20 rooms	110.07
8 rooms	29.38	21 rooms	144.17
9 rooms	36.25	22 rooms	62.50
10 rooms	46.36	23 rooms	83.33
11 rooms	50.51	24 rooms	133.33
12 rooms	55.01	32 rooms	100.00
13 rooms	61.56	Average for all sizes of tenements	17.26

Source: MBLS, *Twenty-second Annual Report*, 1891, 512.

PLACE OF BIRTH

The relative proportions of the different nationalities comprising the tenement-renting population are most clearly seen from the following analysis table in which the numbers are brought to the basis of percentages [Table 37].

Table 37. Birthplace of tenement residents, 1891.

Countries	Population	Percentages
The City of Boston	311,396	100.00
Massachusetts	152,449	48.96
Other States	40,449	12.99
Canada	29,391	9.44
Great Britain and Colonies	12,286	3.95
Ireland	47,864	15.37
Germany	6,454	2.07
Norway and Sweden	3,210	1.03
Portugal	1,000	0.32
Italy	5,922	1.90
Russia	7,911	2.54
Other Foreign Countries	4,460	1.43

Source: MBLS, *Twenty-third Annual Report*, 1892, 190.

"Why," Wadlin asked in conclusion, "do the tenants of the poorer houses remain in them?"

It is not always poverty that compels them, although this is generally the first conclusion. A special inquiry covering 475 families, comprising 2,140 persons, residing in tenements or neighborhoods classed as poor or bad, was undertaken for the purpose of securing definite information upon this point. The result is presented in [Table 38].

In tabulating the results, the principal cause which led the family to occupy the poor tenement has been selected, although in some cases more than one cause was found. For instance, if poverty and intemperance were both found to be operative, and intemperance was, after investigation, deemed to be the leading cause, and poverty a result, rather than itself the main cause, the families have been classed under the head of "intemperance" in the table. The question of choice or necessity in regard to the

Table 38. Reasons for residing in less satisfactory tenements, 1891.

Causes	Number of Families	Population	Percentages	
			Families	Population
Intemperance	205	912	43.16	42.62
Low rent	74	290	15.58	13.55
Poverty	22	103	4.63	4.81
Choice	53	240	11.16	11.22
Necessity	117	572	24.63	26.73
Nearness to work	4	23	0.84	1.07
TOTALS	475	2,140	100.00	100.00

Source: MBLS, *Twenty-third Annual Report*, 1892, 435.

tenancy of these worst places was frequently difficult to determine. The word "necessity," as used in the table, implies that the families classed under this head were obliged to occupy the tenements in which they were found for various reasons different from the five other causes named. This explanation is required in order that the reader may not assume that where persons are classed under this head the necessity was a pecuniary one. If this had been the case, the family would have been classed under the head of "poverty" or "low rent" as might have been found most proper. The necessity in most cases was hardly capable of distinct definition. Sometimes it was due to the inability of families with large numbers of small children to obtain tenements in better localities; sometimes it was attributable to the unwillingness of landlords, for reasons peculiar to the case, to admit the family to better tenements; the nationality and occupation of the family were sometimes found to be factors in determining the tenancy, and sometimes the necessity of residing near the place of employment obliged the family to occupy the tenement. When proximity to the place of employment was distinctly the controlling cause, however, the families have been included under the head "nearness to work." As to the matter of "choice," one of the causes specified in the table, it should be said that while it may seem strange that any one should deliberately choose a tenement of this class, it is nevertheless true that many recent accessions of certain nationalities prefer to live in proximity to neighbors of the same nationality, and are not unwilling to occupy poor tenements or tenements in poor neighborhoods to gratify this preference. . . .

The ... average monthly rent for ... absolutely bad tenements was $8.44 and the average number of rooms per tenement was 2.88. ...

[I]n general, as compared with tenements of the same size, the rent of these unsanitary tenements is lower than the average, yet this was not always found to be the case. Very frequently in the course of the investigation it was found that a comparatively high rent was obtained for a very poor tenement. The reason for this is obvious. The tenants who were found in occupancy were of a class which would not be admitted to better tenements, and being obliged to secure accommodations were therefore obliged to pay high rents. (MBLS, *Twenty-third Annual Report*, 1892, 435–37)

Although he disclaimed any remedy for inferior quarters in congested slums, Wadlin did not, in the end, forgo a parting prescription that echoed ideas of his mentor, Carroll Wright. Wadlin's final paragraphs here imply that more fortunate Americans ought to make a greater effort to provide tenement dwellers the uplifting influence of refined society, a solution that reflected Wright's occasional patronizing of working people and foreshadowed later efforts of progressives to impose their own standards on those perceived to be less fortunate.

Stringent sanitary regulations properly enforced and supplemented by continuous tenement inspection will go far toward improving the environment of the dwellers in the tenement house districts. These, however, are in the nature of police regulations. There can be no question as to the need of elevating the social plane of the dwellers in the crowded sections of the city, and this can be accomplished only indirectly through such regulations. Take the most obvious evil which is met with, that of uncleanliness. Even superficial investigation will convince any one that there are many families, especially among recent accessions, who do not regard dirt as particularly disagreeable and who contentedly live under conditions that would be considered absolutely filthy by those on a higher social plane. As long as this spirit of contentment continues there can be no real improvement, and only a perfunctory compliance with the simplest sanitary requirements. An effective remedy for the evils which grow out of tenement house life, and accompany the concentration of population in certain districts of our large cities, must strike deeper than any merely statutory requirements. Left to themselves, the immigrants who come into these districts simply reproduce here the social conditions out of which they came, and far too often they have been left largely to themselves. In our industrial life we deal with them without coming into direct contact. Our social life does not include them. As long as they commit no overt act we have permitted them to live in their own way in their wretched tenements.

It seems to be felt that they are most dangerous on account of certain theories and beliefs which they may possibly hold. In reality they are dangerous because of their condition. To permit them to remain untouched by the refining influences of society is not only ethically wrong, but it is also economically wrong. They are not entirely responsible for the fact that they are found under such conditions, that they are wedded to class prejudices or that they easily acquire dangerous social theories; nor are they responsible for the miserable tenements which public opinion has permitted to exist. When we cease to regard the immigrant as merely so much cheap labor or as only an impersonal factor in production, then we shall have found the real solution of the problem. (MBLS, *Twenty-third Annual Report*, 1892, 438)

CHAPTER EIGHT

Criminals, Paupers, and Strong Drink

After a career spent observing and measuring American society, toward the end of his life Carroll Wright wrote a friend that "intoxicating drink" was "the cause of poverty and misery."[1] Perhaps that mature judgment rested on data collected in decades of research. But it was also Wright's personal conviction before he became a social scientist, and it was central to the reform orthodoxy of his day. As a young man, he had written poems on temperance themes and preserved them in his scrapbooks. Although he realized later that drunkenness might be only a symptom of some other distress, he nevertheless concluded that alcohol frequently caused it. Tension in the lives of working families, mounting crime and prostitution, diminished intellectual capacity of American workers—any of these phenomena might in specific cases have other explanations. But drink, Wright thought, more often than not was at the root of the problem.

That belief not only shaped some of Wright's work but also comforted middle-class Americans uneasy about the labor question. If economic hardship resulted from profligate spending for liquor, rather than from inadequate wages or the unchecked power of employers, then individual workers could stop drinking and that aspect of the labor question would vanish; regulation of saloons and intoxicants, not of wages and employers, was all that was required. If drinking indicated

1. James Leiby, *Carroll Wright and Labor Reform* (Cambridge: Harvard University Press, 1960), 42.

17. Haverhill Italian saloon, 1890. Courtesy of the Trustees of the Haverhill Public Library, Special Collections Department.

individual indulgence, not social pathology, then reformers need not interfere with established family relationships and existing patterns of housing, employment, and governance. And since drunkenness was illegal, the incidence of lawbreaking in the Commonwealth would dramatically decline if the consumption of alcohol were checked.

Control of the "liquor traffic" was a staple of political controversy in Massachusetts after the Civil War while legislators and local authorities unsteadily sought a regulatory compromise between total prohibition and unrestricted access. Yankees, many of whom still presumed that governing the state was their birthright, associated alcohol with "others": Catholics, immigrants, slum dwellers, the poor. These groups, in turn, resented efforts to dictate their leisure activities and to forbid some in which the dominant society professed no personal interest. Closing neighborhood saloons, for instance, would not only weaken ethnic bonds but also eliminate a male refuge from factories and crowded apartments, where the influence of women seemed to be increasing. This clash of cultures, classes, creeds, nationalities, and sexes was the context for Carroll Wright's effort to inform public policy with research about the connections among intoxicants, poverty, and crime.[2]

In the course of the comparative study of Lowell, Lawrence, and Fall River, Wright's staff had asked "leading citizens" to specify "the chief need (morally, socially, or industrially)" of the city's working people.[3] Observations from Fall River, where industrial unrest was greatest, confirmed Wright's own view of the link between alcohol and disorder. In an earlier study, Wright had also found evidence that alcohol caused poverty.

OPINIONS OF LEADING CITIZENS

The foremost need, as gathered from the replies received would appear to be *temperance*. Sixty-four per cent of the answers specifically name the use of intoxicants as the greatest evil, and abstinence therefrom the chief need of the industrial population of the city.

A mill treasurer says, "If I say that the laboring part of our population spends annually $700,000 for beer and alcoholic liquors, it will be very near the amount of their disbursements for such purposes. This fact alone will account, to the mind of any reflecting person, for many of the evils from which that part of our population suffers. The same class of persons who are not addicted to the use of stimulants are generally prosperous and happy."

A superintendent writes, "375 rum shops to a population of 50,000, and half of them supported by 15,000 operatives, speaks for itself as to what they need."

A resident of the city not connected with the mills, but fully acquainted with the habits of the operatives, and possessing unusual opportunities for

2. For an account of the battle to control leisure in one Massachusetts city, see Roy Rosenzweig, *Eight Hours for What We Will* (Cambridge: Cambridge University Press, 1983).

3. MBLS, *Thirteenth Annual Report* (1882), 366.

knowing whereof he speaks, remarks, "The almost universal custom of spending idle hours about rum shops is the parent of most of the troubles."

A physician, in the following, takes a more philosophical view of the cause and the tendency of the evil: "I must admit that the system of overworking the operatives is so debilitating as to seem to make necessary the use of some kind of stimulant, and, could that necessity be met by a very moderate use of beer or spirits, all might be well. But, alas! all experience goes to prove that this is delusive. The use of alcoholic stimulants defeats the object sought, for they undermine the system, bringing on premature old age, and unfitting any man or woman for effective labor."

While thus recognizing the need of temperance on the part of the operatives, there are but few practical suggestions contained in the replies. Nearly all recommend personal abstinence; several think that prohibition of the sale of intoxicants would prevent the intemperance now so prevalent; while one, a clergyman, advocates the establishment of "reading-rooms and well-conducted coffee rooms where evenings can be spent free from temptations now found in places of social refuge."

He presents no theory as to how these coffee rooms shall be provided but another correspondent would have the need supplied "by the effort on the part of capitalists to place within the reach of the 15,000 operatives counter attractions (to the liquor saloons), such as free scientific and literary entertainments, coffee houses, and reading-rooms." (MBLS, *Thirteenth Annual Report*, 1882, 366–68)

Causes of Pauperism

Pauperism is a disease of the body politic, and being so, no statistics concerning it can be more interesting and valuable than those which show the causes for requiring public or private charity. We present the following table [Table 39] in which the "causes" are given, as returned by the individual, but little condensation having been made. The sexes are designated and a classification by age made.

It is to be regretted that 939, or 21 + per cent, failed to give the cause, but the returns of 3,403, or 78 + per cent, can be relied on. If from these returns we eliminate those suffering from mental or physical infirmity, we find that the idiotic number 306; the insane, 668; the physically infirm, 775; the

Table 39. Causes of pauperism, 1877.

	Under 10		10 to 15		Above 15		Total		
	M	F	M	F	M	F	M	F	Total
Abuse	—	—	—	—	1	—	1	—	1
Bad company	—	—	—	—	1	—	1	—	1
Bad conduct	—	—	—	—	2	6	2	6	8
Bereavement	—	—	—	—	—	3	—	3	3
Convict father	2	2	—	—	—	—	2	2	4
Convict mother	3	1	—	—	—	—	3	1	4
Cruelty of parents	—	—	—	—	1	—	1	—	1
Death of husband	—	—	—	—	—	8	—	8	8
Dependency	2	1	—	—	—	3	2	4	6
Desertion	1	2	—	—	—	7	1	9	10
Desertion of children	—	—	—	—	—	1	—	1	1
Desertion of father	6	5	5	—	4	—	15	5	20
Desertion of husband	—	—	—	1	—	9	—	10	10
Desertion of parents	5	—	3	1	—	1	8	2	10
Disappointment	—	—	—	—	1	1	1	1	2
Discharged prisoners	—	—	—	—	9	3	9	3	12
Family trouble	—	—	—	—	2	1	2	1	3
Fatherless	2	3	5	2	2	2	9	7	16
Father a pauper	6	—	3	2	2	—	11	2	13
Friendless	—	—	—	—	—	4	—	4	4
Grandmother a pauper	—	2	—	—	—	—	—	2	2
Hereditary	—	—	—	—	2	—	2	—	2
Idiocy	4	2	3	7	158	132	165	141	306
Ignorance and loss of head of family	1	—	—	—	2	2	3	2	5
Illegitimacy	9	5	2	1	—	9	11	15	26
Immorality	—	—	—	—	1	6	1	6	7
Infancy	1	2	—	—	—	—	1	2	3
Infirmity	—	—	—	—	12	9	12	9	21
Injury	—	—	—	—	6	2	6	2	8
Insanity	1	1	1	—	213	452	215	453	668
Insanity of father	—	—	—	—	—	1	—	1	1
Insanity of mother	—	—	—	2	—	—	—	2	2
Intemperance	—	3	—	—	362	108	362	111	473
Intemperance of husband	—	—	—	—	—	18	—	18	18
Intemperance of father	11	10	8	3	4	4	23	17	40
Intemperance of mother	—	1	—	—	—	—	—	1	1
Intemperance of parents	25	11	7	5	3	1	35	17	52
Large family, bad management	—	—	—	—	5	2	5	2	7
Loss of property, and business trouble	—	1	—	1	10	5	10	7	17
Mental infirmity	—	—	—	1	26	43	26	44	70
Mental infirmity of parents	—	—	1	—	—	—	1	—	1
Misconduct of parents	1	—	—	—	—	—	1	—	1
Mismanagement	—	—	—	—	12	12	12	12	24
Motherless	3	2	2	—	—	—	5	2	7
Mother a pauper	51	52	4	—	—	1	55	53	108
Neglect	—	—	1	—	—	1	1	1	2
Neglect of father	—	—	1	—	—	—	1	—	1

Table 39. Continued.

	Under 10		10 to 15		Above 15		Total		
	M	F	M	F	M	F	M	F	Total
Neglect of parents	1	—	1	—	—	—	2	—	2
No home	—	—	—	—	—	1	—	1	1
Not given	168	182	226	98	256	9	650	289	939
Old age	—	—	—	—	119	154	119	154	273
Orphan	14	13	10	12	1	2	25	27	52
Parents paupers	13	23	5	3	1	5	19	31	50
Physical infirmity	11	11	6	5	354	264	371	280	651
Physical infirmity of husband	—	—	—	—	—	1	—	1	1
Poverty	6	5	4	—	18	41	28	46	74
Shiftlessness	—	—	—	—	27	7	27	7	34
Shiftlessness of husband	—	—	—	—	—	2	—	2	2
Shiftlessness of parents	1	5	2	3	—	2	3	10	13
Shiftlessness of father	—	2	—	—	—	—	—	2	2
Sickness, disease	—	1	1	—	102	88	103	89	192
Sickness of father	6	4	1	—	—	—	7	4	11
Sickness of husband	—	—	—	—	—	5	—	5	5
Sickness of parents	5	2	—	1	—	—	5	3	8
Sickness of child	—	—	—	—	—	1	—	1	1
Spent all his money	—	—	—	—	1	—	1	—	1
Spiritualism	—	—	—	—	—	1	—	1	1
Unable to work	—	—	—	—	5	8	5	8	13
Want of employment	—	—	—	—	1	2	1	2	3
War	—	—	—	—	1	1	1	1	2
Wife of convict	—	—	—	—	—	1	—	1	1
	359	354	302	148	1,727	1,452	2,388	1,954	4,342

Source: MBLS, *Eighth Annual Report*, 1877, 190.

aged, 273; the sick, 192, making a total of 2,214. These persons are undoubtedly unable to work, and are legitimate objects of public or private charity. Of the remaining number, 1,189, who give the causes, 584 attribute their pauperism, directly or indirectly, to intemperance. Deducting the intemperate, 584, from 1,189, we have left 605, of which number 422 give the actions of others as cause, and, of course, deem their state of pauperism as a circumstance beyond their control. This leaves but 183, besides the intemperate, who are, presumably, responsible for their present condition and likely to make an exertion to better it; but, of this number, 32 are under 15 years of age. These figures would seem to indicate that intemperance is the great and "unsatisfactory" cause of pauperism, while the great majority give what may be called "satisfactory" causes. (MBLS, *Eighth Annual Report*, 1877, 189–91)

Table 40. Illiteracy of paupers, 1877.

Place of birth	10 to 15 Yrs. (both inc.)		Above 15 Yrs.		Total Illiterates	Can not Read	Can not Write	Can neither Read nor Write
	Males	Females	Males	Females				
Born in town named	4	18	127	140	289	—	61	228
Born in other towns in Mass	4	7	105	99	215	—	106	109
Born in other States	2	3	25	38	68	—	31	37
Born in England	—	—	6	19	25	—	16	9
Born in Ireland	1	5	112	251	369	—	111	258
Born in other for'n countries		1	32	38	71	—	30	41
TOTALS	11	34	407	585	1,037	—	355	682

Sources: MBLS, *Eighth Annual Report*, 1877, 197.

Later in the same report, Wright pointed out that poverty had other important causes as well.

Those who can read but can not write amount to 34 + per cent of the whole number of illiterates, and the balance, 65 + per cent, are wholly uneducated. Of the male illiterates, 116 can read but can not write, and 302 can neither read nor write. Of the female illiterates, 239 can read but can not write, and 380 can neither read nor write [Table 40].

Considering the whole number of paupers, less all children under ten, and the idiotic and insane paupers above ten, we secure the following tabular result [Table 41].

The preponderance of illiteracy among the females is remarkable. The general result is that a little over one-third of the sane paupers, above ten years of age, are illiterate.

Comparing the native and foreign born paupers with the native and foreign born illiterates, we obtain the subjoined statement [in Table 42].

If we confine our attention to those born in Massachusetts, we find that

Table 41. Sex and age of illiterate paupers, 1877.

Sex and Age	Number of Sane Paupers	Number of Illiterates	Percentage of Illiterates
Males above 10	1,654	418	25 +
Females above 10	1,009	619	61 +
TOTALS	2,663	1,037	38 +

Source: MBLS, *Eighth Annual Report*, 1877, 197.

Table 42. Birthplace of illiterate paupers, 1877.

Place of Birth	Number of Paupers (All ages)	Number of Illiterates	Percentages of all Ages	Percentages of those above 10 (Estimated)
Native born	3,063	572	18 +	30 +
Foreign born	1,279	465	36 +	59 +

Source: MBLS, *Eighth Annual Report*, 1877, 198.

out of 2,672 paupers, 504 are illiterate, 337 being wholly uneducated. . . .

The exhibit is surely not a gratifying one. Pauperism, in itself, is an evil. If a town allows its children to grow up in ignorance, and afterwards become a burden upon it, the evil is magnified. With our school facilities such an exhibit should have been impossible. . . .

The commonly expressed and received opinion that our pauper class is almost entirely composed of persons of foreign birth receives no support from these statistics. Out of 4,342, the whole number, 1,583 were born in the very towns in the State in which they are now paupers, and 1,089 were born in other towns in Massachusetts. The number born in the State, 2,672, is 61 + per cent of the whole number of paupers. If we add those born in other States of the Union (391), we find of American births, 3,063, or 70 + per cent. (MBLS, *Eighth Annual Report*, 1877, 197–98, 200)

In his investigation of poverty, Wright at least entertained the hypothesis that poor people were not themselves responsible in every case for their condition. The actions of criminals, on the other hand, seemed to him usually the result of addiction to drink. But when Wright studied the state's convicts in 1877, he found insufficient evidence to establish a firm link between liquor and criminal behavior that was not simply a violation of the alcohol regulations themselves. A conviction for burglary or assault, Wright thought, might stem from a desire for, or consumption of, intoxicants as surely as did an arrest for drunkenness. To determine "what part intemperance played in the commission of . . . crime" in which liquor itself was not part of the charge, the bureau monitored every criminal case in the courts of Suffolk County during the year beginning September 1879. The county, which included Boston, was not typical of the entire state. But Wright believed the study would provide "an important basis for computation

Table 43. Crime and intemperance, 1879–1880.

Offences	Was the Criminal under the influence of liquor at the time the Crime was committed?				Was the Criminal in liquor when the intent to commit the Crime was formed?				Did the intemperate hab of the Criminal lead to condition which induce the Crime?		
	Yes	No	Not Ans.	Totals	Yes	No	Not Ans.	Totals	Yes	No	Not Ans.
Aggregates	2,097	2,318	193	4,608	1,918	2,414	276	4,608	1,804	2,566	238
Males	1,732	1,892	133	3,757	1,626	1,928	203	3,757	1,495	2,092	170
Females	365	426	60	851	292	486	73	851	309	474	68

Source: MBLS, *Twelfth Annual Report*, 1881, 494–95.

and conjecture" about the influence of drink on criminal conduct.[4] The introductory paragraph below, more forceful than was Wright's custom, illustrates both the faith and the fervor that sustained state and local efforts to curb alcohol use and that eventually led to national prohibition in the Eighteenth Amendment.

This investigation was inaugurated and conducted in the interest of all who are a prey to the sin of intemperance, but more especially in the interest of the youth of our State, with the ardent hope of revealing to them, stripped of prejudice and sentiment, the naked proportions of an evil, prolific in poverty and prodigality, waste and want, the expense of which, while a burden to all classes, falls in a greater degree on the workers and chief consumers of society. Temperance and frugality will relieve them of the greater part of this burden.

The total number of sentences for the year of our investigation—the distinctive rum offences included—was 16,897. 12,289 were directly due to rum causes; 12,221 being for sentences for the various grades of drunkenness, and 68 for liquor keeping and liquor selling without license, etc.

Thus, for the year, the sentences for rum causes alone constitute 72 + per cent of the whole, leaving a small balance of 27 + per cent. Now, to discover what was the influence of intemperance in the commission of this balance, formed the object of this investigation.

We sought to compass the object of our investigation by ascertaining the connection between rum and the criminal in five directions: 1. Whether the criminal was under the influence of liquor at the time the crime was committed; 2. Whether the criminal was in liquor at the time he formed

4. MBLS, *Twelfth Annual Report* (1881), 481.

Did the intemperate habits of others lead the Criminal to a condition when induced the Crime?			Habits of the Criminal as regards liquor drinking				
No	Not Ans.	Totals	Total Abstainer	Moderate Drinker	Excessive Drinker	Not Answered	Totals
3,404	383	4,608	1,158	1,918	1,317	215	4,608
2,860	286	3,757	940	1,611	1,047	159	3,757
544	97	851	218	307	270	56	851

the intent to commit the crime; 3. Whether the intemperate habits of the criminal were such as to lead to a condition which induced the crime; 4. Whether the intemperate habits of others led the criminal to a condition which induced the crime; 5. What were the drinking habits of the criminal, whether total abstainer, moderate drinker, or excessive drinker? . . .

The facts thus gathered are presented in the following tabular statements. The number 4,608 represents the 27 + per cent balance of crime during the year of our investigation. . . .

It appears that 2,097 of the 4,608—which constitutes the 27 + per cent balance of crime—were in liquor at the time of the commission of the various offences of which they were found guilty [Table 43]. This number is equal to 45 + per cent of the 27 + per cent balance, or to 12 + per cent of the sum of all offences for the year, the distinctively rum offences included; that 1,918 were in liquor at the time of the formation of the criminal intent; that the intemperate habits of 1,804 were such as to induce a moral condition favorable to crime; that 821 were led to a criminal condition through the contagion of intemperance; that, of the 4,608 convictions, the total abstainers numbered 1,158, the moderate drinkers 1,918, and the excessive drinkers 1,317. . . .

And finally, in the grand total of sentences for all offences within the scope of this investigation, the whole number of total abstainers constitutes 25 + per cent, while that of the excessive drinkers alone is equal to 28 + per cent.

Table [44] exhibits the connection between rum and the criminal; and the facts are classified with reference to his condition at the time the offence was committed, whether sober or in liquor, and also whether native or foreign born. Of the 4,608 sentenced, 2,638 were native, and 1,813 foreign born. While there were 1,064 native criminals in liquor at the time

Table 44. Crime, intemperance, and birthplace, 1879–1880.

Offences	Native Born			Foreign Born			Birthplace Unknown			Males	Fe-males	Totals
	Males	Fe-males	Both Sexes	Males	Fe-males	Both Sexes	Males	Fe-males	Both Sexes			
Aggregates	2,294	344	2,638	1,322	491	1,813	141	16	157	3,757	851	4,608
In liquor	946	118	1,064	724	245	969	56	4	60	1,726	367	2,093
Sober	1,274	202	1,476	552	213	765	73	11	84	1,899	426	2,325
Not answered	74	24	98	46	33	79	12	1	13	132	58	190

Source: MBLS, *Twelfth Annual Report*, 1881, 499.

of the commissions of their respective offences, there were 969 of foreign born criminals in liquor also at the time of the commissions of their respective offences; i.e. 40 + per cent of the native criminals and 53 + per cent of the foreign born criminals were under the influence of liquor at the time they became such.

It is a singular and suggestive fact, that all the criminals in the manslaughter cases were foreign born, and also in liquor at the time their high crime was perpetrated.

Table [45] presents the connection between rum and crime, the facts being classified with reference to the nativity and drinking habits of the criminal, whether native or foreign born, and whether total abstainer, moderate drinker, or excessive drinker.

Of the native criminals 862 were total abstainers, and 621 excessive drinkers. Of the foreign born criminals, on the other hand, 256 were total abstainers, and 669 excessive drinkers. The number of the native total abstainers is equal to 32 + per cent of the whole number of criminals born in this country, and the number of the native excessive drinkers to 23 + per cent of the same; while the number of the total abstainers of those criminals born out of the country is equal to 14 + per cent of all the foreign

Table 45. Crime, drinking habits, and birthplace, 1879–1880.

Offences	Native Born			Foreign Born			Birthplace Unknown			Males	Fe-males	Totals
	Males	Fe-males	Both Sexes	Males	Fe-males	Both Sexes	Males	Fe-males	Both Sexes			
Aggregates	2,294	344	2,638	1,322	491	1,813	141	16	157	3,757	851	4,608
Total abstainers	732	130	862	173	83	256	30	6	36	935	219	1,154
Moderate drinkers	939	113	1,052	621	189	810	54	4	58	1,614	306	1,920
Excessive drinkers	540	81	621	481	188	669	27	5	32	1,048	274	1,322
Not answered	83	20	103	47	31	78	30	1	31	160	52	212

Source: MBLS, *Twelfth Annual Report*, 1881, 504.

born, and the number of the excessive drinkers of foreign birth to 36 + per cent of the same. So that the native total abstainers sentenced for crime are 18 per cent *pro rata* in excess of the total abstainers of foreign birth sentenced for crime; while the excessive drinkers of foreign birth sentenced for crime exceed *pro rata* the excessive drinkers born in this country and sentenced for crime, by 13 per cent.

The . . . figures indicate the enormity of rum's share in the commission of the 27 + per cent balance of crime in Suffolk County for the year of our investigation. They show that to the 72 + per cent for distinctively rum crimes must be added 12 + per cent, representing the criminals who were in liquor at the time of committing other crimes,—making a total of 84 + per cent of all crime due directly or indirectly to the influence of liquor.

These figures paint a picture, at once the most faithful and hideous, of the guilt and power of rum. Men and women, the young, the middle-aged, and the old, father and son, husband and wife, native and foreign born, the nightwalker and manslayer, the thief and adulterer,—all testify to its ramified and revolting tyranny. Therefore the result of this investigation, in view of the disproportionate magnitude of the exclusively rum offences, and considered in connection with the notorious tendency of liquor to inflame and enlarge the passions and appetites, to import chaos into the moral and physical life, to level the barriers of decency and self-respect, and to transport its victims into an abnormal and irresponsible state, destructive and degrading, calls for earnest and immediate attention at the bar of the public opinion and the public conscience of Massachusetts. (MBLS, *Twelfth Annual Report*, 1881, 481–83, 485, 487)

The bureau represented graphically criminal activity in the Commonwealth between 1860 and 1879 in a chart published in 1880 (Diagram B [p. 186]). The large area under line *C* illustrates the predominance of offenses associated with alcohol; the tiny area between lines *B* and *C*, showing felonies, suggests the preoccupation of courts and law enforcement officials with the liquor traffic.

Fifteen years and a couple of industrial depressions later, the General Court asked the bureau to return to research on "the relation of the liquor traffic to crime, pauperism, and insanity in this Commonwealth."[5] In 1896, Horace Wadlin responded to that assignment in four

5. MBLS, *Twenty-Sixth Annual Report* (1896), 3.

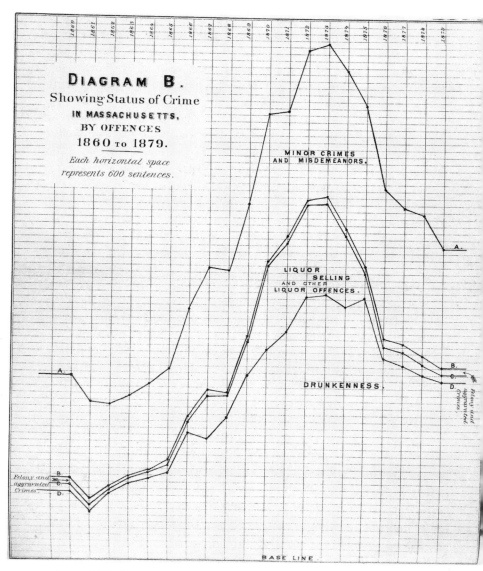

Source: MBLS, *Eleventh Annual Report*, 1880, 178–79.

hundred pages of tables that appeared to require little revision of earlier conclusions.

The following summary presents in condensed form some of the main points derived from the investigation.

PAUPERISM

Out of 3,230 paupers, this being the total number found in the State institutions during 12 consecutive months, 2,108, or about 65 in every 100 (65.26 per cent), were addicted to the use of liquor. The excessive drinkers numbered 505, or about 16 in every 100 (15.63 per cent), of all the paupers. The total abstainers numbered 866, or about 27 in every 100 (26.81 per cent), of all the paupers.

Of the total abstainers, however, 429 were minors; 281 being under 10 years of age. There were also 31 minors addicted to the use of liquor. Excluding all the minors, whether total abstainers or not, we have 2,752 paupers of adult years, of whom 2,077, or about 75 in every 100 (75.47 per cent), were addicted to the use of liquor, including 504 excessive drinkers and 1,573 drinkers not classed as excessive.

Of the whole number of paupers, 47.74 per cent, or nearly 48 in every 100, had one or both parents intemperate.

Of the whole number, 39.44 per cent, or about 39 in every 100, attributed their pauperism to their own intemperate habits; about five in every 100 considered their pauperism due to the intemperance of their parents, one or both; and about one in every 100 attributed their pauperism to the intemperance of those upon whom they were dependent, other than parents. . . .

Of the whole number of paupers (without discriminating as to sex) 2,005, or about 62 in every 100, used tobacco. Of the males (no discrimination being made as to ages) nearly 75 in every 100, used tobacco. Only three paupers were found among the whole number who used drugs intemperately.

Of the whole number of paupers (3,230) 1,019, or about 32 in every 100 (31.55 per cent), were citizen born; 320, or about 10 in every 100 (9.91 per cent), were naturalized; and 1,867, or about 58 in every 100 (57.80 per cent), were alien. The number having both parents native was 305, or about nine in every 100 (9.44 per cent), while 2,652, or about 82 in every 100 (82.11 per cent), had both parents foreign. The others were either of wholly or partly unknown parentage, or had father or mother foreign.

CRIME

Out of 26,672 convictions for various offences during 12 consecutive months, 17,575, or about 66 in every 100 (65.89 per cent), were convictions for drunkenness; and 657, or about two in every 100 (2.46 per cent), for drunkenness in combination with other offences. Hence 18,232 convictions, or about 68 in every 100 (68.36 per cent), included drunkenness either wholly or in part.

In 21,863 cases, about 82 in every 100 (81.97 per cent), the offender was in liquor at the time the offence was committed.

In 8,440 cases in which drunkenness did not form part of the offence, that is, in which the offender was convicted of a crime other than drunkenness, 3,640, or about 43 in every 100 (43.13 per cent), were cases in which the offender was in liquor at the time the offence was committed. Of these 8,440 cases, 4,852, or about 57 in every 100 (57.49 per cent), were cases in which the offender was in liquor at the time the intent was formed to commit the offence.

Out of the whole number of cases, namely 26,672, there were 22,514 in which the intemperate habits of the offender led to a condition which induced the crime. These constitute about 84 in every 100, or 84.41 per cent, of the whole number of cases. Disregarding convictions connected with drunkenness there remain 4,294 convictions for other crimes, committed under conditions created by the intemperate habits of the criminal. These constitute 50.88 per cent, or nearly 51 in every 100, of the total number of convictions for crimes other than drunkenness.

In 16,115 cases, 60.42 per cent of the whole number, or about 60 in every 100, the intemperate habits of persons other than the offender were said to have been influential in the commitment of the offence, and 3,611, or 42.78 per cent, about 43 in every 100, of the total convictions for crimes other than drunkenness were of this class.

Of the whole number of convictions, namely 26,672, the number of offenders addicted to the use of liquor (no discrimination being made as to sex) was 25,137, or about 94 in every 100 (94.24 per cent). The excessive drinkers numbered 4,516, about 17 in every 100 (16.93 per cent), and the total abstainers numbered 1,535, about six in every 100 (5.76 per cent).

Of the total abstainers, however, 632 were minors. There were also 680 minors addicted to the use of liquor. Excluding all the minors, whether total abstainers or not, we have 25,360 offenders of adult years, of whom 24,457, or about 96 in every 100 (96.44 per cent), were addicted to the use of liquor, including 4,482 excessive drinkers and 19,975 drinkers not classed as excessive.

Of the whole number of offenders 57.89 per cent, or nearly 58 in every 100, had fathers who were addicted to the use of liquor, while 20.49 per cent, or about 20 in every 100, had mothers addicted to the use of liquor. . . .

Of the whole number of offenders (without discriminating as to sex), 22,738, or about 85 in every 100, used tobacco. Of the males (no discrimination being made as to ages), nearly 94 in every 100 used tobacco.

Of the whole number of offenders (26,672) 14,131 or about 53 in every 100 (52.98 per cent), were citizen born; 3,726, or about 14 in every 100 (13.97 per cent), were naturalized; and 8,815, or about 33 in every 100 (33.05 per cent), were alien. The number having both parents native was 4,089, or about 15 in every 100 (15.33 per cent), while 21,204, or about 80 in every 100 (79.50 per cent), had both parents foreign. The others were either of wholly or partly unknown parentage or had father or mother foreign. . . .

It is of course true that no investigation of this kind can deal with the psychological aspects of the drinking problem, or with the social conditions which have an important influence upon it. It may be determined, for example, as we have shown, that the use of liquor is a direct cause of a given number of cases of pauperism, crime, or insanity. It may be shown that the drinking habit once formed transmits itself from parent to offspring, and that the sins of the father are visited upon the children, not merely in fastening the appetite upon the child, but in subjecting him to pauperism, crime, or insanity. The converse proposition is perhaps often true, namely, that pauperism and other evils, to say nothing of peculiar mental states, or inherited peculiarities of constitution, lead, in the first instance, to intemperance; and the facts upon this point are neither clear nor easily obtainable.

Many of the paupers canvassed in this investigation were deficient in mental stamina, and while this is by no means so largely true with respect to the criminals, it is impossible to determine what peculiarities of brain exist among them, until criminal pathology has progressed much farther than at present. How far the use of liquor is directly responsible for the

18. Workers of the Haffenreffer Brewery, Boston, 1891. Courtesy of the Boston Public Library, Print Department.

present condition of numbers of these persons may be shown by the statistical method. How far the mental and physical deficiencies of the individual may have led to his use of liquor is another question, and this can hardly be shown by statistics. The causes which lie back of the drinking habit are equally as important as the results of the habit itself, but their determination is obviously outside the limits of such an investigation as this. (MBLS, *Twenty-sixth Annual Report*, 1896, 406–10, 416)

Labor unions forming in the nineteenth century worried less about the drinking habits of criminals than about the unfair competition they presented, once they were prisoners, to workers outside the walls. That perspective, contrasted with the preoccupation with alcohol that characterized the bureau and the legislature, illustrates one difference between middle-class reformers and those with associations in factories. The temptation to use convicts, or to lease their labor to contractors and thereby reduce the cost of incarceration, appealed to taxpayers, not to poor people seeking jobs. And when legislators took up the question of convict labor in 1878, their focus was on competition among entrepreneurs, rather than that among laborers.

The General Court directed the bureau "to make a full investigation" and "to recommend such legislation ... as is advisable to prevent competition" between prisons and private businesses.[6] Since convicts produced shoes, hats, brushes, and other items sold in interstate commerce, the bureau determined that research had to extend beyond the state. The more inclusive report, published in 1880, confirmed conclusions tentatively reached after consultation with Massachusetts factory managers the year before.

> The examination of the boot and shoe interest will enable the legislature to see more clearly the relation of the statistics presented to other facts gathered during the investigation. This industry is taken for illustration, because it is the largest in this State, the product being $90,000,000 per annum; because it is from this trade the most complaint comes; and because the elements essential to a close analysis of the manufacture of goods in prisons are more easily obtained from boot and shoe manufacturers. . . .
>
> At the present time the relation of the cost of labor to the value of the product in the manufacture of boots and shoes outside of prison is as 1 to 3; that is, of every dollar's value of product, 33⅓ per cent goes to labor. This statement is the result of the experience of many of our leading manufacturers, although some of the most prominent proprietors put the value of labor at 27 per cent of the product. It is safe to say, as the result of combined experience and of the testimony received, that the weight of evidence is in favor of the proportion first stated,—that 33⅓ per cent of the product goes to labor; and labor includes the wages or salaries of foremen.
>
> The ratio of labor to product in prison work is 31¼ per cent. This includes the same elements used in obtaining the ratio outside, the wages and salaries of foremen, instructors, etc.; the expense of the latter being much greater in prison than out.
>
> These statements, which are given us as facts by reliable parties, although they are denied, show that the advantage to the prison contractor is really about 2 per cent in the production of goods, on the average. . . .
>
> Parties who write or speak upon convict labor are apt to take it for granted that the product per man is the same for the prisoner as for the

6. MBLS, *Tenth Annual Report* (1879), 17.

outside worker. In this they err. The product of each person employed in the manufacture of boots and shoes in Massachusetts is $1,858 per year; that is, 48,090 operatives—the number of persons so employed in 1875—produced $89,375,792 worth of goods. The product of prison work per man is $1,142 per annum. The 200 men employed on boots and shoes at Concord produce $228,575 worth of goods per year, on an average: the same number outside would make $371,600 worth of goods. . . .

The contractors claim, that if out of prison work, with their experience, they would not enter it. An extensive manufacturer of boots and shoes, who runs a large prison force, and also several factories outside, testifies that he makes larger profits from his outside factories than from his prison contract; and that, if he was out of it, he would not again take a contract for prison labor. No contractor will object to the abolition of the contract system on personal grounds. . . .

One large manufacturer (A) stated that he had at one time believed that prison labor must, of necessity, injure outside labor. He knew, he said, that Rice & Hutchings had the labor of 100 prisoners in the State Prison for 40 cents a day,—a very small sum to pay for labor, and at first glance would seem to give them great advantage; but the great drawback is, that, by the terms of their contract, they are obliged to pay their men all the year round, whether they are employed or not. There are other drawbacks; for instance, prison-made goods will not sell so readily—buyers are shy of them; as a rule, they cannot feel sure of the goods being well made. The partner of the gentleman referred to remarked that he did not see how prison labor in Massachusetts could much affect the shoe business one way or the other. If all the convicts at Concord were put to making shoes, he would not care. It would only amount to one more large factory; and the shoe business of the State could stand that, in his opinion. In answer to the question, "Do you know of any instance where your own business has been affected by prison labor?" Both partners answered, "No." And to the question, "Has it ever caused you to reduce the pay of your employés?" they answered, "Never."

Another large dealer and manufacturer (B) said "that he knew of no injurious effects to his business from prison labor; was very glad the subject was being investigated, as he was satisfied that the most erroneous ideas were entertained in regard to it by many who ought to know better; in his opinion it has been too much of a handle for small politicians to use for their own advantage; and that so many preposterous and ridiculous statements have been made, it was time the real facts were known." . . .

One of the heaviest firms in the United States (the factories located in this State) gave positive statements to the effect that several hundred thousand dollars of trade had been withdrawn from their house on account of the prison shops of Illinois and other Western States, and that their help had been, or would be, cut down at least 10 per cent through the direct influence of prison-made goods. . . . [But] it is rare to find a man in the shoe trade who is willing to assert that prison labor works any great injury; and those who assert that it does have no facts to give as a rule, only opinions, often growing out of local sentiment.

If there is any undue or injurious competition in the shoe trade resulting from prison labor, it is so small, manufacturers, with few exceptions, have not felt it to any great extent; but the State is bound all the same by the principle involved,—that is, that the interests of the industries of the State make up the interests of the Commonwealth, and that the system should be adopted which, on the whole, works the least injury to its industries. This injury we have endeavored to find; for the investigation was started with the idea, on the part of the writer at least, that it existed. So far as the statistics presented or the testimony quoted, or the opinions received, are concerned, the injury to the shoe trade has not assumed the proclaimed proportions; yet it exists, and should be recognized. (MBLS, *Tenth Annual Report*, 1879, 25–30)

Returning to the topic a year later, the bureau first reiterated conclusions reached in 1879 and then added several new suggestions.

That Massachusetts has no right to expect to make profit, or permit others to do so, out of the labor of convicts, at the expense of their reformation.

That, whatever evils may result from convict labor, they cannot be remedied by State legislation, but should receive the attention of the national legislature. There can be no systematic regulation by States alone.

That there is a certain amount of competition arising from prison manufactures that works injuriously at times and in localities, but no general or alarming injury affecting the industrial interests of the State. . . .

The conclusions arrived at least year, as well as the recommendations made, have not suffered by another year's study and research; on the contrary, they have been emphasized. Three other suggestions have, however, either been made or brought out by reflection, and are well worth consideration. They are,—

1. That the Legislature should limit by law the number of convicts to be employed in any one branch to ten per cent of the number employed in the same branch outside.

2. That the use of all power machinery be prohibited in prison shops, and the convicts be employed upon hand work, as upon hand made boots and shoes, hand woven goods for prison wear and other State purposes, etc.

3. That all idea of making prisons self-supporting be abandoned, and the convicts be taught . . . to turn their hands to any trade requiring skill and training. . . .

It is gradually being conceded by many who thought they saw in convict labor a serious evil, and a matter of alarm for the welfare of workingmen, that the question under consideration is one more thoroughly of prison reform and prison administration, and of the methods of treating actual crime, than belonging exclusively, or largely even, to economics. When this idea has obtained sufficient strength, the proposition to educate technically our accidental convicts, without special regard to products, will find hearty response; and then, with efficient prison administration, the State will find its reward in a treasury unaffected by prison deficiencies. The public will demand, probably, that convicts shall, if possible, always support themselves, and yet it will insist upon reformatory effort on the part of the government. . . .

One thing is evident, we have not yet reached the right methods for treating crime. It is not our province here to discuss the matter in this light, and yet we feel that the workingmen are more affected directly and indirectly by the presence of crime itself than by all the labor performed by convicts. The reduction of the number of criminals is of vastly more importance than the regulation of their work. (MBLS, *Eleventh Annual Report*, 1880, 75–76, 78, 80)

CHAPTER NINE

Arbitration, Cooperation,
Legislation, and Organization

"Work," in the folk idiom of the nineteenth century, was financially and spiritually rewarding, and differed in both compensation and status from "labor." "Labor" was what the unskilled performed and often bespoke an inferior social position. Hard "work," on the other hand, was the key to progress in an open society and earned the individual a share in the nation's fabled economic bounty. Implicit in clichés about the "land of opportunity" was the unarticulated notion that factory employment and other "labor" were not careers but only temporary expedients adopted to escape need while awaiting the future rewards of diligence. Consequently, some reformers interested in the labor question promoted programs that promised to elevate workers to another socioeconomic level instead of, or occasionally in addition to, seeking to prevent exploitation and to make working conditions more tolerable.

The establishment of cooperative manufacturing companies and retail stores seemed initially a superb way to advance all these reform goals. In factories owned by those who worked in them, the roles of employer and employee would merge. In profit-sharing cooperative shops, purchasers would become merchants as well as customers. The Massachusetts Labor Reform Party urged in 1871 that "all encouragement shall be given by law to co-operation in all branches of industry and trade." In that same year, the shoeworkers' union encouraged "our brothers to use their utmost endeavors to build up ... a system of co-operation in both trade and manufacture," which would "lift the order into a position of the highest respectability and influence."[1] Apparently, great "respectability and influence" accompanied managerial and entrepreneurial responsibility, which suggests that shoeworkers and their employers had a common understanding of hierarchy.

Most cooperative ventures proved fragile and collapsed without markedly reducing industrial strife. Struggles between employers and employees, of course, had ramifications beyond a factory's gates, as tension built in communities and profits and payrolls abruptly dropped. Civic leaders not involved in strikes and lockouts, including Carroll Wright, tended to disparage them as senseless wastes of resources; believing themselves distinterested, they promoted impartial arbitration as a rational alternative. With rare exceptions, neither workers nor their bosses trusted the professed impartiality of proposed arbitrators, and arbitration was therefore a theoretical solution proposed by outsiders rather than a practical remedy embraced by participants.

For arbitration to succeed and for cooperatives to prosper, individuals had to subordinate self-interest to what someone else defined as the interest of a larger entity. To expect to accomplish that goal voluntarily, in an age Mark Twain called "gilded," with all the get-rich-quick competition that phrase conveyed, was almost certainly naive. The Massachusetts Bureau of Statistics of Labor had been established, after all, because the General Court knew the labor question was one of public policy as well as of private enterprise. The state government never developed a single comprehensive answer or grand design. But bit by bit, the General Court did narrow the freedom of individuals to act on answers of their own.

The first excerpts below show the enthusiasm behind early experiments in cooperation. The strike in connection with the introduction of Chinese contract labor is treated in Chapter 10.

COÖPERATIVE PRODUCTION IN GREENFIELD

The Greenfield Coöperative Machine Company was organized July 1, 1870. Its superintendent is a young man of 26 years, who commenced to

1. MBLS, *Eighth Annual Report* (1877), 90.

learn his trade in Providence at the age of 14. The shop, $50 \times 40 \times 12$ in dimensions; the machinery and the power are all hired. Seven men are at work. All share in the profits equitably. Job work is done better than is usual, and somewhat under current prices. The superintendent is inventor of a planing-knife grinder, blacksmith's drill, and a bolt-cutter, which are made in the shop. Orders have been constant, and the prospects ahead are good. There is unity of feeling among the members, and all are more industrious and steady than before entering upon the experiment. Pay is drawn on the 15th of the month, and the men work on the ten hour system.

COÖPERATIVE PRODUCTION AT NORTH ADAMS

Incidental allusion has already been made to the manufacture of shoes by coöperation at North Adams, and its connection with the strike there about the time of the introduction of Chinese labor. Organization was effected July 25, 1870, with a paid-up capital of $6,000 at $100 per share. An established factory, not far from that of C.T. Sampson, was leased at a rental of $300 per annum.... Women's, misses' and children's balmoral shoes of the best quality are made. Number employed, 44; 35 men and 9 women. Nearly all are shareholders or are taking the place of sharehold-ers. With increase of capital it is expected that outsiders will be admitted to ownership. Current wages are paid, and profits are divided upon the shares. Wages are paid monthly, though at the beginning the men drew as little of their pay as possible. The buying and selling are done by one of the officers, his action being subject to approval or otherwise by the board of management.... No difficulty is found in marketing goods, and orders have been abundant.... The men at work speak with pride of their new feelings of self-reliance and freedom, as well as of the quality of their work and the tendencies developed toward a more economical production than before. Hours of labor, 59 per week. (MBLS, *Second Annual Report*, 1871, 455–56)

FALL RIVER

Foremost among associations operating under this system, is the "Fall River Workingmen's Co-operative Association," organized in 1866.... Its members are people of many nationalities; the larger portion, however, are

English, many of whom were members of similar organizations before coming to this country. The capital of the association is made up by shares, at ten dollars each; every member being required to take at least one, and being restricted to thirty. The store sells groceries, provisions, dry goods, ready-made clothing, boots and shoes, and such other articles as are usually required by families. In the sale of these articles, cash is always demanded. . . .

At the close of its first year's experience, it had sixty-five members, and a share capital of $3,600; at the close of the year 1874, its membership had increased to two hundred and sixty, and the share capital to $19,734, while its assets were about $50,000. During the year 1874, the sales amounted to $79,615, and the net profits for the year were $9,155. During the last quarter of the year, the distribution of profits was, on members' purchases, ten per cent; on non-members', six and two-thirds per cent. In addition, interest on members' capital was paid at the rate of ten per cent per annum; the combined dividends and interest to members, being at the annual rate of about forty-two per cent on the share capital. The average share capital to each member is seventy-five dollars. During the eight years of the existence of the association, it has sold goods to the amount of $425,277; has paid as interest and dividends to members $38,179; and has divided to purchasers, not members, $4,757. As it not required of those who become members that they should at once pay the entire value of the share or shares purchased, cases are quite numerous where the member has paid but one dollar upon admission, allowing the profits on his purchases to remain in the fund, and now has an ownership of twenty shares in the association; connection with the society having encouraged a *desire* to save, and economy in management made it possible.

Strikes and hard times, instead of affecting its business disastrously, have resulted in a notable increase, as the closing quarters of 1873–74 were the most successful business terms of the association. . . . (MBLS, *Sixth Annual Report*, 1875, 456–57)

By 1877, Director Carroll Wright was less sure that cooperation provided an answer to the "labor question." The historical account in that year's *Annual Report* included more analysis of failure than descriptions of success, and the bureau's previous optimism seemed muted.

It appears, from a careful review of the past, of which this article is but a brief outline, that there has been for the past twenty-five years in this State an annual investment of from one hundred thousand to a quarter of a million of dollars in co-operative experiments; that the average duration of their existence, omitting such as have had but a normal life, has been from about three to five years. . . .

It has been shown that they have their origin in the most benevolent and statesmanlike motives,—the good of the human race. The founders in most instances . . . were the men who were agitating for ten hours, the institution of lyceums or institutes, for making the militia system less burdensome to the laboring classes, for legislative regulation of factories, education for all, abolition of imprisonment for debt, the adoption of a national bankrupt law, the extension of the right of suffrage, the enactment of a mechanics' lien law, the abolition of capital punishment, slavery and war.

They organized and worked. They called conventions, wrote appeals, published tracts, weighed out justice and sugar with even balances, and measured men, government, and cotton cloth by the golden rule.

Their weekly meeting was the oasis in the desert of their lives; for there, in their upper room, they discussed the affairs of State and the affairs of their union, the tariff and the price of tea (many of them were free-traders), cotton cloth, slavery and the excessive hours of labor.

With the increasing cares of the organization and of their families, the lesser overcame the larger. Tea was discussed more and tariff less. Men joined the store who never attended the meeting, or cared for aught but low prices and large dividends. Then other stores were started whose meetings were wholly for business purposes, the electing of a storekeeper, and the needed committees. The selfish became the majority. The Utopians were retired from the command, and the store that seemed a portion of the coming kingdom became the arena for a competition that never scrupled at a trade that would bring dividends.

For a time the New England Protective Union . . . held the principle of each to help the other [; . . . it] ended with that of each to help himself. It is not surprising that, in many cases, the storekeeper having more time and opportunity than the rest, often profited by their example, and, at last, helped himself to the sole control.

This experiment demonstrated that a number of men could unite and buy goods at wholesale, and distribute them at less cost among each other, than under the old system; and it further demonstrated that they could not co-operate to make that fact of any use to themselves nor to posterity. . . .

As with this experiment, so with the others. In their inception they were managed by men energetic and disinterested, willing to work, but not always ready for the martyrdom that such efforts demand. When risk or loss was the rule, and dividends an unknown factor, co-operation was easy. But with success came the selfish. . . .

The failure of these experiments is not so much due to methods as to men. . . . Men are often selected to important positions because they are affable, agreeable persons, qualities to be encouraged, but of little avail if methods of business are unsound. . . . The men are masters of the method. When it is said that a store failed because it allowed credit, it only half states the fact. Who allowed credit? Not the storekeeper. He was the servant, subject to the majority. It was a failure to co-operate; for co-operation needs an intelligence equal to the settlement of such a question. . . .

The possibility of inaugurating co-operative distribution has been proven. The small amount of capital required, and the simplicity of the plan, render it financially practicable. . . .

To render co-operative efforts of use in the solution of the labor problem, requires the existence of those moral elements that come from enlarged views of life and duty, but must follow increased opportunities for thought.

The narrowness and selfishness that looks only to the wants of the present, that ignorantly boasts of its superiority in skill, that causes the mechanic of one trade to ignore the claims of his fellow-laborer of another calling,—these must disappear before co-operation can be possible. (MBLS, *Eighth Annual Report*, 1877, 122–24, 127–28, 137)

About a decade later, as part of a study of profit sharing and stock ownership by employees, the bureau again examined the state's co-operative manufacturing enterprises. The summary and conclusions derived from ten example of foundries, furniture factories, and shoe companies (Table 46).

In two of these ten co-operative companies there is a strong opposition to a mixture of nationalities, and care is taken to keep the stock in the possession of men and women of American birth. In three other companies it has happened, without any distinct effort to have it so, that all or most of the members are of American birth. In the other five, nationalities are

Table 46. Cooperative manufacturing companies, 1885.

Name of Co-operative Association	Capital	Annual Product	Stockholders Employed		Employés not Stockholders		Individual Wages per Month	Aggregate Salaries per Year	Average Dividends
			Males	Fe-males	Males	Fe-males			
									Per cent.
American Shoe Co	$30,000	$50,000	11	11	14	9	$43	$900	—
Athol Furniture Co	5,000	15,000	8	—	3	—	32	626	—*
E. Templeton Chair Co	20,000	45,000	14	—	9	—	44	1,220	1.83*
Franklin Shoe Co	20,000	50,000	20	6	2	8	41	1,000	—
Kingston Foundry Co	11,900	20,000	11	—	9	—	30†	782	0.75
Leonard Foundry Co	25,000	75,000	40	—	10	—	60	2,400	3.62
Middlesex Shoe Co	15,000	90,000	21	3	6	12	42	1,880	10.35
Somerset Foundry Co	30,000	75,000	30	—	10	—	76	2,280	7.60
Stoneham Shoe Co	20,000	150,000	20	5	15	20	42	2,400	14.15
Wakefield Shoe Co	15,000	35,000	11	1	—	8	39	2,000	8.00

Source: MBLS, *Seventeenth Annual Report*, 1886, 228.
*Losses by fire.
†Working part time.

indiscriminately mingled. The managers of these latter affirm that the fact causes no inconvenience and that success is in no way impaired by it.

There is a more general agreement that co-operative stockholders should be picked men in regard to character and efficiency. One dissatisfied man can make an amount of trouble altogether disproportionate to his investment.

One of the "outs" of co-operation, in the experience of one agent, is that if business is dull unemployed stockholders think it hard that they cannot have work. Again, in dull times it would often be economy to work in a cheap man to do certain kinds of work while learning the trade, but it will hardly do to substitute the cheap man for a stockholder.

Another agent expressed the judgment that the fewer female stock-holders in the stitching room of a shoe factory the better. They are carried away, he said, by the idea that as stockholders they should be permitted to do as they please; and they are too independent. In the stitching room it is desirable, to economize machinery, to have stitchers change off, doing one kind of work a part of the day, and something else at other times. If they are stockholders young women object. No other agent made this criticism, but on the contrary one said that the trouble would not arise under good management. . . .

19. Textile workers' outing, early twentieth century. Courtesy of the Museum of American Textile History.

From the data gathered from all sources we derive these cardinal principles of industrial partnership:

Participation by workmen in profits in addition to wages is a true harmonizer of the interests of capital and labor. It does in fact identify the interest of the employé with the interest of the employer. It converts the industrial association of employer and employés into a moral organism, in which all the various talents, services, and desires of the component individuals are fused into a community of purpose and endeavor.

The dividend to labor is not usually an increase of pay, services remaining the same, but a form of extra pay for extra services and an inducement calling them out. The extra services called out, and the manner in which they are called out, constitute an invaluable educational discipline. They develop the whole group of industrial virtues: diligence, fidelity, caretaking, economy, continuity of effort, willingness to learn, and the spirit of co-operation. . . .

In general, success in profit sharing depends on a definite understanding, insistence that the bonus must be earned and not expected as a present, and patience in working and waiting for results. . . .

Co-operative manufacturing corporations have been successful in this State in the degree that they have conformed to the conditions to which other manufacturing corporations find it necessary to conform.

It has been necessary to give to managers large powers and to maintain unity and continuity of management.

It has been necessary to subordinate the labor relation to the stockholder relation. The best success is attained when the management has power to hire and discharge labor with sole reference to efficiency and regardless of any supposed claim to employment constituted by stockholding . . . .

It is not shown that an admixture of nationalities or of male and female stockholders is necessarily a disadvantage. If other conditions are conformed to and the management is efficient, sex and nationality may be disregarded.

Failure to separate wages from profits in the aggregate rewards of stockholding workers and to pay wages for labor performed, and to pay them regularly, may be set down as leading to certain failure.

Ample working capital—capital beyond what goes into plant—is of utmost importance. The most frequent mistake of intending co-operators is in underestimating the amount required.

Stock-owning by workmen with participation in management gives a training in prudence, economy, and business affairs. It changes the whole current of the worker's thought and feelings, and economic conduct. He ceases to think of himself as a worker standing over against the capitalist employer in an antagonistic relation. He thinks of himself always as a proprietor and dignifies himself as such, and as such puts new zest into his work. . . . Industrial partnership instituted by capitalist employers, and co-operation instituted by capital owning workmen, work toward the same result from different directions. Each has its own proper field and each will probably acquire increasing prominence in social economy. (MBLS, *Seventeenth Annual Report*, 1886, 228–29, 231–35)

"Industrial arbitration," Carroll Wright thought in 1877, might complement "industrial co-partnerships and co-operation" and reduce friction between employers and their employees. Efforts to settle industrial conflict through negotiation, he believed, demonstrated that "capital and labor are in large degree interchangeable terms" and that each was "dependent upon the other." "The age of lockouts and strikes is fast passing away," he wrote optimistically, to be replaced by reference of disagreements to decision-making boards nominated by the contending parties.[2]

Although Wright asserted that arbitration was "one of the simplest methods of restoring harmony" to contentious labor relations, the examples of this promising development he cited came almost entirely from Great Britain.[3] The American exception was a short-lived arrangement in Lynn that ended when shoe manufacturers decided they had the power to impose settlements without consulting their workers.

By the final decade of the century, cooperation and arbitration no longer held any realistic promise of lifting labor's standard of living or equalizing the bargaining power of employers and employees. When the competitive "free market" that was presumed to exist did not enable workers themselves to check an employer's advantage in power and income, labor reformers invoked the aid of the state. Although the legislative response frequently was a comparatively minor or ineffectively enforced restriction, over two decades the cumulative total of labor legislation was significant, as the bureau's summary in 1891 demonstrated.

At the beginning of the present century trade was subjected to stringent legal regulations. Subsequent legislation has favored the removal of restrictions upon the interchange of commodities. During the same period, however, there has been a marked tendency toward governmental regulation of exchange of services. In the first case the principle of *laissez faire* has ruled; in the other the principle of State regulation of the employment of labor has prevailed. These two tendencies in modern legislation seem opposed to one another. They have really been mutually dependent. The movement which in one direction has aimed at unrestricted competition has in another direction necessitated governmental interference with individual action.

2. Ibid., viii, 3, 4.
3. Ibid., 4.

The development of the factory system following the introduction of machinery immediately changed the conditions surrounding production. It made possible the employment of classes previously unproductive. Skill was no longer essential to such employment. The income of the family might be increased by the aid of child workers, and the employment of women on an extensive scale became one of the features of industrial life. The system of isolated household industry gave place to the modern town in which masses of factory workers are congregated. These changed industrial conditions were practically revolutionary. They have resulted, on the whole, in immense social advantages, by no means confined to any particular class in society; but, at the same time, they have introduced grave social problems. It was very soon felt that the preservation of society demanded the establishment of rules under which the new relations between the employer and the employed might continue. These rules expressed in legal phraseology, with such changes as experience has shown to be necessary, constitute the labor laws now in force. . . .

At every step the assertion of the principle underlying [labor legislation] has been strenuously resisted, the argument taking the general ground of opposition to State paternalism, or to interference on the part of the State with the so-called freedom of contract. Yet it would be difficult to point out, as the result of such legislation, any of the evils which, before its enactment, were predicted by its opponents. In point of fact such legislation is identical in character with statutes which aim to establish and maintain favorable moral and sanitary conditions in society. It is perfectly true that men cannot be legislated into health or happiness, but it is also true that the social conditions surrounding them have much to do with their mental, moral, and physical development. If it is proper to guard against the maintenance of nuisances which may endanger the health of a community, it would seem equally proper to guard against such industrial conditions as tend either to illiteracy, physical degeneracy, crime, or pauperism; and labor legislation as a rule has had no other object. Indeed, this seems at last to be generally recognized. Opposition to labor legislation is now seldom based upon the assumption that the State should not deal with such matters, but it is more frequently urged that the proposed action is inexpedient. . . .

The principal labor legislation passed in this Commonwealth is the work of years subsequent to 1874. . . .

As the grand result of labor legislation, the legal hours of employment in factories for women and for minors under eighteen years of age are fixed at sixty per week with the provision that neither women nor minors can be employed between the hours of ten at night and six in the morning; no child under thirteen years of age can be legally employed at any time in any factory, workshop or mercantile establishment, nor in any indoor work for hire during school hours, nor in any manner during such hours unless he has had thirty weeks' schooling during the year preceding as required by law; no child under fourteen can be employed between the hours of seven at night and six in the morning, nor in any factory, workshop or mercantile establishment, except during school vacations, unless able to read and write in the English language or a regular attendant at a public evening school; nor employed in any indoor work for hire during school hours unless as aforesaid, nor legally employed in any manner for hire during school hours unless he has had thirty weeks' schooling during the year preceding as required by law. No minor over fourteen can be regularly employed if unable to read or write in the English language, except in certain contingencies; no minor under sixteen can be legally employed in any factory, workshop, or mercantile establishment unless his employer keeps on file an age and schooling certificate respecting such minor as required by law; no minor under eighteen can be legally employed more than sixty hours per week in any mercantile establishment; imprisonment for debt is abolished; a lien law is provided; necessary tools of the mechanic are exempt from attachment; the trustee process is curtailed; co-operative associations and banks or building societies are authorized; regulations for the protection of life and health in factories are provided, and the inspection of factories required; and, finally, while perhaps not strictly in the line of labor legislation, educational facilities have been broadened and made perfectly free as regards instruction and text books. Without specific legislation, ten hours has come to be the maximum day's work in most industries, while the tendency is toward a shorter working day. (MBLS, *Twenty-first Annual Report*, 1891, 107–9, 111,112)

Legislation, arbitration, and cooperation, whatever their appeal to working people, were not objectives they could accomplish alone. Labor did not possess the dominant voice in the General Court; arbitration required the willing participation of both parties to an industrial disagreement; support for cooperative production and distribution among the consuming public was too shallow. These efforts to improve the condition of workers—to answer the labor question—depended on the aid and understanding of people who did not themselves earn a living in factories. In a sense, then, these were reforms *for* labor, rather than *by* or *of* labor.

A labor union, on the other hand, usually provoked suspicion or hostility, rather than assistance, outside the ranks of the working people who were enrolled and whose interests were championed. Middle-class reformers, even if sympathetic to workers' aspirations, deplored social discord and mistrusted organizations that appeared to pit classes against one another. Defenders of unrestricted property rights and the economic orthodoxy that protected them associated unions with un-American ideologies. The fact that many factory workers were foreign-born reinforced that association, and the secrecy with which some unions guarded their ritual and membership lists made them appear conspiratorial and perhaps subversive.

The secrecy that helped preserve jobs and shielded union members from the retaliation of hostile employers also kept the general public, including the Massachusetts Bureau of Statistics of Labor, from a fully informed view of these organizations.[4] Although the bureau's reports contain scattered references to unions, much of the material is anecdotal. Before 1900, the bureau devoted more analytical effort to identifying depositors in savings banks than to explaining the programs of unions, and more pages to a discussion of ventilation in factories. Carroll Wright's initial interest in labor organization arose from his concern about the social and economic waste he associated with strikes; only after he left Massachusetts did Wright endorse collective bargaining.

The first excerpts here are responses to the earliest questionnaires that the bureau distributed in 1870 and 1871; they document the hostility of employers and the contrasting attitude of working people. The bureau used case numbers to provide identification while preserving confidentiality.

4. The perceived need of the Knights of Labor for secrecy did not prevent the New Jersey Bureau of Statistics of Labor and Industry from attempting to survey the union's membership. See Kim Voss, *The Making of American Exceptionalism* (Ithaca: Cornell University Press, 1993), chap. 4.

Office No. 159. An Iron Nail Manufacturer states, that they had a strike in the nailing department which lasted from three to four months; that the object of the strike was to obtain increased pay; that the result was "no increase;" that the loss of time and aggregate earnings to the parties participating in said strike, were thirteen thousand dollars. He also states that he has refused employment to parties for participating in *labor reform movements.*

Office No. 235. A Boot and Shoe Manufacturer. There has been a strike among the sewers, lasters and finishers of this establishment, but that the object was neither for increased pay or shorter time. He says: "They claimed the right to dictate to the employers who should and who should not be hired or discharged." He also states, as a result of the strike, that the strikers (Crispins) were not employed; that workmen not belonging to the Crispins were employed in their stead. He, moreover, states, that workmen in their employ have been discharged for participating in *labor movements*; and adds, "No Crispin need apply!"

Office No. 230. An Iron and Steel Manufacturing Company . . . says: "We have never known of our operatives being engaged in any labor movement. We should never employ men belonging to societies that attempt to regulate pay, or hours indiscriminately, if we knew it." . . .

Office No. 151. An Employer in Iron Works says: "A few years ago we had some trouble among the moulders. A delegation called upon Mr.——, and demanded that certain moulders, not members of the moulders' union, should be discharged. Mr.——refused, when quite a number quit work; but in a short time everything went along smoothly. Since that time, we have generally refused employment to members of the moulders' union."

Office No. 18. A Boot Maker says: "I think it (the trade union) has had a practical tendency to prevent a reduction of wages. It has profited me, educationally and socially. As to the habits of members, I think they have improved *very much indeed.*"

Office No. 13. A Shoemaker says: "We have an organization, called the 'Knights of St. Crispin.' The expenses are about six dollars a year. It has been a good thing for all who work at the trade, as far as my judgment goes; especially in habits of temperance."

Office No. 29. A Plasterer says: "I belong to the 'Boston Plasterers' Union.' We pay twenty-five cents per month for dues; funeral assessments, twenty-five cents; and we have often been assessed to help disabled members, orphans, widows, &c. It has reduced the hours of labor on

Saturdays, increased my earnings, and made plasterers more temperate, in general, than they ever were before."

Office No. 107. A Carpenter remarks: "My experience in the 'trades-union' has convinced me of their efficacy in increasing wages, improving its members, morally, socially and intellectually, making them more temperate, better workmen, and better citizens." (MBLS, *Annual Report*, 1870, 207, 246, 254, 280–81)

The session of the General Court that established the Bureau of Statistics of Labor denied a charter to the Knights of St. Crispin. At the time, a majority of legislators held that the labor question demanded a more general and more informed answer than the routine approval of the petition of one union. Study by the new agency was supposed to provide time and information to that end. As the next excerpt reveals, that soft answer failed to deflect the wrath of some disappointed members of the order. The following account from Marlborough illustrates local support for the organization.

A Boot Maker remarks: "Now there was a large number so situated that they could not get away from their circumstances, in many instances having large families, and homesteads on their hands, mortgaged. It became evident that something should be done to prevent this class from falling a prey to capitalists, or taking the first step towards a system of serfdom from which there could be no backward steps. But how to unite upon a plan, was the important question. We could not adopt a scale of prices, because we had not faith enough in one another to make the attempt. We were told that this plan had been tried many times, and failed, and it was folly to think of adopting, for a national policy, that which had failed at home. Thus, within our own lines, avarice was arrayed against us like a mountain-wall, and our petitions to legislators were ridiculed and trampled under foot. But at a time when we had almost given up hope, the idea was started by a workman in the West, that if we could agree to pledge ourselves not to take apprentices, we could grow into a system wherein we could get even more than could be acquired by any other system, and eventually open the door to a coöperation in trade, as well as in political economy. The plan was eagerly seized upon and adopted. In a few months from this time, nearly every boot maker in the country was enrolled in this noble Order, and here we are to-day knocking at the door of every workman's heart to assist us in helping ourselves. We now desire coöperation in this trade. The first step is a charter from the legislature of the State. But this body saw fit to treat our petition as King George III did the American colonies. But Great Britain lost her colonies; and the capitalists of Massachusetts may profit by her example. We do not ask for a 'Bureau of Labor' to look into our condition; we propose to take care of ourselves, and this we will do. We are determined to know why privileges are denied to us that are granted to moneyed associations. 'We enact,' says the statute, 'this law, looking to the permanent prosperity of the industry of the Commonwealth.' It looks to us as though it was intended to find out who to bribe, and how much more we could endure. Do you question our rights to a charter? If you do, you certainly have given us no reasons why it should not be granted. If it is the industry and prosperity you seek, can it not be better carried out by allowing the workmen to receive good wages, which will be used in taking off the productions of industry, than to have wealth conferred upon the few, to be used in building up greater monopolies? The application for this charter has revealed the fact, that capital holds labor in a system of slavery, and we the toilers are determined to make a square fight for independence, charter or no charter. We are marching on! Rights or no rights, we are determined to cease work, or else have the profits of our labor!" (MBLS, *Annual Report*, 1870, 281–82)

Testimony of a Citizen of Marlborough Concerning the Local Influence of the Crispin Organization in That Town

"There are those who think the organization of Knights of St. Crispin works to the injury of our town. I think otherwise. During the seven years I have lived there, real estate has doubled in value, and during the two years of Crispinism, there have been more houses built than during the five previous years. This comes from the fact that our laborers are confined to Malborough more than they used to be. This organization rather controls labor. Instead of folks coming from Canada, Maine, New Hampshire, and other places abroad, to work a few months and then carry their money away, the work is done by those who live, or propose to live there. The money earned is therefore spent in town. The interest of the working people in the town is increased. Little places are bought, and Marlborough is every way more prosperous than it would have been but for this labor movement. I am well acquainted with most of the members of the Crispin body. They are as orderly as could be expected of a mixed society, composed of different nationalities. As a class they are temperate. Many of them belong to temperance organizations. The Irish society and the two divisions of the Sons of Temperance are mostly patronized by the laboring classes. It has stimulated an interest in town affairs. The general effect of the society upon its individual members has been good. Should judge that it had improved their earnings, those at least of some classes, about 40 per cent."

TESTIMONY OF A CRISPIN

The following testimony of J. R., a Crispin, is corroborative of the claim of the favorable influence of this association:-

"Our organization has given us an advance of 40 per cent. in wages, in the winter season. The bosses used to cut us down then. Indeed some of us think prices are 40 per cent better right through. I certainly think I am a better man, a better citizen, and more interested in the affairs of the country I have adopted as a home, than I should have been but for the organization. This has come through associating with others. I have been brought in contact with smarter men than I ever thought of being myself. I have learned of others, and others have learned of me. The lodge room has given us practice. Three years ago designing men would come into our town meetings and get the crowd to go with them, because we didn't understand the way to put motions. They can't 'pull wool' over our eyes so easy now. A friend of mine who knows says, that eight years ago there was hardly an Irishman or a laboring man who could get up in town meeting and say anything; now there will be one in every four or five of these men who can get up and talk, owing to the practice they have had in the lodge. For myself I can say that I have not drank any liquor for fifteen years, and that I have taken a steady interest in the temperance movement. I can prove, however, that our Crispin organization has done more for temperance than all our temperance societies have done together. Have never known a proposition looking to violence to be brought up in the lodge or talked of in any way. Outside the meetings it has always been discouraged." (MBLS, *Second Annual Report*, 1871, 33–34)

The following historical account of the Crispins, which appeared in 1877, was in effect an obituary for the weakened union. It was also the most detailed discussion of labor organization that the bureau published while Carroll Wright was director. His report notes, but does not stress, an apparent willingness on the part of small-scale entrepreneurs to tolerate or even encourage unions, an attitude in sharp contrast to the hostility of larger producers. Perhaps those who manufactured on a small scale were themselves former shoemakers, more attuned to the concerns of employees than were remote owners of large corporations. In addition, resolution of differences with their workers may have enabled smaller producers to manage their enterprise more efficiently and thus compete more effectively.

Sometime in the year 1864, Newell Daniels, then living in the town of Milford, Mass., conceived the idea of organizing the shoemakers of that place on the plan of not allowing any one to teach the trade to new hands, without first obtaining the consent of the organization. . . .

Before the preliminary arrangements were completed, however, Mr. Daniels left Massachusetts, settled in the West and for the time being the matter dropped.

About two years afterwards, Mr. Daniels, with some others, succeeded in organizing in the city of Milwaukee, Wis., a society of shoemakers, comprising all who had worked at any branch of the shoe-trade for the space of one year, with the restriction that no member should teach his trade to any one unless by consent of the organization. . . .

Circulars setting forth the plan and principles of the order were prepared and sent to all parts of the country where it was known that shoes were manufactured. By these means Crispinism was introduced into Eastern Massachusetts, where it spread with great rapidity through all the shoe towns. . . .

The effects of the revolution, through which, as is well known, the entire shoe business was at that time gradually passing, were nowhere more felt than in Lynn. The complete and final change of methods brought about by the introduction of steam power and labor-saving machinery, and the consequent subdivision of labor whereby production was greatly increased and cost reduced, the employment of unskilled labor being allowed to an extent before impracticable, were of course disastrous to small manufacturers, whose business now began to be absorbed in larger firms.

The small-shop system was mostly abandoned, and the large-factory system adopted in its place. The Lynn shoemaker, hitherto more or less independent in the management of his business, began to sink into the mere operative, and in place of making a shoe throughout, as formerly, was obliged to work continuously and monotonously at one or another of the thirty or forty branches into which the industry, under the new system, was divided. He thus became a cutter, a laster, a heeler, a beater-out, etc., or was set to run a McKay sewing machine, a skiving machine, a pegging machine, etc., in any of which labors the skilled shoemaker found that the knowledge and experience gained by years of practice gave him little advantage over the green hand.

The natural result of this state of things was to give to the large manufacturers, who could command the necessary capital, a manifest advantage over those of smaller means, who were still struggling along in the business. This is, no doubt, one of the reasons why the small manufacturers looked with more or less favor on the combinations of workingmen, and in particular on their efforts, by means of the Crispin organization, to keep up the rate of wages; for there is every reason to believe that these employers sympathized to some extent with the workingmen, and that it was owing largely to their friendly support and encouragement that the Crispin organization attained to such power and wielded so much influence during the years 1868 and 1869; it was a power they might have continued to retain, to a great extent, had the wise counsels of some of their members prevailed in the lodge-room, and certain provisions of the constitution been altered or repealed; as it is now generally conceded, even by members of the order, that at that time some of their rules were arbitrary, and unjustly interfered with the rights of employers.

In the constitution for subordinate lodges which was adopted by the International Grand Lodge, April 23, 1869, and which was binding on the order everywhere, were some provisions which bore injuriously upon the rights of manufacturers, or, at all events, left their interests subject to the caprice of temporary majorities in the lodge-room.

The following is from a printed copy:—

"ARTICLE X.—NEW HELP.

"No member of this order shall teach, or aid in teaching, any part or parts of boot or shoe making, unless this lodge shall give permission by a three-fourths vote of those present and voting thereon, when such permission is first asked: *provided,* this article shall not be so construed as to prevent a father from teaching his own son; *provided,* also, that this article shall not be so construed as to hinder any member of this organization from learning any or all parts of the trade." . . .

Many of the most intelligent Crispins state that they always believed some of these rules to be unjust and arbitrary, and that the order, by their enforcement, was attempting to deal with matters not within its proper province; that they had often urged their repeal, giving it as their opinion, in the course of discussion in the lodge-room, where these matters came up, that employers were only submissive to such restrictions to save themselves from loss, and were determined to free themselves on the first opportunity from restraints under which they were every day becoming more and more restive.

Manufacturers of the smaller class, as we have before remarked, express themselves, for the most part, as having been favorable to the order on its first establishment. They think it might have been made a means of protection to their interests, as well as those of the workmen. But they say that, in the latter part of the year 1868 and during a portion of 1869, when the organization had almost full sway, the Crispins became exacting, presumptuous and insolent in their demands upon employers, often interfering with matters they did not understand, and which, at any rate, were not their concern; that, by the operation of the special laws, manufacturers were subject to loss and continual annoyance; that they could not discharge a man for any reason but he was almost sure to make complaint to his lodge, calling it a grievance and asking for a committee of arbitration; that there were many instances where they felt such committees had not treated manufacturers with even a shadow of justice; that it sometimes happened that an employer had reasons for his action, which he was not willing or even justified in unfolding to the committee; that, in all such cases, the committees were apt to be influenced by the most narrow views, and almost certain to decide against the employer; and that, even when the matter was fairly investigated and fairly reported to the lodge, it was always easy for a few demagogues or a small faction, by specious talk, to carry any vote they desired, sometimes ordering manufacturers to take men back into their employment whom they did not want, and sometimes to discharge men they needed and were anxious to keep, and who, on their part, were contented and willing to stay.

Manufacturers who are conducting a large business and employ many hands, express themselves as having always been opposed to Crispinism, and indignant at its claims. They have no objection to combinations of workingmen to keep up the rate of wages, in any fair and legitimate way; but, they say, "These men assumed to control our whole business. We claim the right to employ any who are willing to work for us, for as long as we please, and to discharge them when we please, without giving outsiders any reason." . . .

Factories were opened in Pittsfield, N. H., where the proprietors felt themselves safe from the effects of Crispin authority, and could command the advantages of cheap rents and cheap labor. In consequence, a large part of the work was done out of the city, which in other years had been retained there, for there was so much sharp competition among manufacturers, that each was on the watch continually to gain, if possible, any advantage over others; thus, though the workmen did receive more for their labor while at work, there was so much less work done in Lynn, that it is believed they really earned less money than they would have done had there been no organization. (MBLS, *Eighth Annual Report*, 1877, 19–25)

CHAPTER TEN

"A State of War"

The labor question of the later nineteenth century came most insistently to general attention when strikes and lockouts moved disagreement from factory floors and corporate offices into city streets. The ripple effect of economic distress, rarely mitigated by charity or relief funds, and the possibility of disorder and violence transformed private disputes over wages or union recognition into threats to the public's prosperity and safety. The Bureau of Statistics of Labor was founded partly to furnish accurate information, collected without preconception and presented without bias, to assist the larger community in its effort to limit these conflicts to contending employers and their employees.

Probably Henry K. Oliver never decided whether strikes were symptoms of an inequitable economic system or the result of temporary, local circumstance; both explanations inhere in the bureau's early treatment of the topic. In the volumes he edited, Oliver included an essay on the wage system, for instance, that suggests a more inclusive explanation for discord than do his narratives of particular struggles. But he also had the staff interview extensively and submit detailed reports of specific incidents, an approach that emphasized the uniqueness of each event and implied that generalizations about industrial injustice or agitating outsiders did not contribute to industrial peace. The bureau's investigators inquired about wages, hours, and shop conditions, not about abstractions; they attributed settlements to compromise, conciliation, or surrender, not to the operation of economic laws. Eventually, Carroll Wright identified elements common to many industrial disagreements, but his tabular treatment of causes and consequences did not inspire a revision or even a forceful critique of the economic principles that were the conventional wisdom of his day.

Although many Massachusetts strikes had similar elements, one in 1870 was distinctly unusual. Members of the Knights of St. Crispin, working at C. T. Sampson's North Adams shoe factory, attempted to protect their craft from machinery and unskilled competition. Like union members elsewhere, they limited apprenticeship and refused to work where nonmembers were employed. Since the Daughters of St. Crispin enrolled women who were engaged in the trade, a union shop was theoretically possible. That and other Crispin aims seemed to Sampson an intolerable infringement of entrepreneurial discretion and led him to replace his workers with Chinese contract laborers.[1]

This singular solution provoked considerable controversy and the cautious interest of the bureau. To ensure a credible account, the bureau's investigators made "phonographic" transcripts of conversations in North Adams, rather than relying on their customary notes. This tactful effort neither soothed the prickly proprietor nor altered his determination.

STRIKE AT NORTH ADAMS, AND INTRODUCTION OF CHINESE WORKMEN

This strike may be considered worthy of notice more than any others that have occurred in Massachusetts, not indeed for its magnitude, but for the fact of its leading to the introduction of a new element into our laboring population. This consideration, and the conflicting accounts that reached us, induced a visit to North Adams, and to make personal examination and inquiry, the result of which is given below. The testimony was reported phonographically by Mr. Slade.

---

1. See Frederick Rudolph, "Chinamen in Yankeedom: Anti-Unionism in Massachusetts in 1870," *American Historical Review* 53:1 (1947), 1–29.

Testimony of C. T. Sampson

... Two years and a half ago, the Crispin order here struck against the employment of persons not members. That was my first introduction to them.... The facts about the strike two years ago last May, are these: I employed a man, who was an excellent shoemaker, to make up a certain class of work. He could make a very nice shoe, and I wanted one of that kind made; so I set him to work in the room with other bottomers, not knowing anything about the Crispins. A few days after, my foreman notified me that there was a man at work up stairs that the help did not like to have there. When I asked why, he answered that he believed they had an order called the Knights of St. Crispin, and that it was so constituted that they could not work with a man not belonging to it. I replied that that was nothing to me; that I employed him, and I employed them. The matter rested until the next day, when they applied to the foreman to know if I wasn't going to turn the man off. He said he guessed not; and they, in turn, said they would not work in the room with any such man as that; his morals were too bad. They made that an excuse. Finally, I told the foreman to inform them that if they were not satisfied they could leave; the man would be kept at work anyhow.... Speaking to the leader of the crowd, I said, "That man will not be turned off." "Well, then," said they, "we shall not go back to work." "Very well," said I, and told them to take out their benches and kits. So they hustled them out and piled them in front of the building. I kept my factory running with that man for three weeks. One day I had occasion to go away, and they whipped him while going to or coming from dinner. We had the persons who committed the violence bound over. After the man got well he was missing, and I have not seen or heard of him since ...

... We filled up our shop then with green hands. Mr. Chase, my superintendent, went to Maine, the foreman of the sewing rooms went to Canada, and the foreman of the bottoming room to Worcester County, to find help that did not belong to the order. We found them, and once a month, for some time, required them to sign a writing that they did not belong to the order and would not join it while in my employ. Very soon I found they all belonged to the order; but they kept very quiet until last winter.... The shoes began to come out very poor.... Goods were returned frequently.... I found I could not govern my own business, so ... I said to Mr. Chase: "Now I guess we will get some workmen." He says: "What shall we do?" In answer I said: "Mr. Batchelder, of North Brookfield, is not doing much, and the prospect is he will not do much for some time. It strikes me as very probable that we can get a quantity of American help there, and make it just such help as we want." He says: "Shall we hire those that belong to the order?" I said, "Oh! certainly. . . ." On Monday quite a number came on, looked the shop over, and said it appeared as though they could make money here. . . . They were nice-looking fellows, and we were pretty well pleased. That night a lodge meeting was called, a committee waited upon the men with an invitation to attend, and they went up. The lodge men objected to the others going to work, as there was a strike on hand. The Brookfield men remained about four days, and during the time three lodge meetings were held. The men here said: "There are plenty of workmen in town; you are not needed here and must not go to work." And they did not. . . .

I waited until sure they were aboard the cars, then came to the shop and called Mr. Chase into the office. . . . I told him to go to San Francisco and hire me seventy-five Chinamen. If he could not get men experienced in making shoes, he was to engage those who had a natural turn for mechanism. . . .

The following Wednesday the men were on the way. They had been placed in charge of Charley Sing, and the first time Mr. Chase saw them altogether was at the ferry landing, where he was introduced to them informally. Each man had a roll made up of his bed, blanket and clothing. . . . They also brought along tea, rice, and Chinese merchandise. . . . The railroad journey lasted from the evening of June 1st to the evening of June 13th. . . . When the cars stopped for an hour or two, they would cook rice, and at the stations would sometimes buy Bologna sausages. There was no difficulty on the way to speak of. Mr. Chase would telegraph to the station agents ahead where there was any likelihood of trouble, and policemen would be on hand. Where the trains stopped but five minutes at a station, no one was allowed to get out of or into their cars. . . . We had no serious trouble, though it was anticipated. Previous to their coming we were notified that if the Chinamen stepped their feet into North Adams they would be shot, and that if I showed my head I should meet the same fate. There was a great crowd of people at the depot. We were twenty-five minutes coming from it to the factory, a distance of less than a quarter of a mile. There was every chance for the execution of threats. A few spirited with whiskey pitched in. Two of them, Frenchmen, who had worked for me, were put in the lockup at once, and nothing more transpired. . . . At the depot Mr. Chase introduced me to Sing, and Sing gave the boys to understand that I was their "boss-man." They were . . . taught everything connected with the business, to which they were total strangers. We communicated with them as you would with a deaf and dumb person. The work at first was about the average work of beginners. My agreement or contract was not made with the men personally, but was made and signed with Kwong, Chong, Wing & Co. . . . They are held to me for a certain number of years; at the end of the time they are at liberty to dispose of themselves as they see fit, or renew the contract. *I decline to show the contract.* . . . The money is put in the hands of the foreman (Sing) monthly. He keeps their accounts. . . .

Since the Chinamen have got to work, there have been threats of blowing up the mill and destroying Mr. Chase and myself. . . . The first threats came through the Crispin lodge, from a man who said he would shoot the first Chinaman that came here. . . . I have suffered no violence. . . . Stones have been thrown through the windows once or twice. . . . The Chinamen don't seem to be afraid to go about town at all, though they have been waylaid once or twice, and kicked several times. Men have slapped them in the face, but they don't say anything about it, and when you ask about it you cannot find who has been struck. They are out almost every evening. Their ordinary food is meat and vegetables. They use tea, taking a few swallows before and after meals, but not drinking it with their food. Their tea comes from their own people. Coffee is not drank by them. Rice is their bread and butter. They have it at every meal, together with beef, pork, mutton and fish, or something of the sort, and vegetables. Sing buys their food, and they have two cooks of their own. Besides their tea they have some preserved things from China, ginger, etc. It will be cheaper to manufacture shoes with these than with other workmen. When this kind of labor becomes general, the consumer will reap the benefit.

Testimony of Daniel Luther

Am a shoemaker but not a Crispin; have never been one. I have worked for Mr. Sampson a good deal, but left his employ in September, three years ago. There was no strike while I was with him. . . .

When I worked for him, the hands were mostly American and French. Their general character was good. They were as temperate and honest as the average of citizens. Once I went to Stoneham for him to get new hands. I got some men and brought them on. According to his instructions I promised them a case a day for a year. When I brought them to his office and turned them over I repeated to him my statement to them, and he said it was correct. They worked five weeks according to agreement, and then he put them down to three cases a week, and said he never promised them any more. It made trouble, but there was no strike. One team left. The reason I left Mr. Sampson, as I said before, was on account of unfair treatment. He never kept a single bargain with me that he ever made. I judge that the weekly pay-roll in the department where the Chinamen are employed, amounts to almost $643, and that the average production is sixty cases a week. On that basis his shoes would cost him not less than $9 a case, estimating upon three kinds of work made, which price is as high as is paid by any one in town. Mr. S. has said in the street that when he got sixty cases made by the Chinamen, he should have twenty cases made for nothing, at the rate other bosses were paying, which I think is far from being the case.

Testimony of Oliver A. Brown

Am a shoemaker, of French Canadian parentage, and have been here, off and on, since 1844. Have worked for Mr. Sampson, but not at the time of either of the strikes in his shop. I have had good chances to know about them, however, from the parties engaged. When the Chinese came into town I did not leave my work to go and see them. . . . I thought Mr. Sampson had the right to get the Chinese if he wanted, and I had no disposition to interfere. The proposition of Mr. S. to his men, as presented to the lodge, was, that if they didn't wish to go to work, they could lay still until the first of July, when he would give the same price—a course which would be better for him. . . . When the committee told Mr. Sampson of our action, he said it would suit him better than to continue to work; he would make more money in the end. The next day I saw Mr. Chase on the street. He asked me if I didn't think the men missed it, and added that Mr. Sampson was very much tickled over it. The same day Mr. Chase went to Brookfield, and it was found, when the men from there came, that Mr. Sampson had made an agreement to wait, and had then sent off and got other men. One reason why the Brookfield men did not go to work was, because of misrepresentation; Mr. Sampson having given them to understand that there was no trouble. . . . Finding there was trouble here, they did not wish to go to work. . . . Nearly a quarter of a year previous to this trouble I met Mr. Sampson, while working in Albany, and in the course of the conversation he said: "I will show the Crispins that they can't control my business. I will have the Chinese here the first thing you know." Mr. Sampson and I belong to the same church. I have nothing against him whatever.

Testimony of Lucius A. Ellis

Am in general trade in North Adams, keeping boots, shoes, hats, caps and a full line of provisions. Have been in business since 1864. My customers have largely been among the laboring class, perhaps one-fifth of them shoemakers. . . . The tendency of the coming of the Chinamen has been to make trade dull. My trade has been some two hundred dollars a month less. The displaced seventy-five American laborers would spend at the stores from ten to fifteen dollars a week each, say from $750 to $1,100 in all; while the new comers buy very little. From a third to a half of the old set have left town with their families. The trade of a family, say of four persons, would amount, with me, to from $20 to $40 a month. The wages of a Chinaman are understood to be only about $20 a month, while the men displaced earned from $45 to $60. When the Chinamen came I saw no violence. I heard "rats" hallooed. Saw nothing specially out of order. Have heard the Crispins say they would countenance nothing in the shape of violence. For instance, a man came into my store one day, and represented that as I was in business, it was for my interest that the laboring man should get the largest wages he could. He then said, "I can get a hundred men to go down and take that factory, and clean it out." There were one or two Crispins present, who spoke up at once and said they would not countenance any violence. I never heard anything else in the nature of a threat against Mr. Sampson or the Chinamen. (MBLS, *Second Annual Report*, 1871, 98–107, 109–12, 115–16)

Henry Oliver drew no conclusion from his initial inquiries in North Adams. A second interchange with C. T. Sampson a year later brought accusations of misquotation and distortion. An irritated Sampson demanded to know who had suggested contact with employees whose remarks the bureau had published and declined to discuss the matter further. (The fact that some of his managerial associates confirmed the bureau's version of disputed conversations did not enhance Sampson's willingness to cooperate.) After consulting local law enforcement officials, Oliver decided that Sampson could furnish additional evidence in writing, a decision probably made easier by his uncertain legal authority to compel anyone to testify in any medium. In replying to Oliver's questions, Sampson repeated in brief the grievances he had previously recited at greater length to the bureau's stenographer. Oliver concluded with a description of living conditions for the Chinese shoeworkers.

REMARKS BY MR. SAMPSON

In your report for last year, there was published as "sworn testimony" the statements of several persons. In these statements, the principal object seems to have been, to underrate my standing as a man of honesty and integrity, in business transactions. Especially concerning transactions with my employés. Now as this testimony is in *many respects untrue*, and as it, in each case, came from men who are *prejudiced* against Chinese immigration, and against myself, men who have openly opposed me since I began employing the Chinese in my manufactory, I consider it as very unfair and one-sided. I can give you testimony, besides my own, which will prove to the contrary all statements, showing that I have broke a contract with my employés. Except it may be an instance when the contract was made between one person and myself alone, and no witnesses were present, in which case I cannot, of course, bring forward additional testimony.

The bureau responded:

In our Second Report we gave what information, we could obtain upon the history of the introduction of Asiatic labor into Massachusetts, its influence upon other labor and its method of operation. The information, however, was more that of historical detail, than anything else, since the recentness of its introduction had not permitted any development, either of the success or the failure of the new laborers, or of the expediency or inexpediency of further introduction. We at that time decided that it would be advisable to wait, and to renew our visit and inquiries after the lapse of a year. Accordingly, in the month of October, 1871, we returned to North Adams to make further inquiries. The particulars of this visit are given below. We found the Chinese, as we found them at our visit in 1870, both living and working in the same building, the factory of Mr. Sampson.

20. North Adams contract laborers, 1871. Courtesy of the North Adams Historical Society.

Their sleeping quarters are a large hall adjoining, fitted up with sleeping bunks, one over the other, on the sides and in the centre. These are furnished each with a mattress and bedding, the whole resembling the barrack arrangements of soldiers. The area of ground about the building is large and ample for exercise or amusement, the locality healthy, and the rooms within favorably situated for ventilation and heating. How far their sanitary condition was affected by the occupancy of one hall as their general living and sleeping room, we are not informed. Their eating room is a hall between their sleeping quarters and the main factory and general shop. This room is fitted up with small tables and with seats, each table accommodating six or eight persons. These several messes constitute one grand mess for the whole number of about 75, under the charge of one of their number, who acts as commissary, making the purchases and settling the bills, and keeping all the necessary accounts. The men are held for a certain number of years, at the end of which, they become their own masters, and may or may not renew their contract, as they please. After payment of their bills, whatever balance is due each individual, he disposes of as he sees fit. It is said that they have become somewhat assimilated to our habits and fashion of dress, and an interest is taken in them by people in the town, in the way of ordinary and religious instruction, an interest that was never taken in any other foreign laborers. Were they single individuals, and not a group, their assimilation would be more rapid, and national habits more rapidly ignored; but collectively, they will the longer retain the habits and the feelings which bind them to their own country, and which may eventually carry them back. The whole experiment is an important one, and its denouement will be waited for with much interest. (MBLS, *Third Annual Report*, 1872, 401–2, 408)

Commenting on a strike in Worcester in 1870, the city marshal remarked that "talk of having Chinamen hired" as strikebreakers had agitated people in the city and perhaps stimulated the violence that marked the confrontation.[2] In 1881, the bureau quoted informants who disparaged French Canadians as "the Chinese of the Eastern States." The outraged reaction to that comparison forced the agency to provide a public opportunity for French Canadians to rebut the characterization.[3] Although the adjective "Chinese" became a rough synonym for "cheap" or "exploited" in the idiom of the day, other Massachusetts manufacturers apparently did not adopt Sampson's union-busting tactic.

Oliver's investigations of labor disputes resulted in narratives—less detailed than the Sampson example—in which his impatience with employers and his identification with the aspirations of working people, if not avowed, were undisguised. Carroll Wright intended to shift the bureau's focus from specific strikes to a general consideration of the causes and consequences of industrial disharmony. His reports contained fewer journalistic paragraphs and many more tables than had Oliver's; Wright rarely discussed the practices of particular employers and almost never mentioned unions. His research demonstrated the social cost of industrial argument, especially to workers,

2. MBLS, *Second Annual Report* (1871), 129.
3. See Chapter 4 above.

21. Textile spinning room. Courtesy of the Museum of American Textile History.

rather than the intransigence of employers that was implied in Oliver's words. Oliver examined a strike and found injustice; Wright found social and economic waste.

That difference in perception reflected contrasting political attitudes as well as divergent research techniques. Wright did not excuse the exploitation of working people. But until after he left Massachusetts, he did not endorse unions as a remedy; like progressives later, he regarded any organized interest group as a potential threat to the public's welfare. Nor could he ignore the institutional jeopardy to the bureau that Oliver's earlier advocacy had caused. Scholarly detachment was for Wright both temperamentally congenial and politically prudent.

He displayed his continuing concern about strikes and lockouts in tables that showed days and dollars lost, winners and losers, reasons and results (Tables 47–52). Explicating his quantitative survey of the topic in 1880, Wright concluded that labor appeared to bear a dispro-

Table 47. Strikes and lockouts, 1825–1879.

Occupations Affected by Strikes and Lockouts

Occupations	Number of Strikes and Lockouts	Occupations	Number of Strikes and Lockouts
Bleachery, employés in	1	Nail and tack makers	6
Building trades, employés in	10	Navy yard, employés in	5
Calkers	1	Riggers	1
Cigar makers	3	Shoe factory operatives	34
Coal heavers	1	Tailors	4
Coopers	3	Tanners	1
Cordage makers	1	Textile factory operatives	59
Grinders	1	Sailors	1
Hatters	2	Soap makers	1
Horseshoers	1	Stone cutters	2
Laborers	7	Waiters	1
Locomotive engineers	1	Wire makers	1
Machinists	2	Wood workers	1
Miners,	3		
Morocco dressers and finishers	5	TOTAL	159

Causes of Strikes and Lockouts

Causes of Strikes and Lockouts	Number of Strikes and Lockouts
To secure better wages	118
To secure shorter days	24
To enforce trade union rules	9
Resistance to employers' rules	5
Against introduction of machinery	3
TOTAL	159

Source: MBLS, *Nineteenth Annual Report*, 1888, 4–5.

portionate share of the cost of struggles with management. Even when workers achieved their objectives, success rarely replaced lost wages, restored lost jobs, or renewed the lost prosperity of families and communities dependent on manufacturing. The income that workers "voluntarily forfeited," Wright wrote, had it been saved instead, might have become an investment in housing or a small business. The fact that employers sometimes welcomed, and even induced, strikes suggested to Wright that interrupted production provided a convenient, occasional means of trimming production and expense in a bad market. His concluding hope that contending parties would substitute for

Table 48. Summary of strikes, by year and industry, 1881–1886.

	Years and Industries	Ordered by Labor Organizations		Establishments			
		Yes	No	Number	Number Closed	Aggregate Days Closed	Avera Days Cl
	Years						
1	1881	4	31	35	27	129	4.8
2	1882	28	50	78	67	1,122	16.7
3	1883	26	7	33	21	288	13.7
4	1884	25	21	46	27	1,700	63.0
5	1885	80	17	97	75*	2,755	36.7
6	1886	652	54	706	570	13,297	23.3
7	Totals	815	180	995	787	19,291	24.5
	Industries						
8	Boots and shoes	161	10	171	113	4,037	35.7
9	Brick	—	1	1	1	1	1.0
10	Building trades	459	33	492	478	10,291	21.5
11	Carpeting	1	2	3	3	90	30.0
12	Clothing	76	2	78	47	971	20.7
13	Cotton and woollen goods	—	2	2	2	199	99.5
14	Cotton goods	11	40	51	26	1,206	46.4
15	Food preparations	5	—	5	—	—	—
16	Furniture	2	2	4	1	77	77.0
17	Glass	7	1	8	5	246	49.2
18	Leather and leather goods	10	5	15	8	297	37.1
19	Machines and machinery	1	—	1	—	—	—
20	Metals and metallic goods	3	27	30	13	484	37.2
21	Printing and publishing	1	2	3	—	—	—
22	Public ways construction	—	3	3	—	—	—
23	Public works construction	2	1	3	2	8	4.0
24	Rubber goods	2	8	10	10	201	20.1
25	Shipbuilding, etc.	20	5	25	25	275	11.0
26	Silk goods	1	1	2	1	7	7.0
27	Stone quarrying and cutting	3	21	24	21	490	23.3
28	Telegraphy	—	1	1	—	—	—
29	Tobacco	32	—	32	24	307	12.8
30	Transportation	4	4	8	2	2	1.0
31	Woollen goods	—	5	5	3	71	23.7
32	Miscellaneous	14	4	18	2	31	15.5
33	Totals	815	180	995	787	19,291	24.5

| Duration (Days) | | Results | | | Employés— | | |
Aggregate	Average	Succeeded	Succeeded Partly	Failed	Loss	Assistance	Employers' Loss
363	10.4	15	12	8	$ 50,779	$ 12,265	$ 39,235
204	15.4	66	1	11	941,183	14,007	524,245
491	14.9	19	1	13	78,090	6,735	27,720
341	50.9	12	1	33	691,416	36,024	139,380
587	47.3	69	4	24	1,053,499	42,149	352,885
520	30.5	170	438	98	1,385,522	155,528	887,416
506	30.7	351	457	187	$4,200,489	$266,708	$1,970,881
540	49.9	107	15	49	$1,623,530	$162,293	$ 478,519
1	1.0	—	—	1	53	—	200
305	20.9	47	423	22	246,916	5,055	429,080
126	42.0	—	1	2	106,000	1,950	90,000
724	60.6	74	—	4	73,590	7,030	20,500
213	106.5	1	—	1	822,990	10,500	505,000
659	32.5	14	2	35	635,350	27,866	74,177
5	1.0	5	—	—	54	—	100
132	33.0	1	—	3	40,262	1,400	3,000
262	32.8	3	—	5	68,505	5,734	25,425
366	91.1	7	1	7	102,579	13,598	22,900
33	33.0	—	—	1	15,000	3,000	30,000
932	31.0	9	1	20	178,494	2,010	46,500
20	6.7	1	1	1	1,498	142	750
7	2.3	1	—	2	656	—	110
9	3.0	1	—	2	1,632	—	700
222	22.2	2	2	6	145,446	3,400	141,000
275	11.0	25	—	—	5,748	—	1,000
14	7.0	1	—	1	3,292	800	8,000
519	21.6	22	—	2	25,189	65	1,400
3	3.0	—	—	1	80	—	—
358	11.2	25	1	6	36,862	8,215	19,270
66	8.3	2	—	6	11,495	—	4,950
245	49.0	2	—	3	23,476	150	23,800
470	26.1	1	10	7	31,792	13,500	44,500
,506	30.7	351	457	187	$4,200,489	$266,708	$1,970,881

Table 48. Continued.

		Number of Employés					
		Before Strikes			After Strikes		
	Years and Industries	M	F	T	M	F	T
	Years						
1	1881	4,264	870	5,134	4,279	876	5,1
2	1882	8,783	5,550	14,333	8,393	4,300	12,6
3	1883	2,734	1,889	4,623	2,662	1,843	4,5
4	1884	7,989	6,935	14,924	7,730	6,873	14,6
5	1885	16,957	7,854	24,811	16,706	7,497	24,2
6	1886	35,543	15,121	50,664	33,949	14,184	48,1
7	TOTALS	76,270	38,219	114,489	73,719	35,573	109,2
	Industries						
8	Boots and shoes	23,670	8,130	31,800	22,207	7,697	29,9
9	Brick	52	—	52	48	—	
10	Building trades	7,761	—	7,761	7,779	—	7,7
11	Carpeting	1,197	2,425	3,622	1,210	2,384	3,5
12	Clothing	1,521	1,364	2,885	1,408	1,281	2,6
13	Cotton and woollen goods	2,563	3,192	5,755	2,247	2,043	4,2
14	Cotton goods	13,863	18,041	31,904	13,765	17,719	31,4
15	Food preparations	58	19	77	58	19	
16	Furniture	1,767	320	2,087	1,719	305	2,0
17	Glass	1,291	124	1,415	1,212	124	1,3
18	Leather and leather goods	1,578	1	1,579	1,359	1	1,3
19	Machines and machinery	650	—	650	640	—	6
20	Metals and metallic goods	7,842	277	8,119	7,726	277	8,0
21	Printing and publishing	207	151	358	202	161	3
22	Public ways construction	445	—	445	448	—	4
23	Public works construction	256	—	256	323	—	3
24	Rubber goods	4,417	2,333	6,750	4,275	1,994	6,2
25	Shipbuilding, etc.	185	—	185	185	—	1
26	Silk goods	149	326	475	95	280	3
27	Stone quarrying and cutting	887	—	887	900	—	9
28	Telegraphy	40	—	40	40	—	
29	Tobacco	646	492	1,133	602	447	1,0
30	Transportation	3,546	—	3,546	3,653	—	3,6
31	Woollen goods	460	216	676	460	217	6
32	Miscellaneous	1,219	808	2,027	1,158	624	1,7
33	TOTALS	76,270	38,219	114,489	73,719	35,573	109,2

Source: MBLS, *Nineteenth Annual Report*, 1888, 46–49.

ployés aged in rikes	Employés Engaged and Involved in Strikes			New Employés After Strikes			Employés Brought from Other Places
	M	F	T	M	F	T	
538	1,861	483	2,344	147	6	153	78
781	7,701	4,538	12,239	1,263	—	1,263	1,209
417	1,793	1,490	3,283	102	39	141	50
047	5,777	5,821	11,598	481	261	742	246
818	14,877	6,299	21,176	638	69	707	341
094	22,880	7,534	30,414	2,642	538	3,180	1,239
695	54,889	26,165	81,054	5,273	913	6,186	3,154
587	16,998	5,870	22,868	1,879	453	2,332	909
19	52	—	52	—	—	—	—
429	7,568	—	7,568	79	—	79	37
365	1,197	2,425	3,622	57	—	57	40
343	1,226	1,254	2,480	72	72	144	12
910	2,563	3,192	5,755	13	12	25	25
420	7,536	9,550	17,086	543	149	692	65
28	28	—	28	—	—	—	—
307	772	100	872	86	6	92	15
333	884	69	953	—	—	—	—
760	1,451	1	1,452	124	—	124	110
200	270	—	270	150	—	150	100
139	4,163	16	4,179	85	—	85	22
116	120	4	124	8	10	18	8
445	445	—	445	98	—	98	58
231	246	—	246	90	—	90	90
351	4,395	2,333	6,728	357	119	476	318
185	185	—	185	—	—	—	—
56	149	326	475	—	—	—	—
598	598	—	598	39	—	39	—
40	40	—	40	5	—	5	—
859	592	425	1,017	63	35	98	10
516	2,516	—	2,516	1,323	—	1,323	1,265
173	261	153	414	82	26	108	50
285	634	447	1,081	120	31	151	20
695	54,889	26,165	81,054	5,273	913	6,186	3,154

Table 49. Distribution by sex of employés involved in strikes and lockouts, by year, 1881–1886.

| | | Strikes | | | Lockouts | |
| | | Percentages of— | | | Percentages of— | |
Years	Employés Engaged and Involved	Males	Females	Employés Locked Out	Males	Females
1881	2,344	79.39	20.61	—	—	—
1882	12,239	62.92	37.08	—	—	—
1883	3,283	54.61	45.39	1,212	60.31	39.69
1884	11,598	49.81	50.19	132	98.48	1.52
1885	21,176	70.25	29.75	1,285	60.31	39.69
1886	30,414	75.23	24.77	11,699	78.71	21.29
Totals	81,054	67.72	32.28	14,328	75.68	24.32

Source: MBLS, *Nineteenth Annual Report*, 1888, 81.

strikes some more socially responsible method of resolving industrial disputes was not demonstrated in the bureau's subsequent reports. In 1888, another survey concluded with the notion that compulsory arbitration might be a route to harmonious labor relations, a proposal that echoed one the bureau had advanced earlier without evoking a discernible response.[4]

Conclusion

The statistical side of strikes is easily presented. The facts brought together in these pages will enable any town which has suffered in the past from industrial disturbances to estimate the economic results of the contests, and the lesson taught by them should have its effect upon public opinion in the future. There are, however, other phases of the subject, equally important, that cannot be shown in figures. . . .

A strike is a state of war, and like war is, in its tendency and immediate results, wasteful and destructive. As long as war is in certain exigencies justifiable upon reasonable grounds, so long, probably, upon similar

4. See Chapter 9 above. In "The Commissioner of Labor's *Strikes and Lockouts*: A Cautionary Note," *Labor History* 32:3 (1991), 432–40, Gary L. Bailey warns that in at least one instance Wright's method understates the incidence of strikes and lockouts. Bailey's assessment rests on data Wright collected as the U.S. commissioner of labor, and not on a Massachusetts case study. And Bailey concludes that, whatever their shortcomings, Wright's reports "have been and will continue to be an invaluable tool for the investigation of the world of the 19th century worker" (p. 440).

Table 50. Results of strikes and lockouts, by year and industry, 1881–1886.

Results of Strikes for Employés

Years and Industries	Employés Engaged and Involved in Strikes That—					
	Succeeded		Succeeded Partly		Failed	
	Number	Percentages	Number	Percentages	Number	Percentages
YEARS						
1881	796	33.96	321	13.69	1,227	52.35
1882	4,048	33.07	800	6.54	7,391	60.39
1883	362	11.03	96	2.92	2,825	86.05
1884	2,452	21.14	20	0.17	9,126	78.69
1885	10,606	50.09	2,497	11.79	8,073	38.12
1886	9,882	32.49	6,893	22.66	13,639	44.85
TOTALS	28,146	34.73	10,627	13.11	42,281	52.16
INDUSTRIES						
Boots and shoes	13,580	59.38	1,338	5.85	7,950	34.77
Building trades	983	12.99	6,426	84.91	159	2.10
Carpeting	—	—	700	19.33	2,922	80.67
Clothing	2,313	93.27	—	—	167	6.73
Cotton and woollen goods	500	8.69	—	—	5,255	91.31
Cotton goods	3,014	17.64	178	1.04	13,894	81.32
Furniture	35	4.01	—	—	837	95.99
Glass	197	20.67	—	—	756	79.33
Leather and leather goods	504	34.71	49	3.38	899	61.91
Metals and metallic goods	1,770	42.35	17	0.41	2,392	57.24
Rubber goods	1,546	22.98	1,767	26.26	3,415	50.76
Tobacco	632	62.14	6	0.59	379	37.27
Transportation	1,100	43.72	—	—	1,416	56.28
Other industries	1,972	49.82	146	3.69	1,840	46.49
TOTALS	28,146	34.73	10,627	13.11	42,281	52.16

Results of Lockouts for Employés

Years and Industries	Employés Involved in Lockouts That—					
	Succeeded		Succeeded Partly		Failed	
	Number	Percentages	Number	Percentages	Number	Percentages
YEARS						
1883	—	—	—	—	1,212	100.00
1884	132	100.00	—	—	—	—
1885	1,285	100.00	—	—	—	—
1886	5,213	44.56	300	2.56	6,186	52.88
TOTALS	6,630	46.27	300	2.10	7,398	51.63
INDUSTRIES						
Boots and shoes	3,962	35.74	—	—	7,123	64.26
Building trades	—	—	300	100.00	—	—
Food preparations	700	100.00	—	—	—	—
Leather and leather goods	1,530	92.45	—	—	125	7.55
Woollen goods	425	100.00	—	—	—	—
Other industries	13	7.98	—	—	150	92.02
TOTALS	6,630	46.27	300	2.10	7,398	51.63

Source: MBLS, *Nineteenth Annual Report*, 1888, 87–88.

Table 51. Outcomes of successful strikes and lockouts, 1881–1886.

Percentages of Establishments having Strikes that Succeeded, etc.,
for Principal Causes or Objects of Strikes

Causes or Objects	Number of Establishments	Percentages of Establishments Having Strikes That—		
		Succeeded	Succeeded Partly	Failed
Against adoption of proposed scale of prices	40	100.00	—	—
Against discharge of employés	6	66.67	—	33.33
Against reduction of wages	62	20.97	6.45	72.58
Disagreement among employés regarding new scale of prices	18	—	—	100.00
For adoption of union scale of prices	7	14.29	—	85.71
For discharge of foremen	7	57.14	—	42.86
For employment of union men only	5	100.00	—	—
For increase of wages	351	72.65	10.83	16.52
For increase of wages and reduction of hours	5	60.00	20.00	20.00
For reduction of hours	425	0.24	96.94	2.82
For reinstatement of discharged employés	8	37.50	—	62.50
In sympathy with strike elsewhere	6	—	—	100.00
Other causes	55	40.00	3.64	56.36
TOTALS	995	35.28	45.93	18.79

Percentages of Establishments having Lockouts that Succeeded, etc.,
for Principal Causes or Objects of Lockouts

Causes or Objects	Number of Establishments	Percentages of Establishments Having Strikes That—		
		Succeeded	Succeeded Partly	Failed
Against demand for discharge of non-union employés	42	—	—	100.00
Against demand for increase of wages	4	50.00	—	50.00
Against union men	58	98.28	—	1.72
To enforce reduction of wages	16	25.00	—	75.00
To resist strike for increase of wages in another establishment	24	100.00	—	—
Other causes	3	33.34	33.33	33.33
TOTALS	147	59.86	0.68	39.46

Source: MBLS, *Nineteenth Annual Report*, 1888, 89.

grounds strikes will be justifable. But while this may be conceded, both parties to an industrial controversy may well hesitate to resort to war before exhausting other and more civilized modes of adjusting differences. Wherever, as in Massachusetts, an equitable tribunal has been established for the purpose of settling labor controversies every employer and certainly all employés should be interested in testing its efficiency and

Table 52. Days required for employés to recover wage losses in succcessful strikes, 1881–1886.

Years and Industries	Localities	Average Wages Lost per Employé during Strikes	Average Daily Wage Gain per Employé by Strikes	Average Days Required to Meet Loss
1881				
BUILDING TRADES				
Plasterers	Boston	$11.25	$0.50	23
Painters	Fall River	2.05	0.46	4
METALS AND METALLIC GOODS				
Puddlers and helpers (iron works)	Fall River	1.98	0.01	198
TOBACCO				
Cigar makers	Springfield	8.10	0.03	270
1882				
BUILDING TRADES				
Masons and tenders	Fall River	12.87	0.19	68
SHIPBUILDING, ETC.				
Employés (shipbuilding yard)	New Bedford	7.52	0.50	15
Calkers	Boston	34.75	0.50	70
STONE QUARRYING AND CUTTING				
Marble cutters	Boston	58.00	0.50	116
TRANSPORTATION				
Longshoremen	Boston	1.80	0.20	9
1883				
TOBACCO				
Cigar makers	Springfield	6.13	0.12	51
Cigar makers	Springfield	10.44	0.11	95
Cigar makers	Springfield	13.35	0.08	167
Cigar makers	Springfield	15.76	0.15	105
Cigar makers	Springfield	18.50	0.15	123
Cigar makers	Westfield	5.00	0.17	29
Cigar makers	Westfield	11.07	0.17	65
Cigar makers	Westfield	25.00	0.18	139
1884				
BOOTS AND SHOES				
Buffers and beaters	Lynn	$2.85	$0.15	19
COTTON GOODS				
Employés	Taunton	22.40	0.10	224
1885				
BOOTS AND SHOES				
Employés	Spencer	24.02	0.06	400
Lasters	Rockland	49.83	0.04	1,246

Table 52. Continued.

Years and Industries	Localities	Average Wages Lost per Employé during Strikes	Average Daily Wage Gain per Employé by Strikes	Average Days Required to Meet Loss
1885—Con.				
GLASS				
Employés	Boston	73.91	0.11	672
LEATHER AND LEATHER GOODS				
Curriers	Peabody	32.52	0.15	217
METALS AND METALLIC GOODS				
Stockers (steel works)	Worcester	3.00	0.02	150
1886				
BOOTS AND SHOES				
Employés	South Weymouth	23.24	0.02	1,162
Lasters	East Stoughton	3.75	0.06	63
Lasters	North Weymouth	4.87	0.04	122
Lasters	Quincy	29.45	0.02	1,473
Cutters	Stoneham	41.78	0.04	1,045
Cutters	Stoneham	13.13	0.03	438
Cutters	Stoneham	46.28	0.03	1,543
Lasters	North Abington	41.13	0.05	823
BUILDING TRADES				
Masons and tenders	Worcester	28.61	0.38	75
CLOTHING				
Tailors	Boston	48.00	0.18	267
Employés (clothing factory)	Boston	18.50	0.17	109
SILK GOODS				
Employés (silk mill)	Canton	5.14	0.11	47
Aggregates		$20.09	$0.15	134

Source: MBLS, *Nineteenth Annual Report*, 1888, 93–94.
Note: The strikes included in this table are those successful ones for increase of wages in which all employés in the several establishments joined in the strike. The strikes for increase of wages in which but a part of the help joined are excluded on account of the difficulty of determining upon a method of computation that would be just and exact, and at the same time susceptible of tabular presentation. Fractions of cents and of days are omitted.

supporting its decisions. If arbitration is to be commended, and all will agree that it is to be commended, as a substitute for war among nations, it should be equally commendable as a substitute for industrial warfare. In our present complex social organization no strike can be confined in its results to the particular industry, or locality, or establishment in which it occurs. Its effect is perceptible in every part of the social structure. It has a public as well as a private significance. It is a social no less than an individual or personal affair. The loss to employés or to employers may be readily estimated and presented in statistical form, but this loss must be only a fraction of that which other interests inevitably suffer. Every limitation of consumption on the part of wage workers, whether brought about by enforced idleness during the period of the strike or lockout, or by subsequent retrenchment of expenditure made necessary by loss in wages, limits in equal degree the market upon which all producers depend. The wage earners in any of our factory towns provide a home market, the preservation of which is essential to the prosperity of the town. A strike or lockout in any of our industrial centres, if long continued, paralyzes every business enterprise. If it were otherwise both capital and labor might be left to abide the issue of the contest unmolested. But because the social or public welfare is involved in every such contest, public sentiment ought to demand the submission of the personal questions involved to the tribunal established by public authority to deal with them. (MBLS, *Nineteenth Annual Report*, 1888, 115–16)

Index

DOCUMENTS IN AMERICAN SOCIAL HISTORY
Edited by Nicholas A. Salvatore

---

*Their Lives and Numbers: The Condition of Working People
in Massachusetts, 1870–1900*
edited by Henry F. Bedford

*We Will Rise in Our Might: Workingwomen's Voices from
Nineteenth-Century New England*
by Mary H. Blewett

Dutch American Voices: Letters from the United States, 1850–1930
edited by Herbert J. Brinks

*Peter Porcupine in America: Pamphlets on Republicanism
and Revolution*
by William Cobbett, edited and with an
Introduction by David A. Wilson

*Invisible Immigrants: The Adaptation of English and Scottish
Immigrants in Nineteenth-Century America*
by Charlotte Erickson

Keepers of the Revolution: New Yorkers at Work in the Early Republic
edited by Paul A. Gilje and Howard B. Rock

News from the Land of Freedom: German Immigrants Write Home
edited by Walter Kamphoefner and Ulrike Sommer

History of My Own Times
by William Otter, edited by Richard B. Stott